D0323155

Rereading Molière

Mise en Scène from Antoine to Vitez

Jim Carmody

Ann Arbor

THE UNIVERSITY OF MICHIGAN PRESS

Copyright © by the University of Michigan 1993
Published in the United States of America by
The University of Michigan Press
Manufactured in the United States of America

1996   1995   1994   1993   4   3   2   1

Library of Congress Cataloging-in-Publication Data

Carmody, James Patrick.
    Rereading Molière : mise en scène from Antoine to Vitez / Jim
Carmody.
        p.   cm. — (Theater—theory/text/performance)
    Includes bibliographical references and index.
    ISBN 0-472-10466-7 (alk. paper)
    1. Molière, 1622–1673—Stage history—1950– 2. Molière,
1622–1673—Stage history—1800–1950. 3. Molière, 1622–1673—
Dramatic production. 4. Theater—France—History—20th century.
I. Title. II. Series.
PQ1871.C37 1993
842′.4—dc20
                                                    93-9065
                                                    CIP

A CIP catalogue record for this book is available from the British Library.

For Michael and Ellen

Acknowledgments

Research for this book was funded by the Georges Lurcy Foundation, by the Mrs. Giles Whiting Foundation, and by grants from the Chancellor and the Committee on Research of the University of California at San Diego. I thank them for their generosity.

I also wish to thank the Johns Hopkins University Press for permission to use material in chapters 5 and 6 that first appeared in *Theatre Journal* in a somewhat different form.

On a more personal level I wish to thank Charles Lyons, Bill Eddelman, and the late Doug Russell for their invaluable comments on the earliest versions of these ideas.

I have been fortunate to be able to discuss Molière with Jean-Marie Apostolidès and Judd Hubert. I have learned a great deal from their work and from their comments.

Finally, I owe a debt beyond measure to my wife, Laurie Edson. Her astute comments and the exemplary clarity and audacity of her own critical work have helped greatly at every stage of this project.

Contents

A Note on Translations

All translations in this book are by the author unless indicated otherwise in the list of Works Cited.

Chapter 1

Reading Molière in the Theater: Mise en Scène and the Classic Text

Since the 1949 publication of Will Moore's seminal book, *Molière: A New Criticism,* English-speaking critics of Molière have accepted the premise that Molière's texts should be interpreted in the context of the theater. In France, René Bray's 1954 book, *Molière: homme de théâtre,* exerted a similar kind of influence.[1] Although Moore and Bray were pursuing very different, even fundamentally opposite, intellectual agendas, they agreed that the *theatrical* aspects of the plays had been far too long ignored, and that when interpreting Molière's writings, scholars should remember that Molière wrote for the theater.

As a corrective, Moore offered a reading that discussed some of Molière's major plays under such rubrics as "Mime," "Mask," and "Scene," thus creating a prototype for what has come to be known as "metadramatic criticism." Moore's readings of individual plays, however, are less sensitive to the material aspects of performance than they appear to be. Although he advocates a consideration of Molière's plays as works written for the theater, Moore is principally interested in the elucidation of Molière's *morale,* like those critics who precede him and whose methods he contests. In his discussion of *Tartuffe,* for example, Moore remarks that Molière wore a mask while performing some of his roles, then goes on to discuss *Tartuffe* as a play about the unmasking of Tartuffe. In the course of this discussion, Moore turns an actor's *commedia* mask into a metaphor without exploring the connection between Molière's use of *commedia* masks in performance and Moore's own description of the "unmasking" of Tartuffe, and without acknowledging that neither Molière nor the other actors wore masks during performances of *Tartuffe.* Instead of investigating Molière's writings as the product of a historically specific artistic and cultural practice, he devotes his attention to the philosophical issues that the critical tradition had already identified in the plays.

Rather than address the material aspects of theatrical production,

Moore affirmed the importance of studying Molière's aesthetics as the best means of arriving at an appreciation of the playwright's ethics, an emphasis that encouraged scholars to turn their attention to the text itself after a long period of focusing on Molière's personal life.[2] The frequent, often explicit, linking in recent decades of aesthetics and ethics in the titles of books and articles on Molière indicates the extent of Moore's influence. Following his example, writers employ terms such as *actor, mask,* and *scenic space* to discuss what they take to be the ethical issues raised by Molière's dramaturgy; like Moore, they, too, never discuss actual actors, masks, or scenic spaces. For Moore and those who have adopted his methods, the language of the theater provides a range of useful metaphors that enables a metadramatic critique of a range of issues.[3] It is important to note, however, that these are precisely the same issues that earlier generations of *moliéristes* had discussed using different vocabularies.

A recent book by Nathan Gross, one of the prominent ethics/aesthetics critics of the 1980s, reveals the extent to which the methodology pioneered by Moore continues to ignore the material aspects of performance. In *From Gesture to Idea: Esthetics and Ethics in Molière's Comedy,* as the title of his book implies, Gross selects "gesture" as his theatrical point of reference:

> Each of these essays . . . develops from the observation of a specific detail of language and gesture, more apparent in a staged performance than in a reading of the printed text, into an exploration of the underlying ethical values that the play in question urges upon an audience's attention. . . . These gestures recur within episodes of plot arranged in parallel cycles. Organization of the dramatic text . . . guides the spectator's pleasurable response; it furnishes a series of contexts that allow him, by virtue of his knowledge of similar earlier incident, vocabulary, and gesture, to anticipate the comic protagonist's behavior and to appreciate ironies of situation and language. (1–3)

Although he refers to gestures that are "more apparent in a staged performance than in a reading of the printed text," Gross never discusses actual performances. And although the details that interest Gross could indeed be made apparent in performance, he does not take into account the very real possibility that individual directors might choose to ignore, alter, or even suppress those details.

While an individual actor may perform gestures such as those indicated by Gross, it is unlikely that any performance would provoke on the part of the spectator the kind of systematic moral reflection that Gross finds in Molière's plays. The dramatic text (synonymous here with the printed text) may guide the reader's "pleasurable response," but the spectator is not sitting in the theater reading a book. The spectator's experience of a play is quintessentially different from that of a reader. Whereas the reader can suspend the flow of action to consider and reconsider whatever strikes his or her fancy, rereading the same passage or passages in whatever order seems most productive, the spectator can see a mise en scène only once. Whatever limited kind of "rereading" is possible in the theater, it simply cannot be the same as that which the reader takes for granted. Unlike the reader, the spectator cannot stop the performance to consider the ethical implications of a single gesture, line, exchange of lines, or sequence of events; in other words, the spectator cannot perform any of the analytical operations that Gross's reading fundamentally depends on in the time frame allowed by performance. It is useful to remember, too, that the vast majority of spectators are not professional humanists and do not pay very much attention to the kinds of ethical considerations that this kind of criticism claims to find *systematically* explored in these plays. This is not to say that a spectator with the angle of vision of an ethics/aesthetics critic such as Gross will not be able to discern in a certain mise en scène the very pattern he or she has already identified in the play. Clearly, there are many directors who approach Molière's text looking for precisely the kind of patterning of behavior that interests Will Moore and Nathan Gross.

I shall return to the question of Molière's *morale* in later chapters. What is important, for the moment, is not whether the ethics/aesthetics critics have anything of value to contribute to Molière studies (they do); what I want to contest is their claim to be dealing with Molière in the context of the theater. What Gross has to say about the repetition of gesture is valid but only in the most general, abstract way. The gestures that Gross describes are not performed by a living actor on a stage before a live audience, although Gross's discussion probably draws on unacknowledged performances that he has attended. Like other ethics/aesthetics critics, and like other scholars who adopt a metadramatic mode of commentary, Gross never addresses the question of which kind of mise en scène he has in mind. Is he thinking of a realist or nonrealist, modernist or postmodernist mise en scène? Or does he have in mind the kind of classical mise en scène that offers a judicious blend of "classical" acting values and suggestions of contemporary "relevance"? Does he, for instance, prefer Jouvet's *Tartuffe* or Planchon's, Vilar's *Dom Juan* or Chéreau's, and for what reasons? Like most literary scholars, Gross is far more comfortable citing a printed document than a theatrical performance, even though the failure to deal with actual theatrical performances calls his critical methodology into question.

It is useful to remember, however, that the work of Moore, along with that of the critics who have investigated the fields of research that he opened up, is itself determined by the discursive practices within which it emerges and which gives it its specific forms. Molière scholars such as Moore are first and foremost devoted to the humanist study of literature. Consequently, their work on the writings of Molière and on the cultural production of seventeenth-century France reflects the interests of that discipline. As a result, in their professional writings they inevitably privilege the text over theatrical performance, no matter how much they may appreciate and take pleasure in attending performances of Molière's plays. The fact that Molière scholars have, relatively speaking, almost entirely ignored the *comédies-ballets* (almost half of Molière's plays) for over three and a half centuries is perhaps not irrelevant in this context.

Like other ethics/aesthetics critics who take their lead from Moore, Gross avoids any discussion of the material aspects of the theater. René Bray, on the other hand, researched the working habits and environments of seventeenth-century French theater that he believed conditioned, if not actually determined, Molière's development as actor, director, company manager, and playwright. In place of detailed readings of individual plays, Bray offered what was, in effect, a revisionist historiography of French seventeenth-century theater. Bray thus opened up lines of inquiry that have led not only to significant shifts in perspective in Molière studies but also in studies of the work of other dramatists and theaters of the period.

Bray's work is perhaps less frequently quoted than Moore's for a number of reasons. In the first place, Bray offers few interpretive comments on individual plays in his *Molière: homme de théâtre*. (The Bray and Scherer edition of the plays, while listed in many bibliographies, is also seldom discussed.) In the second place, and more significantly, Bray undertakes a sustained assault on the humanist tradition of reading Molière as a *moraliste*. With considerable energy, he contends that Molière is not a systematic thinker and that no significant moral philosophy can be deduced from a reading of the plays. He devotes an entire chapter to posing the question, "Is Molière a Philosopher?" a question he answers unequivocally with a resounding "No." Unsurprisingly, Bray's rejection of Molière as a moral philosopher made his work difficult to assimilate into discussions of the interrelationships between Molière's ethics and aesthetics. Ironically, while his work provided scholars with potentially valuable insights into the practices of the French theater industry during Molière's lifetime, none of the scholars interested in developing a "theatrical reading" of the plays has been willing to set aside his or her interest in Molière's moral philosophy.[4] It is not surprising, therefore, that Laurence Romero, in his 1974 survey of Molière criticism, offers the disappointing assessment that Moore's and Bray's most important contribution has been that they persuaded critics to look for Molière's thought in the entire play and not simply in the speeches of the *raisonneur*.[5]

Bray's questioning of the kind of philosophically oriented humanistic research that has consistently informed Molière studies (the revelation and explication of Molière's moral "philosophy") emerges as a radical break not only with almost every element of established Molière criticism but also with the humanistic discipline of dramatic criticism itself as it had been practiced until that time. (Indeed, Bray's critique of traditional Molière criticism may perhaps be seen in retrospect as being somewhat akin to poststructuralist critiques of the Author.) Bray insisted on the purely theatrical origin and destination of Molière's text. No satisfactory understanding of those texts could be arrived at, he believed, in the absence of an understanding of the signifying practices within which they emerged.

In *La Formation de la doctrine classique en France,* Bray made substantial contributions to our understanding of classical dramaturgy as it evolved in the real world of seventeenth-century France. Subsequently, other scholars turned their attention to the day-to-day realities of Molière's theater, notably Georges Mongrédien and Roger Herzel. In addition to his *Daily Life in the Theatre at the Time of Molière,* Mongrédien published in 1965 the first anthology of seventeenth-century French documents relating to Molière. Herzel produced a number of influential articles on Molière's stagecraft prior to his 1981 book, *The Original Casting of Molière's Plays.* Other scholars have significantly increased our understanding of seventeenth-century theater architecture and scenography.[6] Along with Henry C. Lancaster's monumental history of French classical drama and Jacques Scherer's equally exhaustive *La Dramaturgie classique en France,* this research provides us with a better understanding of Molière's work as actor, director, and company manager—and how that work formed the context for his playwriting. While this research has resulted in significant gains in our understanding of the theater of Molière and his contemporaries, it has also reminded us, time and again, of how very few accounts exist of the performances of Molière's plays.

As an author, Molière was influenced as much by his director's imagination as by his actor's experience; while his experience as an actor nourished his ability to create rich, theatrical characters, his experience as a director taught him to think in terms of the interplay of character, décor, and spectator. Molière's contemporaries acknowledged him as a superbly talented and innovative director. Donneau de Visé, for example, one of the first commentators on *School for Wives,* complimented Molière on the degree of aesthetic control manifested in his mise en scène, remarking that Molière had set a new standard: "Never was a play so well performed with so much attention to detail; each actor knows exactly how many steps to take and every wink is measured" (qtd. in Mongrédien *Recueil* 1:177). While Molière's experience as a performer undoubtedly helped him create effective scenes between characters at both the moment of writing and the moment of staging, it is his directorial imagination that gave birth to the complex, hybrid form of the *comédie-ballet.* A mixture of different modes of theatrical performance that combines verbal, musical, scenic, and choreographic elements, the *comédie-ballet* demonstrates Molière's ability to think in terms of what the modern era calls the poetry of the stage.

Indeed, much of the scholarly disinterest that has greeted the *comédies-ballets* over the years can be attributed to the fact that Molière's texts quite obviously do not provide an adequate sense of the scenic life of these plays. Accordingly, the texts of the *comédies-ballets* have been relegated to the same secondary status as opera librettos or the "books" of musicals. It is hardly surprising that such creations should have been denied critical approval in the doctrinaire neo-Aristotelian climate of French neoclassicism, or that subsequent generations of scholars and theater artists should have felt embarrassed by the nonliterary (i.e., nonverbal) elements of Molière's texts. Nevertheless, the fact that Molière was capable of creating such works for the stage, often at alarmingly short notice, suggests that his theatrical imagination was directed toward creating works of theater principally at the level of performance or mise en scène. In other words, we can see Molière as the author of two quite distinct texts, the verbal text and the scenic text, only one of which has survived.

At a distance of more than three centuries, it is unlikely that we will ever be able to reconstruct Molière's original mises en scène in anything but the most fragmentary manner; it is therefore possible to propose only the most conjectural readings of Molière's writings in the context of seventeenth-century theater.[7]

Unfortunately, we know very little about the day-to-day work of seventeenth-century theater artists: we do not know how plays were rehearsed, what the acting values were, or what the production values were. What little we know about production values has been gleaned from sources such as Mahelot's *Mémoire,* seventeenth-century graphic reproductions of décors or scenes from a relatively small number of plays, and the manuals of scenography by experts in scenic illusion. Our information about acting styles, especially Molière's personal technique, is considerably less reliable than the documents on scenic practices, for it is based on comparisons with the extravagantly rhetorical style associated with the tragedians of the Hôtel de Bourgogne, a style about which we know equally little. While Molière was praised for the "natural," realistic quality of his acting, we should not assume that those who praised him shared our modern notions of naturalistic or realistic acting. If Molière was praised for being "natural" onstage, more "lifelike" than his tragedian colleagues at the Hôtel de Bourgogne, he was also simultaneously acknowledged as the most gifted *farceur* of his time, applauded for his extraordinarily flexible facial expressions and talent for grotesque silliness.[8]

If we do not possess sufficient information to discuss Molière's plays in Molière's own stagings, it is possible to consider Molière's work in the context of twentieth-century mises en scène, as many of the most influential mises en scène have been relatively well documented. Fortunately, we have not only critical accounts of the different performances but also texts written by directors and their collaborators that shed considerable light on the problematics of staging French classic drama in this century. No single book, however, can hope to discuss all of the important productions of every Molière play. Perhaps no single book can even hope to undertake a comprehensive discussion of every significant production of one of the major plays. Rather than trying to focus on the entire oeuvre or on every important production of a single play, this book focuses on productions of two plays that proved to be turning points in the twentieth-century staging of Molière's plays, *The School for Wives* and *Tartuffe*. The productions in question are André Antoine's and Jacques Arnavon's 1907 *Tartuffe*, Arnavon's 1936 notebook production of *The School for Wives*, Louis Jouvet's 1936 *School for Wives*, Roger Planchon's two productions of *Tartuffe* in the 1960s and 1970s, and Antoine Vitez's Molière tetralogy of 1978.

These productions are not, by any means, the only important Molière productions of this century, nor are the directors who staged them the only individuals who have achieved significant results with the plays in question. These productions are, however, representative of the best stagings of Molière in this century. More significantly, perhaps, they represent key moments in the history of French theater: each of these productions marks an important development in the ways that plays from the classical period were staged in France. Indeed, I hope to show that, taken together, these productions reveal an almost century-long exploration of the status and identity of "the classics" in twentieth-century French theater. These productions also reveal an abiding interest in exploring the ever-shifting understanding of the "Grand Siècle" as a value in modern and contemporary French culture.

This book, then, is an attempt to take up the challenge of Bray and Moore in a new way by writing about Molière's plays, not in the context of a generalized notion of the theater but, rather, in the context of specific moments of theatrical production. The following chapters offer a synthesis of theater history and dramatic criticism. They attempt a necessarily partial reconstruction of certain productions as a way of examining how Molière has been "read" in the French theater during this century.

The mises en scène that are the focus of this book are the products of a response both to the individual plays in question and to the extraordinarily complex cultural identity of Molière himself. In a sense these directors respond as much to what Molière represents as to the scripts he wrote. Their individual responses are themselves products of the forces of French culture (forces that collide with one another as often as they coalesce) operating within the theatrical and other artistic spheres at a given moment; the same mise en scène may, accordingly, appear conservative from one perspective and revolutionary from another. I have not attempted to map out all of the forces that may have operated on any one of the productions I shall be discussing but have, instead, chosen to concentrate on a nexus of issues: the relationship between director and playwright as manifested in directors' attitudes to the classic text; developments in directors' strategies for adapting the dramaturgy and scenography of the 1660s to the aesthetics of the twentieth century; and developments in directors' responses to the ideologies of "fidelity" and "realism."

Molière, Classical Author

The director's goal is the creation of a mise en scène that his or her contemporaries will find theatrically compelling. In order to create a theatrically compelling mise en scène of a play by Molière, the director must first address two related problems: he or she must find a means of reconciling Molière's seventeenth-century dramaturgy with the poetics of contemporary mise en scène; he or she must also find a satisfactory way of addressing the cultural status of Molière's play as a classic, for the play is being revived in the modern theater precisely because it is a classic. In short, a compelling mise en scène of a classic text must contain both a theatrically exciting performance of the drama in question and a persuasive treatment of the play's identity as a classic.

Since Molière's text exists as a material product of a certain place and time (Paris in the 1660s), the director must choose how to explore the relationships between the text and the society in which it was created, a relationship that is complicated by the double identity of the play as both a script and a recognized literary classic. Whereas the script is but one element, however important, of the technology of the theater, the mere fact of the play's publication as a book by an important author immediately "elevates" the play to what literary scholars have regarded as the higher cultural status of Literature.[9] (It is useful to remember that theater scripts need not take the form of a book. Molière's actors never read the complete text; instead, each actor was given a "side" or copy of his or her own part only, a practice that continued into the present century.) Molière's scripts are products of seventeenth-century French theater; Molière's "classic plays," on the other hand, are as much, if not more so, products of more recent periods of French and other cultures.[10] As classics of French culture, they have been identified as containing timeless truths about the human condition, truths that are fixed for the reader and the spectator in perfect models of dramatic form. But this notion of the classic is not a seventeenth-century one. For Molière's contemporaries, the "classics" were Greek and Roman. Although Molière and other artists of his day were consciously attempting to create their own art based on Greek and Roman models, they did not label themselves Neoclassicists. That labeling occurred much later.

Molière's status as a classic author has significantly influenced the direction of both Molière studies and productions of his plays. This influence is perhaps best seen in the tendency to treat Molière's comedies as serious dramas and to pay a great deal less attention to his farces and *comédies-ballets*. Since tragedy as a genre has traditionally been seen as representing a higher level of aesthetic and indeed moral achievement, scholars have tended to privilege the more serious, darker aspects of Molière's drama. Similarly, generations of directors have shown a marked preference for a "tragic" Molière.[11]

Theater is an ephemeral art and, as such, is notoriously difficult to describe and evaluate. Productions not only eventually end their runs and literally disappear forever, but as every theater artist acknowledges, no two performances are ever alike. The published text, however, remains as a permanent trace of the original production and becomes available to each successive generation of readers and potential directors. In a culture that prizes the "timelessness" of the work of art, it is not surprising that the book of the play has superseded the performance of the play as the privileged mode of being for the dramatic work of art. Indeed, until the advent of the theatrical avant-garde at the end of the last century, the relationship between dramatic literature and its performance onstage was relatively unproblematic. With the rise to prominence of the stage director, however, the staging of the production, which I shall be referring to from a semiotic perspective as the scenic text, eventually came to rival the playwright's text as a focus of interest.

For the scholar of drama, the written text understandably remains the primary source of interest, and he or she usually tends to consider both performance and scholarship as sharing a common goal—producing the most convincing, "faithful," or otherwise satisfactory interpretation of the text. Theater artists and spectators, however, are not primarily interested in the written text. As a playwright, actor, and director, Molière wrote his texts with the knowledge that they were to be used as only one element among many that would go into the preparation of a performance.[12] The institution of dramatic literature notwithstanding, theater scripts are not written to be read outside the theater: the potential for performance dictates the content of every line, the shape of every scene, and the identity of every character.[13] Even the plays of Jean Racine, which are generally acknowledged as the greatest literary achievements of seventeenth-century

France, were written to take advantage of the possibilities offered by a specific kind of theatrical performance.[14] Arguing for the primacy of performance over text even in the case of an apparently literary theater such as Racine's, Bernard Dort writes:

> On the surface, it seems to be a theater that is exclusively a theater of text. Few, if any, stage directions. Racinian tragedy seems never to have had any existence other than literary. But that is obviously not correct. In fact, the exact opposite was true. The text existed only to fulfill the requirements of an already existing form: the form of tragic performance. And the *palais à volonté* of the Hôtel de Bourgogne was more than a mere décor; it was, properly speaking, a symbolic location, the very image of how a certain society saw itself. The text did nothing more than furnish the ingredients for a ritual that these individuals produced for their own pleasure. ("Les Classiques" 158)

Dort's semiotic analysis of the theatrical event is usefully comprehensive in that it avoids restricting "theatrical performance" to the narrow sense of what transpires on the stage. Instead, he proposes that we examine plays and their performances not only as purely aesthetic events abstracted from the influences of the cultural and political environment but also as responses to an identified, socially circumscribed desire. In the case of Racine, Dort suggests, the playwright was responding to the desire of a certain segment of the aristocracy to see its own experiences figured on a tragic scale.

   Like Dort, theater semioticians see all scripts as, in part, responses to the signifying potential present in theatrical performance during a given period.[15] In *The Semiotics of Theatre and Drama*, for instance, Keir Elam writes:

> Since, chronologically, the writing of the play precedes any given performance, it might appear quite legitimate to suppose the simple priority of one over the other. But it is equally legitimate to claim that it is the performance, or at least a possible or "model" performance, that constrains the dramatic text in its very articulation. (208–9)

The script, then, need not be seen as a writing that exists before the performance but, instead, as a writing that is completed in performance.

In a 1985 article, "Theatrical Performance," Marvin Carlson has suggested that we should see the relationship between script and performance not in terms of an adaptation, a translation, or a realization but, rather, in terms of a Derridean complementarity.

Surprisingly enough, semioticians often neglect to consider what actually happens to the script in the theatrical production process: the script (especially an unproduced script) that remains unchanged by the rehearsal process is the exception, not the rule—the dialogue the actors read at the first rehearsal is rarely the dialogue heard by spectators at the first performance.[16] The script, then, represents a certain provisional conception of the dramatic potential of the stage itself, for the playwright begins work with an acquired store of theatrical experience and an acquired knowledge of the conventions of the contemporary theater; the script comes into being in the context of that knowledge.

Although Roland Barthes did not explicitly consider the question of the theater script, his celebrated distinction between work and text provides a valuable perspective on the question. Indeed, Barthes's notion of the text as intertext, as a fabric "woven entirely with citations, references, echoes, cultural languages . . . antecedent or contemporary, which cut across and through it in a vast stereophony," applies equally well to both the script and the mise en scène that eventually subsumes it (*Image-Music-Text* 160). It is Barthes's intertextual view of both the script and its mise en scène that informs the following chapters.

In the theater, the author's intention is that the script be used to create something else (given a choice, most living playwrights will choose to be performed rather than understood). Certainly, one can legitimately question the effectiveness of the ways in which the script has been used, just as one can express reservations about the ways in which a certain actor or a certain kind of lighting instrument has been used. The semiotic view of the creative process in the theater should, therefore, not be understood as a means of devaluing the contribution of the playwright; rather, it should be seen as a recognition of the many different sources of creativity that combine to make an effective piece of theater.

This view of the relationship between script and mise en scène has important consequences for the study of what Jonathan Miller calls the "subsequent performances" of plays by Molière or any classic dramatist. If the script comes into being as a kind of proposal for the way the "cybernetic machine that is the theatre," to borrow Barthes's image, can be made to function at a given moment in time, it makes no sense to ask whether or not the mise en scène has been faithful to the intentions of the author (*Critical Essays* 261). More productive questions will address the mise en scène, the play-in-performance, as a complex montage of different signifying systems. Furthermore, this understanding of the nature of the script reminds us that the physical realities of the theater, the personalities and skills of the performing and scenic artists, the economic health of the various theatrical and cultural institutions, as well as the tastes and opinions (aesthetic, moral, or political) of the spectators and critics provide more than a mere abstract context for the creation of the play. In fact, the play emerges from a dialectical interplay between the playwright and each of these environments. In the case of the classic playscript, these environments are precisely what have been stripped away by the passage of time, leaving behind only the "book." As Bernard Dort reminds us, once the passage of time has separated the printed text from the cultural and theatrical conditions from which it initially emerged, insisting on fidelity to the text becomes unproductive:

> One can never, dramaturgically, get away from performance. Cut off from its environment and extracted from the theatrical form in which it was to be realized, a classical text can come to life again only in another form. Let us not speak any more of being faithful to the classics or of betraying them; let us speak about the uses we make of them, uses that will never be truly productive unless they acknowledge their necessary infidelity. ("Les Classiques" 159)

Instead of pursuing a fidelity to "the classic," which amounts to privileging the book, Dort directs our attention to the demands of performance, reminding us of its inevitably contingent nature. Performance occurs only at specific moments and in specific locations, and because it depends on its immediate context for its significance as a cultural event, that immediate context often assumes priority over the classic text, notwithstanding the all too familiar and almost inevitable rhetorical gestures on the part of directors who suggest the contrary. Directors typically speak about their work in one or more of the following ways: as attempts to locate hitherto unsuspected meanings in the text; as attempts to present the author's thinking on issues that, in the director's estimation, are of compelling relevance in today's world; as attempts to realize the author's dramatic and theatrical ideas as fully as possible. Each of these positions appears to subject the director and his associates to communicating an already existing set of meanings. Indeed, with few exceptions directors present themselves as being faithful, first and foremost, to the author's "vision." Such rhetoric, as Dort reminds us, has served to obfuscate the actual practice of directors in the theater. In the course of the following chapters, I shall be considering the ways in which each director articulates a personal understanding of "fidelity" to Molière as well as looking at the notions of "Molière" to which he will attempt to be faithful.

Even though he wrote plays for himself and other members of his company to act, Molière, like other playwrights of the period, prepared his scripts for publication, recognizing that his work would be read and enjoyed as dramatic literature by his contemporaries. When he prepared scripts for publication during his own lifetime, Molière assumed, as a result of his readers' familiarity with his mises en scène and conventions of the theater of the time, that his readers would be capable of mentally theatricalizing his printed words. Three centuries later, however, Molière's readers are no longer aware of the conventions of seventeenth-century theater that provided a frame of reference for Molière's printed text. The linguistic, social, and theatrical conventions adopted (or undermined) by Molière are no longer familiar to us; indeed, Molière may have consciously exploited conventions of which we remain ignorant. Instead, we read his plays in the context of our own experience of twentieth-century theater and in the context of what we *imagine* theatrical performance in the seventeenth century to have been like.

Each of the productions discussed in the following chapters forges a kind of aesthetic compromise between a three-hundred-year-old play and a specifically contemporary theatrical practice. These accommodations between the classic and the contemporary result in the creation, by the director, of a new text, a mise en scène that merges the dialogue of the classic script and a contemporary scenography in the moment of performance. Enveloped in the new mise en scène, the familiar script takes on a new array of possible meanings, meanings that are directly generated by the juxtaposition of the familiar script and its traditional interpretations with a new scenography. The new mise en scène alters the contours of what we imagine we know by creating a fresh set of scenic images that recontextualizes the well-known characters and dramatic events of the classic play. In addition, the new staging often fashions radically different identities for these familiar characters. (Roger Planchon's suggestion, for example, that there exists a homosexual attraction between Orgon and Tartuffe represented a somewhat startling departure from the accepted stage tradition.) The contemporary mise en scène of a classic play may, therefore, be seen as an event in which the past is confronted by the present, the already known becomes the unknown, established interpretations are overturned, and familiar cultural and moral values are contested.

The mise en scène of a Molière play can be seen as a reflection of the individual director's theoretical understanding of the nature of the neoclassical text and of its relationship to the director's culture, of which the critical, scholarly, and performance traditions constitute important parts. Planchon's production of *Tartuffe*, for instance, offers a detailed scenographic evocation of the political and cultural turbulence of Louis XIV's reign that frames the action of the play in an unprecedented way. Planchon's new setting represents a significant departure from the conventionally calm, balanced, and rational neoclassical aesthetic that informs conservative mises en scène of this play. He thus uses his production of *Tartuffe* to offer a revisionist, critical view of the Grand Siècle itself.

Antoine Vitez responds differently to the Grand Siècle and uses his mises en scène of seventeenth-century dramatic texts, both comic and tragic, to explore the extent to which these monuments of French culture, texts that are taught every year in both primary and secondary French schools, are essentially foreign, even indecipherable in terms of their aesthetic form and content to French men and women of the late twentieth century. Vitez thus takes a position completely opposed to that of Antoine's collaborator, Jacques Arnavon, who argues that Molière's thought remains unambiguously present to the reader in his scripts, even for twentieth-century directors or readers. Whereas Arnavon believes that Molière's work communicates to people of every period and is therefore a classic by virtue of its readability (*lisibilité*, in Barthes's sense), Vitez believes that the play's classic status is precisely what blinds us to its real nature as a text that is no longer (re)readable but only (re)writable (what Barthes calls *scriptible*).

The following chapters investigate the attitudes of a number of French directors to Molière's classic texts while considering those attitudes in the context of their responses to the theatrical culture of their various periods (ranging from 1907 to 1978) as well as their individual senses of the general purpose of the theater institution itself. Each of these directors is distinguished not only by the extent of his influence on subsequent generations of directors in France but also by the degree to which his work on Molière is carried out in a self-conscious manner. Each sees his work as both creative and critical: creative in the sense that he is involved in the making of new productions; critical in the sense that his new production articulates a response both to Molière's script and to the received traditions of interpretation as manifested onstage and in the writings of theater critics and scholars. Indeed, each in turn comments, in his mise en scène, on the work of his predecessor. Planchon's productions of *Tartuffe,* for instance, constitute a particularly trenchant critique of the interpretations of both Antoine and Jouvet while, at the same time, showing how much he has learned from these two directors. In a similar vein, Vitez explicitly identifies his tetralogy of Molière plays as a critical response to the kind of "socializing mise en scène best represented by Planchon" (Vitez, Lassalle, and Maréchal 22).

Staging the Classic Text: Evolutions in Theory and Practice

The study of the mise en scène of Molière's plays in the present century must inevitably involve some study of the career of the stage director during the same period. It is a commonplace of theater history that the last hundred years or so have been the era of the director. Edward Braun, for instance, begins his account of the history of the stage director with Saxe-Meiningen and Antoine, although he acknowledges that these two men borrowed extensively from the staging innovations of the Romantic and Realist theater (7). André Antoine, acknowledged by many as the very first modern stage director, shares Braun's sense of the director as a creature of the modern theater. In 1903 he wrote: "Mise en scène is a newborn art, and nothing, absolutely nothing before the last century, before the theater of intrigue and situation, determined its coming into being" (qtd. in Dort, "Antoine le patron" 277).

Most theater historians offer accounts strikingly similar to Braun's: without exception, they assume that the rise to power of the director during the last hundred years or so is tied to the theater's increasingly sophisticated attempts to recreate offstage reality onstage. Such histories invariably see the director as the figure of authority who emerged to impose order on the chaos of proliferating innovations in both scenography and dramaturgy, a kind of super-*régisseur*. The director's rise to power, however, can also be related to the director's emergence as an *auteur* figure of comparable stature to the playwright. From yet another perspective, the history of this same emergence could be related to the rise of the scenographer, or the visual poet of the stage, to a stature equivalent to that enjoyed by the dramatist and the actor in earlier periods.

I use the term *scenographer* here (rather than stage or scenic de-signer) to draw attention to the graphic, textual nature of the design elements of theatrical performance as well as to call attention to the pri-macy of the visual text in modern performances of plays from the classic repertoire. It goes without saying that no mise en scène of a classic text in this century has achieved distinction in the absence of a compelling and often innovative scenography. Certainly, the illusionist scenography of the Baroque theater attracted crowds of admiring spectators to the theater, but nobody has suggested that such visual entertainments ever achieved the cultural status accorded to the leading actors and writers of that period. In the last hundred years, however, mise en scène has become as valued a cultural product as the play itself. In the case of classic plays, the director's staging of the play has increasingly attracted the spectator's and critic's focus away from the playwright and the actor, the traditional centers of attention in the theater. Indeed, Planchon has suggested that the prominence of the twentieth-century director is a result of the emergence of a certain notion of the classic and, paradoxically, that our ideas about the classics have in turn been greatly affected by the interventions of the director:

> The emergence of the classic brings with it the birth of a dubious character. He presents himself as a museum curator; leaning on Mo-lière and Shakespeare, he levers himself into a position where he is running the whole show. We may lament the fact, but the two things are linked: the birth of the classic gives power to the theatre director. In his hands the great theatres of the world become museums and justify their existence by producing *Oedipus, Hamlet,* or *The Miser.* A museum curator "restores" works and puts them on show. And this is where the ambiguities begin. (Qtd. in Bradby and Williams 6)

This brief excerpt from Planchon's preface to the 1986 Livre de Poche edition of *L'Avare* (The Miser) echoes many of the concerns of the present study.

In the eyes of Bernard Dort, founding editor of France's two most important postwar theater periodicals, *Théâtre Populaire* and *Travail Théâtral:* "The history of theatrical practice in France, at least during the period that concerns us [1945–60], could well be written in terms of a number of major productions of classic texts rather than in terms of the first productions of new plays" ("Un Age d'or" 1003–4). Although Dort's focus is the fifteen-year period immediately following World War II, his comment might equally well be applied to the entire postwar period for two reasons. First, the most prominent French directors have devoted a substantial portion of their energies to the staging of classic texts. Second, and perhaps more significantly, these directors have also achieved considerably more recognition for their work on classic texts than for their work on the first productions of new contemporary plays. Although Vilar, Planchon, and Vitez, for example, all directed the first productions (and acclaimed revivals) of plays by respected contemporary playwrights, their reputations as stage directors (rather than as artistic directors of their respective theaters) rests on their work with plays from the classic repertoire.[17] In the period prior to World War II, however, directors' reputations rested equally on their work with new and classic texts. Both Antoine and Jouvet, for example, established their reputations with productions of new plays and did extensive work with classic plays only in the latter part of their careers.

Before directors as we know them today first appeared on the scene of theater history, their predecessors in the early nineteenth century began to rethink the ways in which they set about the staging of classic texts. The impulse to reconsider the established practice of the preceding two centuries finds its origins in the death of the ancien régime following the French Revolution and in the new aesthetic of Romanticism that ushered in the nineteenth century. In "Les Classiques au théâtre ou la métamorphose sans fin," Dort describes three different notions of the classic, each of which corresponds (although not rigorously) to a period in history. In the seventeenth and eighteenth centuries, Dort writes, the classic was seen as an "old" play that had, by virtue of its continued popularity, remained in the repertory. Such plays were performed as if they were no different from the "new" plays of the day. Theater artists felt no need to differentiate between the old and new, Dort suggests, because classics were by definition timeless and could therefore be treated as if they had just been written.

One factor that made the play's age relatively unimportant for eighteenth-century theater artists was that eighteenth-century dramaturgy was not greatly different from that of the previous century. Similarly, eighteenth-century mise en scène differed very little from seventeenth-century mise en scène. For all intents and purposes, then, seventeenth-century plays presented few problems of technique or comprehension to the eighteenth-century theater artists who performed them or to the eighteenth-century spectators who attended those performances. (A similar situation obtains in our own period, when the naturalist/realist dramaturgy and scenography of the late nineteenth century differ so little from their counterparts of today.)

Dort suggests that with the beginnings of modern mise en scène in the nineteenth century, the classic came to be seen as a cultural product of a different place and time. As a result, artists staging old plays no longer felt able to treat the classics as if they were essentially no different from the plays of their own time. Now that the classics were identified with the past ("the past" emerged in this period as a theme in its own right), directors and designers became obsessed with researching and representing their historical context onstage. Dort cites the familiar examples of directors such as von Meiningen, Antoine, and Stanislavski sending researchers to Rome to learn about the Forum and other Roman locations for productions of *Julius Caesar* ("Les Classiques" 155). Like their Romantic predecessors earlier in the century, such directors assumed that the classic play's sociocultural context was that of the time and place in which the dramatic action was nominally located, not that of the culture that produced the play itself. They felt that because the action of *Julius Caesar*, for instance, was set in Rome, *Julius Caesar* was a play "about Rome." That *Julius Caesar* is more a play about Elizabethan England than imperial Rome is a relatively recent perception that owes a great deal to the ongoing critique of realist representation that has played such a large role in the artistic and intellectual life of this century.

Although late-nineteenth- and twentieth-century theater artists were aware of the many technical ways in which texts from the classic period were unlike those produced by their own contemporaries, they nevertheless seem to have sensed no radical cultural otherness in those classic texts. Certainly, for all their awareness of the difficulties of staging Molière's three-hundred-year-old plays, Antoine and Jouvet both felt that they shared with Molière in a common culture. Dort suggests, however, that shortly after World War II the theater's relationship to the classic entered a third phase, as theater artists began to recognize the extent to which those classical texts were products of a theater and a culture quite different and far removed from their own. From this estranged perspective on the classic text, directors began to develop new interpretive strategies that have a great deal in common with the strategies of philosophers and literary theorists engaged in modernist and postmodernist critiques of representation.

In "Le Jeu des classiques: réécriture ou musée?" Anne Ubersfeld focuses on this third phase of the theater's response to the question of staging the classic text. For the purposes of her essay, she defines a classic as a text that was "not written for us" and needs to be "adapted for our ears" (181).[18] Ubersfeld investigates the choice of interpretive strategies available to contemporary directors living in this third phase. She distinguishes two different ways of reading and interpreting the classic text: the director (and the scholar too) can either read the text in the conventional manner (*lire*) or disturb those conventions (*délire*) (182). (Ubersfeld's distinction between *lire* and *délire* recalls Barthes's distinction between work and text: we read a work [*lire*] whereas we "play" with a text [*délire*].) Reading in the traditional manner (*lire*), according to Ubersfeld, implies a reliance on a set of ideologically determined assumptions rooted in a bourgeois appropriation of the cultural production of the Grand Siècle, an appropriation, she points out, that was initiated by Voltaire in his *Siècle de Louis XIV*. Ubersfeld enumerates these assumptions:

> 1) The classics are eternal because they speak to us about the unchanging nature of human passions and human character; 2) their truth is of a psychological nature, a psychology that is concerned with individuals, or more exactly, autonomous subjects; 3) their beauty stems from their formal perfection, [making them] absolute models, a universal system of reference. (181)

The productions discussed in subsequent chapters offer particularly fruitful examples of directors wrestling with these assumptions.

Reading in the traditional manner inevitably raises what Dort calls the question of the "impossible fidelity" of the mise en scène, as such a reading assumes that there is indeed something to which the mise en scène must be faithful. Each of the directors whose work is discussed in the following chapters believed that he was being faithful to Molière. As we shall see, however, both "fidelity" and "Molière" mean something quite different in each case. Though each director claimed a certain degree of authenticity in his interpretation, he in fact staged his own ideas about the text and its sociohistorical or cultural context. Indeed, following Dort and Ubersfeld, I shall be arguing that the director can only stage ideas *about* the classic text. Rather than investigate how closely individual directors hew to Molière's intentions, I shall be looking at how the directors have adapted Molière's classic text to their own needs as twentieth-century theater artists.

New Scenographies for Old: Recoding Molière

In their discussions of the various strategies directors have employed for dealing with the "otherness" of the classic text, Dort and Ubersfeld display a clear preference for what they call "historicization" (a concept borrowed from Brecht). For Dort, the key element of a historicization consists in making the classic text's historically determined difference the "center of gravity" of the contemporary mise en scène:

> While respecting the letter of the work, it is a matter of reinserting it in its historical and social context, and of restoring, to the stage and for today's audience, that unity created by the staging. It is not a matter of attempting, as Antoine did a little naïvely, to reconstitute "the performance of the Cid in 1637" on the stage of the Odéon, but of performing both the play and the distance that separates us from it and from the society from which it emerged and which it reflects in its own manner—indeed, to make of that distance the center of gravity of the performance. ("Un Age d'or" 1012)

Each of the mises en scène discussed in the following chapters reveals just such a self-conscious attempt at a reconstitution that reflects the director's own vision of Molière's period and/or the status of the Grand Siècle in twentieth-century French culture.

Ubersfeld, for her part, discusses historicization in a more explicitly semiotic manner. She suggests that the director's primary responsibility in staging a play that "was not written for us" is to translate what she calls the "scripted unspoken" (*non-dit textuel*) of the earlier period into its contemporary equivalent. The director is thus faced with a semiotic problem of considerable magnitude. But the problem is even more complicated, for, as Ubersfeld points out, the classic text has itself acquired with the passage of time a range of connotations that have to do with its status as a cultural object:

> The director's task is to find an equivalent for connotations that have become evanescent. . . . The twentieth-century spectator imposes on

the text connotations that are those of his own personal culture—not to mention connotations that originate from his cultural relationship with the object itself. The classic [text], read "in class," imposes connotations of its "imaginary" monumentality. ("Le Jeu des classiques" 183)

Ubersfeld is not, however, as her examples will clarify, proposing that we see the director as a kind of supertranslator who can master the cultural and theatrical codes of two distinct historical periods and, through the medium of mise en scène, convey a cultural "message" of some complexity across history. Like Dort, she believes that directors can best deal with the "scripted unspoken" by introducing what she calls "a mimetic frame" into the mise en scène.

As examples of what she considers mimetic frames that effectively historicized some of Molière's classic texts, she cites Planchon's representations of Orgon's house and George Dandin's farm. In his celebrated 1960s production of *George Dandin*, Planchon showed the farm workers toiling in Dandin's farmyard during the action of the play. He thus juxtaposed the behavior of the Dandins and their in-laws with the spectacle of their workers sweating at their labor. Although Planchon's scenography provides a historically accurate rendering of life in a seventeenth-century farmyard, Molière's text makes no reference to Dandin's employees working in the farmyard, nor did Molière's own mise en scène attempt to recreate Dandin's "real-life" environment onstage. But Planchon did not feel obliged to restrict himself to representing only what was explicitly mentioned in Molière's text. In fact, he chose to stage what Molière's text remained completely silent about, to frame Molière's text in a way that would have been quite literally unimaginable in Molière's theater. Planchon elected to juxtapose a theatrical fable with a scenographic evocation of a historical reality; he elected to historicize. In doing so, Planchon made Molière's text signify in a new way. By framing Molière's comic action with images of backbreaking physical labor, Planchon used Molière's play to draw our attention to aspects of life in the Grand Siècle that Molière's classic text never addressed.

Historicization is a means of encouraging the spectator to focus on the way in which the action is framed scenographically as much as on the action itself. It is achieved by creating scenic images that the spectator will recognize as representing something other than the location of the events of the play in the conventional realist manner. In other words, the spectator is encouraged to recognize that the scenography presents a narrative of its own. Planchon calls this scenographic narrative an *écriture scénique* (literally, "scenic writing"). The scenic writing, in Planchon's conception, is a narrative that does not illustrate or realize the play as those processes have traditionally been understood. Planchon developed his concept of *écriture scénique* in response to the experience of seeing Brecht's work with the Berliner Ensemble on their second visit to Paris in the 1950s.[19] Planchon writes:

> The lesson of Brecht is to have declared that a performance combines both dramatic writing and scenic writing; but the scenic writing—he was the first to say this and it seems to me to be very important—has an equal responsibility with the dramatic writing. In fact any movement on the stage, the choice of a color, a set, a costume, etc., involves a total responsibility. The scenic writing has a total responsibility in the same way as writing taken on its own: I mean the writing of a novel or a play. (Qtd. in Bradby and Williams 55)

Thus, in a historicized mise en scène, the spectator is not encouraged to locate the meaning of the play solely in the interactions of the playwright's characters or in the realism-based interactions of character and milieu; instead, the spectator is encouraged to investigate the possible significances of apparent discontinuities between the mise en scène and the classic text.

Chapter 2

André Antoine and Jacques Arnavon: Representing *Tartuffe*'s "True Milieu"

Tartuffe . . . is a play that will remain forever modern. It could be performed in contemporary clothing; we will do better than that: we will set it in its true milieu.

—André Antoine

André Antoine: "Essai de mise en scène"

André Antoine is remembered today as the creator of the Théâtre Libre, where, with a small group of amateur collaborators, he pioneered realistic techniques of acting and scenography that continued to influence the development of mise en scène in France and elsewhere for decades. Antoine's career did not end, however, with the Théâtre Libre: in fact, he continued to work for almost another fifty years. After leaving the Théâtre Libre, Antoine went on to found the Théâtre Antoine. He subsequently served twice as artistic director of the Théâtre National de l'Odéon.[1] After resigning his second artistic directorship at the Odéon (1906–14), he went on to direct a number of films and to write a history of modern French theater as well as influential theater criticism for a number of publications.

During the brief lifetime of the Théâtre Libre, Antoine was most frequently identified as the leading advocate of the Naturalist dramatists, although in his capacity as artistic director he provided a stage for new writing of all kinds by both French and foreign playwrights. The Théâtre Libre presented nonrealist, poetic drama as well as realist and naturalist drama. The majority of theater historians, however, even those especially interested in directing, have concentrated on his experiments with realist mise en scène at the Théâtre Libre and neglected to study a major portion of his career. Edward Braun's *The Director and the Stage,* to mention one standard English-language history of directing, devotes only one seven-

25

line paragraph to Antoine's work after the closing of the Théâtre Libre (35). As a result, historians such as Braun have perpetuated the practice of identifying Antoine as a Naturalist.[2]

Theater historians have preferred to see Antoine as, first and foremost, a director of modern plays by realist or Naturalist dramatists. Although Antoine produced only new plays at the Théâtre Libre, he abandoned this practice when he took over the Théâtre Antoine. Later, at the Odéon, he devoted his energies almost exclusively to the classics. Yet Brockett and Findlay's encyclopedic *Century of Innovation* contains only a single paragraph on Antoine's work with classic texts (199–200).[3] The authors note that Antoine proposed that seventeenth-century plays be set in the seventeenth century and not in the supposed time period of the play's action. As an example, they cite Antoine's 1907 production of *The Cid,* which took the form of a reconstruction of a seventeenth-century performance at the Théâtre du Marais, in which spectators were seated onstage and costumed in the manner of wealthy French spectators of the period. They go on in the next paragraph to criticize Antoine's experiments as "another form of antiquarianism," thus suggesting that the production should be understood as yet another example of the excesses of naturalism.

Antoine's production of *The Cid* has often been ridiculed in precisely this manner by those who prefer to see Antoine as a Naturalist rather than as an innovative director of the classics, although some of the most respected directors of this century have found Antoine's experiment worth repeating. Maurice Béjart, for example, placed a "seventeenth-century" audience onstage at the Comédie-Française for *Les Plaisirs de l'île enchantée,* which included a version of *Tartuffe* (Holmberg). Patrice Chéreau's production of *Dom Juan* (1969) and Roger Planchon's paired productions of *Dom Juan* and Racine's *Athalie* (1980) not only incorporated a number of onstage spectators but also revealed the workings of period scenography. Indeed, what some have dismissed as Antoine's "antiquarianism" can be seen as the indispensable precursor to Planchon's deconstruction of the Grand Siècle in *Tartuffe* and Antoine Vitez's archaeological project that spanned a series of productions, culminating in his 1978 Molière tetralogy.

In an important essay, "Antoine le patron," Bernard Dort offers a reconsideration of Antoine's legacy that is particularly valuable as a corrective to the orthodox versions of French theater history that pigeonhole Antoine as a Naturalist. Most twentieth-century theater historians, adopting the dominant antinaturalist (even antirealist) values of their times, see Copeau as the director who revolutionized the staging of classic texts during his brief career at the Théâtre du Vieux-Colombier. But Dort disagrees with this view and asserts that "we must not seek a common denominator for the most ambitious experiments of contemporary theater in the stylization of Copeau . . . we must look for it in the realism of Antoine" (301). Dort, an early champion of Brecht in France in the 1950s, found in Antoine's work at the Odéon the beginnings of a different tradition:

> Although his early work had been grounded in a naturalist orthodoxy, Antoine rapidly freed himself [from those influences] and it was, without a doubt, at the Odéon, from 1906 to 1910, that he completed the most significant and the least well-known portion of his work. Was he not the first director to experiment with the classics in a systematic manner and to restore them to us, not under the auspices of a fallacious eternity, but inscribed in a specific society, comprehended through the history of their time such as we are able to imagine it today? Some of his notes, some of his suggestions regarding *Tartuffe*, for example, anticipate Jouvet's mise en scène (which was condemned almost unanimously by the critics at the time), even Planchon's. (300)

Antoine never saw or presented himself as a doctrinaire Naturalist, and his experiments with mise en scène ranged far beyond the domain of Naturalist dramaturgy. Antoine was the first director in France to stage an uncut text of a play by Shakespeare (*King Lear*, 1904), just as he was the first to restore the traditionally excised passages of plays by Corneille, Racine, and Molière. Indeed, Antoine's staging of *King Lear* at the Théâtre Antoine broke with the Romantic tradition of nineteenth-century Shakespearian mise en scène by dispensing with the elaborate "realistic" scenography that necessitated lengthy set changes and a number of intermissions (Sanders, *André Antoine* 78). His fast-paced and simplified staging of this play even earned a favorable comment from Copeau, whose "*tréteau nu*" aesthetic is usually defined as the opposite of Antoine's (Sanders, *André Antoine* 76). Antoine was also the first modern director to restore the ballets to Molière's *comédies-ballets*. While it is not difficult to see the ways in which Antoine's experiments with scenic realism informed his work with classic texts, it is almost impossible to discern a

Naturalist agenda in these productions. Pigeonholing Antoine as a man devoted to Naturalism makes a productive understanding of his work—and the ways in which that work influenced other artists—almost impossible. As Denis Bablet reminds us: "Antoine is not the servant of a theory set in stone; he is the proponent of a theatrical politics that implies a moral attitude, an orientation of the repertoire, a particular way of thinking about working on the stage" (13).

What I want to emphasize here are the dangers of looking at Antoine's work from too narrow a perspective. Antoine's influence on the staging of classic texts stems not from his application of a narrowly focused interest in scenic realism but, as Bablet suggests, from his engagement in a significantly more broadly conceived cultural politics. I do not mean to imply that Antoine did not apply what he had learned from his experiments with realist and naturalist mise en scène to his work with classic texts. On the contrary, he was able to approach the classic repertoire in a new and productive manner precisely by applying the theories and practices of modern scenic realism as he had come to understand them.

On October 31, 1907, in the second year of his tenure as artistic director of the Théâtre de l'Odéon, André Antoine staged a production of *Tartuffe* that used, for the first time, four different realistic settings instead of the conventional single décor: a garden for act 1, a ground floor salon for acts 2–3, a small salon-boudoir for act 4, and a vestibule (*galerie*) for act 5. The garden was made to look like a Louis XIV restoration of a Louis XIII design, and the furniture was a mixture of both Louis XIII and Louis XIV, although the house itself was decorated in a pure Louis XIV manner (Sanders, "*Le Tartuffe* d'Antoine" 587). Half a century later, Roger Planchon was to explore this same motif of restoration with striking results.

The theater program for this Thursday afternoon *matinée classique* characterized the production as "an experiment in mise en scène" (*un essai de mise en scène*), an experiment that Edmond Stoullig felt "ought to generate a revolution in the staging of our classic dramas" (186). While some critics agreed with Stoullig, many were offended by Antoine's breaking with the traditional norms of staging. Predictably, the traditionalists condemned what the "moderns" applauded.

When Stoullig published his account of this production in *Les Annales du théâtre et de la musique, 1907*, the *Annales* were in their thirty-third year of publication. In that time, he had seen and written accounts of literally hundreds of productions of both new and classic plays, but no mise en scène of a classic made such a profound impression on him. He describes few productions in so much detail; indeed, he gives most productions no more than a single brief paragraph. Stoullig represents the spectator that Antoine must have wished for, an individual with sufficient knowledge of the theater and its history to appreciate what was different in this staging:

> The first act takes place in Orgon's garden. On the right an attractive house. . . . Upstage, iron railings through which can be seen the road and, farther away, houses spread out on a hillside. The changing hues of an intensely romantic sunset make it difficult to situate the bourgeois action of *Tartuffe* in a modest quarter of Paris. . . . A vast ground-floor parlor provides a frame for the 2nd and 3rd acts. . . . Paintings from the period, comfortable chairs . . . that one would not be afraid to sit in, . . . the frequent use of doors that will make entrances and exits seem realistic—notably two large doors with glass through which appears quite clearly the antechamber, a vestibule, and a staircase that we will see used—all of this gives an impression of real life being lived. Tartuffe will make his celebrated entrance through the antechamber. . . .

> For the 4th act, the traditional single setting makes Tartuffe's audacity seem extremely unrealistic, as he prepares to make love with Elmire then and there, taking no precautions beyond having a quick look around the adjoining room. Antoine shows us a kind of private salon. No doubt people still come into this room without knocking, but because it has something of the boudoir about it . . . it no longer suggests a busy part of the house with people frequently passing through—the heavy drapes and discreet divan might even encourage the nefarious aspirations of the hypocrite. And I could make a similar argument in favor of the scenic advantages of the ground-floor room where the reversals of the 5th act unfold. You have already guessed the objection to all of that. "None of that ever entered Molière's thoughts!" In his time, all attempts at realism were doomed to run up against an insurmountable obstacle: the members of the aristocracy were entitled to seat themselves on the stage. . . . All of the "conventions" that the old state of affairs imposed or authorized in Molière's time are emphasized by Antoine's interpretation. What exactly is the familial or domestic status, for example, of Dorine,

who criticizes Mme Pernelle, Orgon, and Marianne so brusquely? Chambermaid? Cook? Wet nurse? The more this bourgeois life is given to us in detail, the harder it is for us to locate the normal place for such a sermonizing and moralizing servant. The role [of Dorine] is certainly a juicy one; but the character appears in the new version to be what it never seemed in the old: totally artificial. Of course you will also guess how, under Antoine's guidance, the actors' movements will develop in this transformed frame, this atmosphere of living reality. From this moment on, a host of absurd traditions have been rendered obsolete. (186–89)

Although he greatly admires Antoine's achievements in this production, Stoullig shows a swift understanding of the semiotic problems inherent in a mise en scène that seeks to recreate a classic play in today's terms. Dorine, for example, as Stoullig correctly points us, functions extremely well as a character in terms of seventeenth-century dramaturgy and scenography and less so in terms of their twentieth-century counterparts. Once the traditional conventions of performance have been challenged successfully, as they were by Antoine, the problems of reconciling the practices of the modern and contemporary theater with Molière's dramaturgy must be addressed. Indeed, it is precisely by solving those problems in unexpectedly resonant ways that the most influential directors of this century have made their marks.

During his nine years as artistic director of France's second national theater, Antoine continued his experiments with classic texts, which invariably met with a similarly polarized critical response. The revolution that Stoullig anticipated did not occur, although Antoine's innovations were gradually assimilated. Today nobody is surprised when a theater creates a new scenography for a revival of *Tartuffe* or another classic text, or when a director attempts to recreate the colors, lines, and textures of Orgon's house in the Paris of the mid-1660s. We take for granted that environment may shed light on character, even if we no longer accept the scientific validity of such a linkage in quite the same way as the nineteenth-century Realists and Naturalists did.

Jacques Arnavon: Reading Molière in the Theater

When Antoine assumed the leadership of the Odéon in 1906, Jacques Arnavon was a young career diplomat with no previous experience of working in the professional theater. In 1907, in the first of what would become a series of books on Molière, he began to describe what he hoped would become the accepted modern mode of staging Molière, a realistic staging that would employ the technologies of modern mise en scène to create a more complete illusion of the real than could be found in the tradition-bound, conventional stagings of the Comédie-Française.[4] Arnavon sent this proposal for a realistic mise en scène to Antoine. Arnavon chose his director wisely, for Antoine was indeed looking for a new way of staging the classics. Antoine had begun to work with the classics during his tenure at the Théâtre Antoine, where he had staged an innovative *King Lear* and even rehearsed *Tartuffe* for a time during the 1904–5 season before postponing the production. Antoine's son, André-Paul, relates that during the years at the Théâtre Antoine, his father dreamed of modernizing the staging of the classic repertory (*Antoine, père et fils* 100). With his appointment to the Odéon in 1906, Antoine was given the opportunity to realize that dream. In 1907, Arnavon approached him with some ideas about how the staging of Molière might be modernized. Antoine responded enthusiastically to Arnavon's suggestions for a "rational" mise en scène of *Tartuffe* and produced a mise en scène based on Arnavon's ideas a month after he read the proposal.[5]

By the time he took over the Odéon in 1906, Antoine's realism was considerably less controversial than it had been when he opened the Théâtre Libre in 1887. In 1907, realist theater was no longer regarded as a challenge to the established theater; indeed, it had lost its experimental, avant-garde aura and had been assimilated into the cultural mainstream for some time already. There was nothing revolutionary, therefore, about a realist mise en scène in itself; what was revolutionary about the Antoine/Arnavon *Tartuffe* was the application of the techniques of realist mise en scène to the staging of a classic text. Antoine never intended that his work with classic texts should be interpreted as an assault on mainstream culture of the kind enacted by the Théâtre Libre. Indeed, Antoine's appointment as artistic director of France's second national theater was an emphatic sign of approval from the conservative government of the time.

Antoine was conscious of his desire to present the classical repertoire in a modern fashion without, at the same time, permitting the modernity of his approach to appear as the mark of a certain disrespect: "When I was appointed to the Odéon, I staged the classics, not with puppets or statues, but with living, palpitating beings, without stripping them of their grandeur or weighing them down with degrading realities in the process" (qtd.

in Sanders, *André Antoine* 187). Antoine's recognition of the "grandeur" of classic characters and his simultaneous refusal to represent them as being burdened by "degrading realities" both demonstrates his respect for his cultural heritage and the inappropriateness of too closely identifying his work on the classics with his earlier work in the Naturalist theater.

Arnavon fully shared Antoine's sense of the grandeur of French classic dramaturgy and proposed a realistic staging of the classic repertoire because, in his view, such a staging would have the advantages of modernity and familiarity, with the familiarity ensuring intelligibility. Arnavon's realistic model strategically circumvented many of the convulsive changes in the arts that were provoked by the Modernist revolution; no doubt the disruptive formal experiments of early Modernism (which, ironically, included Antoine's early Naturalist productions) appeared quite unsuited to Arnavon as an ideal vehicle for celebrating what he considered the accumulated wisdom of the national culture and for communicating that wisdom to the modern theatergoing public. For Arnavon, the already fully assimilated conventions of late nineteenth-century scenic realism provided the fullest, most truthful (and least tendentious) representation of the world as he believed it to be and to have been. Ironically, Arnavon was proposing as a vehicle for transmitting the core values of the national cultural patrimony the very same kind of mise en scène that had horrified the members of his parents' generation.

Antoine was enthusiastic about the possibilities for staging many of the play's familiar events in startling new ways that the scenography suggested by Arnavon offered:

First, the garden for Orgon's entrance and Mme Pernelle's exit. Then, the formal salon, from which we can see the great staircase that Tartuffe will descend in the third act. Tartuffe's entry, so admirably prepared by Molière during two acts, will be so much more impressive when it is accentuated by the fake holy man coming down the stairs! First we see the feet, then the body, then the head. And after reaching the bottom, he will say, no longer to the fireman on duty [in the wings], but to Laurent, . . . "store my hairshirt with my whip." In the fourth act, Elmire's boudoir, the tempting sofa, and the table, no longer crudely prepared to hide Orgon, but in its natural place. Finally, in the fifth act, the entrance of the Exempt and soldiers filling the gallery, painted by Ronsin—that will make quite an impression! (Qtd. in Genty 106–7)

Antoine's enthusiasm in this passage should not be seen as enthusiasm for visual effects alone. What excites him is, in fact, the possibility of seeing *Tartuffe* as if it were a modern play, a play conceived, like the melodramas and realistic dramas of the previous century, in both verbal and visual terms. Antoine's enthusiasm is a response not only to new scenographic possibilities for *Tartuffe* but also to a new understanding of the play's dramaturgy, for in the new setting, as Arnavon persuaded him, a "new," modern play begins to emerge.

Although the association with Antoine, one of the most respected directors in the world, validated his ideas by demonstrating their viability in performance, Arnavon was not entirely satisfied with Antoine's reading of the play. He was dissatisfied because Antoine had accepted the argument that Molière's play should be staged in a number of realistic settings but had not, in Arnavon's view, taken the next logical step and given characterization and acting style a similarly realistic treatment: Antoine had merely created the scenic representation of a realistic milieu for an otherwise conventional mise en scène. Arnavon disagreed with Antoine's interpretation of the play as a "portrait of a charming family, with gracious characters and noble passions" because it merely echoed the conventional interpretations of the play at the Comédie-Française (Sanders, *André Antoine* 160). Yet, as Sanders points out, many critics at the time responded as if Antoine had, in fact, staged a radical new reading of the play. Sanders is undoubtedly correct when he ascribes this perception on the part of the critics to the overwhelming effect of Antoine's new multiple décors, a scenography that represented a radical break with a tradition that had remained intact for two and a half centuries. Apart from the radical experiment with décor, however, the production offered no noteworthy innovations in the interpretation of Molière's characters.[6]

Two years later, in 1909, Arnavon published a revised version of the proposal he had sent Antoine under the title *Tartuffe: la mise en scène rationnelle et la tradition*. Although the published version of Arnavon's notebook mise en scène was, in some important ways, quite different from Antoine's mise en scène, there is no evidence to suggest that the two men quarreled or that the 1909 book represented a rejection of Antoine's work. On the contrary, numerous letters attest to Arnavon's unwavering support and enthusiasm for Antoine's work, especially with plays by Molière. Consequently, Arnavon's book offers us an opportunity rare in theater history as it provides a detailed presentation of the ideas, both literary and theatrical, that gave birth to a new way of staging Molière's *Tartuffe*.

Like Arnavon's other books on Molière, *Tartuffe: la mise en scène rationnelle et la tradition* challenges the traditional interpretations and stagings in the repertory of the Comédie-Française on the grounds that they represent a false tradition that does not, contrary to popular myth, descend in an unbroken line from Molière himself. In place of the "corrupt" readings and stagings of the tradition, Arnavon offers his own proposals for a modern mise en scène that would, he confidently asserts, be embraced by Molière himself if he were alive.

Arnavon's critiques and proposals are remarkable for their attention to detail. Indeed, his notebook productions are so meticulously described that they can be staged with very few adjustments. This is possible because Arnavon "sees" Molière's characters in very specific environments, wearing historically accurate clothing, and behaving in a manner consonant with those environments and those garments. For Arnavon, as for the Realists and Naturalists of the preceding century, milieu is a more or less determining factor in human behavior. While he was acutely conscious of the degree to which all aspects of interpretation and staging are interdependent, and while he was careful to consider the question of décor in context, he nevertheless privileged scenography and devoted a large percentage of his analysis of *Tartuffe* and other plays to investigating all of its aspects.

Antoine shared Arnavon's perception of the importance of scenography and, unlike other theater artists of the time, designed the set before developing the blocking with his actors. As he put it in his "Causerie sur la mise en scène": "It is the milieu that determines the blocking of the characters and not the blocking of the characters that determines the milieu" (qtd. in Bablet 15). It was with the scenography of his 1907 mise en scène that Antoine made his most significant contribution to the scenic interpretation of *Tartuffe*.

A Critique of Traditions: Molière Our Contemporary?

Throughout *Tartuffe: la mise en scène rationnelle et la tradition*, Arnavon attacked both directors and actors for distorting Molière's "intentions" in the name of what he himself considered a corrupt tradition. But he was reluctant to attack the Comédie-Française explicitly as the established guardians of that tradition. In later years, however, when he himself had become part of the French literary establishment (two of his books were awarded prizes by the Académie Française), he openly criticized the

Comédie-Française in such books as *Notes sur l'interprétation de Molière*.[7] He was particularly irritated by the Comédie-Française's observance of what he felt was the ridiculous principle of unity of décor (and its corollary, unity of costume), a practice that resulted, for instance, in what he saw as an "irrational" mise en scène for the tercentenary production of *Tartuffe* in 1922. Arnavon called the 1922 production "irrational" because it employed a single décor and failed to follow the example of the "rational" scenography provided by Antoine's production of 1907.[8] Arnavon was not entirely unhappy, however, with the tercentenary season, as the Comédie-Française produced new mises en scène of all of Molière's plays that were not in the repertory at that time, and these new productions dispensed with many of the traditional acting techniques that disturbed Arnavon.

In Arnavon's view, the Comédie-Française was turning its back on three centuries of theatrical progress by ignoring twentieth-century mise en scène in favor of the obviously antiquated conventions supposedly inherited from the seventeenth century. Arnavon was determined to stage Molière's plays as he believed Molière would have done had he been alive in the early 1900s. *Tartuffe: la mise en scène rationnelle et la tradition* is, as the book's subtitle implies, both a critique of the established tradition and a reasoned proposal for what ought to replace that tradition. Arnavon attacks the tradition with respect to *Tartuffe* on several specific grounds: (1) it lacks integrity; (2) it offers the public a dull and boring simulacrum of outdated acting techniques that do not accurately reflect either seventeenth- or twentieth-century behavior; (3) it is not faithful to Molière's intentions as reflected in the text; (4) it sets the play in a "ridiculous" décor; (5) it violates the integrity of the text by cutting some lines in performance; and (6) it performs the play on the same bill as other "inferior" works, thereby ignoring what Arnavon takes to be its proper status as a classic of French literature. Arnavon complains, for example, that *Tartuffe* is being slighted by being programmed as only part of an evening's entertainment when other plays (such as those of Victor Hugo) are presented on their own. In his opinion, such programming has a detrimental effect on the reception of the play because it emphasizes the purely theatrical, entertaining aspects of the play at the expense of its pedagogic value as a major element of the national cultural heritage. Including a full-length play such as *Tartuffe* as part of a long evening's entertainment, Arnavon argues, encourages actors to rush through the play, with the result that the audience cannot adequately appreciate the playwright's thought: "What kind of attention can the actors bring to a work thus sacrificed in advance?" (*Tartuffe* 15).

Arnavon attacks the tradition by challenging the methods employed to teach actors how to play roles from the classical repertoire. He questions the value of copying the manner in which an earlier generation of actors performed their roles, particularly when the interpretations of that earlier generation do not derive from Molière's original production but are themselves the result of almost three centuries of the accretion of actors' "bits." Consequently, he argues, the actors at the Comédie-Française cannot be said to be playing Molière's characters at all since their performances derive not from the script but from other actors' imitations of (and improvements on) the performances of their predecessors (*Notes* 1–6).

In addition to criticizing the tradition's reliance on the handing down of interpretations and bits of stage business from master to apprentice, Arnavon criticizes its lack of respect for Molière's script, which he sees as the only authentic trace of Molière's "intentions." For Arnavon, Molière's script should take precedence over any traditions of performance: "All theories of mise en scène, especially where classical comedy is concerned, should take the text as their foundation and obey it" (*Notes* 45). He cites, for example, the habit of playing Orgon clean shaven although the script refers to the character's large beard, the habit of playing Tartuffe as a *neurasthénique* although he is described as "gros et gras" (big and fat), and the habit of setting the play in an enormous interior when the script speaks of a "salle basse" (ground-floor room, usually small) (*Tartuffe* 74; *Notes* 6–7; *Molière* 168). Since the tradition reveals a blatant disregard for the details of Molière's script, and since the tradition is itself suspect, Arnavon proposes that it be abandoned in favor of a new kind of mise en scène:

> Faced with a work from the classical theater that has, by virtue of its perfection, the right to be revived on the modern stage, two positions, and only two, are reasonable. You can either reconstruct with precision and in minute detail the first performance, the *première* of that faraway epoch; or you can start from scratch in staging the play and, having set aside all of the uninteresting stage traditions, take as your sole guides the text, logic and good sense, and the history of manners. (*Tartuffe* 8)

This new mise en scène will be grounded in three principles: a close reading of the script; logic and "good sense" (*le bon sens*); and the history of manners.[9]

Arnavon's decision to accept both his own historical moment and the most advanced theatrical practices of his own time as the principal frames of reference for a new mise en scène, a new reading of the play, is a landmark in theater criticism. He is the first French critic to show *how* a classic might be staged using contemporary staging conventions; he is also the first to mount a sustained challenge to the mythic status of the Comédie-Française, a "living museum" in which the classics were, at that time, "preserved" by a system of passing on interpretations from one generation to the next. As Arnavon observes, however, employing modern staging conventions involves finding equivalents for those implied in Molière's script, a difficult enterprise, since the theater itself has undergone so many changes in three centuries: "Molière never had the slightest idea of mise en scène as we conceive of it, with furniture on the stage, characters constantly moving to illustrate the text, changes of scenery—replicating reality as closely as possible" (*Notes* 8).

While Arnavon distrusts traditional methods of staging Molière's plays and wants to replace them with a more realistic and contemporary alternative, he values the humanist tradition of interpreting the plays. He argues that a fully satisfying mise en scène should incorporate the wealth of commentary that has contributed to our sense of "who" Molière's characters are and "what" the play itself is:

> The works of Molière, like so many from which the world has drawn nourishment for centuries, have acquired a life independent of him, a very clearly defined and indomitable sort of personality. . . . This undefinable ensemble of thoughts and feelings . . . all of those human desires that we apprehend through intuition rather than through reason have, over time, been subsumed into each of the plays, assuring each a kind of life of its own. (*Notes* 10–11)

Somewhat paradoxically, then, Arnavon finds that in attempting to honor the author's intentions as he finds them in the script, he is obliged to incorporate information from the accumulated tradition of interpretations and commentaries on that script:

> It must be performed in a spirit of absolute fidelity to his writings, that is to say, to the several meanings of his text: the meaning that reveals itself or hides itself, the meaning that we glimpse only on occasion—meanings that succeeding generations have often discovered and that the author had not suspected. All of these meanings are fixed forever, layer upon layer like the siltings of glory, in this volcanic stone. This fidelity to a tradition that is of unimpeachable purity calls for a perfect harmony of décor, movement, lighting, costume—a total fusion of the multiple elements of theatrical performance. (*Notes* 37–38)

Curiously, Arnavon neglects to subject this other tradition, the tradition of humanist commentary, to the same rigorous questioning as the staging tradition. He uncritically describes the interpretive tradition as being "unimpeachably pure," free of the kind of innovations introduced by a series of star actors, and concludes that a faithful and realistic mise en scène should reflect this hypothetical purity by presenting onstage an image of complete harmony to echo the complete harmony that Arnavon finds between the play and its generations of commentators.

While Arnavon's books undertake a sustained critique of the conventional stagings of Molière's plays at the Comédie-Française, they accept without question the traditional nineteenth-century vision of Molière as the culture's preeminent *moraliste*.[10] The image of Molière that emerges from Arnavon's books is reminiscent of that propagated by Désiré Nisard, who suggested in 1844 that the characters and events of Molière's dramas offer valuable lessons because they so closely reflect Nisard's own sense of the "real": "These are our ways, our family crises, our setbacks, this is us" (qtd. in Albanese, "Molière Myth" 241).

Déjà Vu: Realism and the Cultural Heritage

In Arnavon's opinion, the traditional stagings of *Tartuffe,* such as those in the repertory of the Comédie-Française, failed to reflect the play's true nature because they were themselves the result of a failure to appreciate its significance as a classic; rather, they reflected the play's importance as a vehicle for virtuoso acting (thus, the Comédie-Française's respect for the tradition of performance in which roles were handed down from generation to generation) instead of its importance as a pivotal humanist text of the seventeenth century. Arnavon would have preferred a national theater that devoted its energies to preserving the culture's literary heritage. He believed that a realistic *Tartuffe* would offer his audience a coherent and compelling picture of seventeenth-century Paris and that the evident authenticity of the representation would in turn facilitate and promote an appreciation of the play's humanistic qualities: "The value of a rational mise en scène consists precisely in permitting the uneducated spectator (*auditeur non lettré*) to escape the present for a time in order to take part in the story, to care about and put himself body and soul into the person of an inhabitant of Paris in 1664" (*Tartuffe* 37). In opting for the modern *vraisemblance* of a realist mise en scène, Arnavon hoped to foreground the play's humanistic, literary values by removing the barrier of Molière's "outdated" stagecraft.

A realistic production of *Tartuffe* allows the audience, Arnavon believes, to behold the events of an evening in Paris in the 1660s, not as it was but as it must have been. His stage is not a window on the world; his proscenium does not mark the simultaneous presence and absence of a fourth wall. Rather, his stage is a picture framed by a proscenium, his mise en scène a succession of *tableaux vivants* populated by actors who by their art "bring to life" a number of personalities from Molière's life and times. Painting provides Arnavon's visual reference of choice: the composition and color palette of his scenery as well as the blocking patterns he describes (movement from one pictorial composition to another) either explicitly refer to paintings (he frequently cites Abraham Bosse) or implicitly suggest the influence of painters such as Courbet and Manet. A typical remark shows Arnavon invoking a painterly aesthetic:

> The adoption of these new set designs [his own], enriched of course by every means that the contemporary theatre habitually uses to hold the spectator's attention and produce emotion (lighting effects, set decoration, the use of color, etc., etc.), is subject to one condition: respect for the text. The mise en scène should at no time exceed its role, which is to set off the tableau. What would people think of a frame that attracted so much attention that it made the coloring of the painting seem dull? (*Tartuffe* 14)

Molière's character portraits exist, for Arnavon, in the collective memory of the French public, merely waiting for a talented actor to lend them his or her body and voice. They are real in the sense that they are already known, *vraisemblable,* or "real-like," because they are recognizable elements of an acquired culture. They are as familiar and as real as the gardens of Versailles, Notre Dame, and the Musée du Louvre; as familiar and as real as the characters of Balzac, Dumas, and Zola. Transplanted from the conventions of the representation of reality in seventeenth-century Paris to the conventions of the latter half of nineteenth-century Paris, these already real characters come to life once again in a contemporary reality, a leap across the centuries that defies the gravity of time and unifies the field of French culture by making the product of another period seem homogeneous with the products of today—thus the title of his book, *Molière, notre contemporain.*[11]

Realist Décor and the Psychology of Scenic Space

Reading Molière's script from the perspective of early twentieth-century realist scenography, Arnavon identifies a need for three different décors: a garden for Molière's act 1, an interior view of the house that reveals other rooms offstage for acts 2–4, and a large *galerie,* or formal hall, for act 5. Bringing Molière's play into line with modern scenographic practice results in a break with the tradition of observing the unity-of-place rule and its unwritten corollary, the rule of unity of décor. At the same time, and without drawing attention to the fact, he performs a more subtle adaptation, for the mere presence of the new décors has the effect of converting Molière's neoclassical five-act structure into the three-act structure favored by late nineteenth-century dramatists, even though Arnavon still respects Molière's designated act breaks. Arnavon thus brings into play three different kinds of realism. Before investigating those realisms, a description of his proposed scenography is in order.

For the first act of this three-act *Tartuffe* Arnavon suggests the following:

> The stage will represent . . . a large, very deep garden in front of Orgon's mansion. . . . In the middle, an old tree . . . will give shade to a wide stone bench. . . . On the right, a perron. This perron includes a balustraded terrace with climbing plants. . . . Facing the audience, a flight of stairs with ten or twelve steps descends to the garden. At the back, a fairly low wall covered with climbing plants. . . . At the back and on the left [he is describing the setting from the audience's point of view] is the gate seen in three-quarter profile. Fine Louis XIV forged ironwork. . . . To the left, hedges

concealing the street wall. A fountain with basin mounted on the wall. . . . The house . . . is in the grand Louis XIV style. (*Tartuffe* 27–28)

A salient feature of this description is that it is obviously not the description of a specific house that existed somewhere in Paris or its environs in the 1660s. It is, rather, recognizably a description of a décor, which goes a long way, perhaps, to explain Arnavon's degree of influence on Antoine: Arnavon communicated his ideas to Antoine in an already theatricalized fashion. Few scholars or critics have been able to claim such a direct influence on a production staged by a major director. One thinks of Jan Kott's influence on productions of Shakespeare or of Roland Barthes's influence on productions of Racine in the 1960s and 1970s. But neither Kott nor Barthes can claim, nor has anyone made such a claim on their behalf, that their written ideas were actually realized in a specific mise en scène to the extent that Arnavon's were in Antoine's *Tartuffe* of 1907.

Arnavon places his second act (Molière's acts 2–4) in the living room of Orgon's house. Again, his description of the room reveals a detailed scenographic imagination. Each detail is designed to provide information about the household and its inhabitants as well as to convince the spectators that they are looking at a historically accurate reconstruction:

In the back wall, which takes up no more than a third of the length of the stage, a wide-open plate-glass window reveals a garden landscape. On an oblique line, two large bays. . . . These bays contain doors with large panes of glass; swagged tapestries hang on the other side of these doors, but as they are raised very high during this act, they allow the large gallery to be seen. . . . A beautiful marble tile floor in two colors, busts, chairs, rich motifs on the walls: the Hall of Mirrors in miniature. This gallery contains the bottom of the great staircase that leads to the other floors of the house. . . . Chairs, armchairs, and a stool form an X. In the angle, on the right, a kind of rotunda. . . . This *loggia* [which will become Damis's hiding place in Molière's act 3] is separated from the stage by a sliding curtain, also a tapestry. The curtain is closed at the beginning of Act II. Towards the front, the classic table with its cover touching the floor. Near the table, at an angle, a beautiful, wide Louis XIV chaiselongue. . . . At the back, between the bay that leads to the staircase and the window, an open clavichord with a score by Lulli. In front of the window a loom with an unfinished piece of weaving. . . . On the walls, glass-covered collector's display cases. Armaments, ceramics, silverwork, silks, enamels. . . . The action takes place a few days after the first act. Acts II, III, and IV will thus be presumed to take place between nine o'clock in the morning and five o'clock in the afternoon approximately. (*Tartuffe* 110–14)

Arnavon's citation of the Hall of Mirrors (Salle des Glaces) at Versailles is, of course, an obvious anachronism, designed to provide the spectators with an instantly recognizable icon of the Grand Siècle. The emphasis on Orgon's acquisitiveness (he is presented as an avid collector, almost a character out of Balzac) may strike us, however, as a somewhat obvious and inelegant way of introducing period objects into the play. On the other hand, this same scenographic motif may be read as an implied (and perhaps unintended) criticism of Orgon's bourgeois morality. The ostentatious accumulation of objects that Arnavon imagines certainly provides an interesting point of comparison with the mises en scène of Planchon and Vitez, who offer us quite different visions of Orgon's house stripped bare.

Although Arnavon uses the same set for Molière's acts 2–4, he nevertheless makes small adjustments between acts 2 and 3 and again between acts 3 and 4. The first of these changes is barely perceptible and involves drawing the loggia curtain halfway to create a hiding place for Damis (*Tartuffe* 171). The second change is rather more obvious: Arnavon repositions the sofa so that it is almost parallel to the footlights and creates a more intimate, enclosed space by dropping the tapestries to close off the gallery and by closing the garden window (225).

Arnavon sets his third and final act (Molière's act 5) in the great *galérie-vestibule* with its red and white marble tile floor, allegorical paintings, tapestries, and the gilded mirrors that deliberately invoke the spectator's memories of the Hall of Mirrors at Versailles (*Tartuffe* 283–84). The garden provides an appropriate setting for the sequence of entrances and exits in the first act; the complex of interrelated interior spaces supplies the different locations needed during the middle three acts; and the large, formal gallery offers an appropriate frame for the fifth act, in which the family's troubles are presented in the context of society at large. Several decades later, Roger Planchon's mise en scène of the 1970s reveals a similar interpretation of the script's scenic requirements: Planchon employs a passageway for act 1, three different rooms for acts 2–4, and a large, open, "public" space for the final act.

In Arnavon's opinion, this modern realist scenography with its wealth of specific period detail will allow the twentieth-century spectator to take seriously elements of Molière's play that a conventional mise en scène will tend to obscure. His discussion of the Tartuffe/Elmire "seduction" scene in act 4 provides a good example of what he takes to be the benefits of the new kind of mise en scène. He begins with a critique of the traditional scenography, arguing that it works to undo any psychological realism in the portrayal of character (*Tartuffe* 108–10; 236–75). He first investigates the problem from the perspective of Tartuffe (whom he treats as an autonomous individual). Unless the scene takes place in a space where a clandestine sexual encounter is a real possibility, Arnavon argues, Tartuffe will suspect a trap. Then he shifts to consider the matter from the perspective of the spectator who, according to Arnavon, cannot be expected to accept that a potential for erotic contact exists if the scene is presented in a less realistic fashion than other "seductions" in boulevard entertainment (*Notes* 180–81). Finally, he suggests that the scene's importance in the play's moral structure (which he sees as an aspect of Molière's moral realism) will be substantially undermined if the audience is not made fully aware of the risk Elmire takes.

Arnavon thus brings into play three different kinds of realism, three different perspectives on the real, all of which he feels must harmonize in performance if the scene is to be both convincing and effective. The first kind of realism relates to the logic of the relationship between the dramatic action and the space in which that action occurs. Arnavon believes that an audience will not accept that Tartuffe can be tricked by the offer of a sexual encounter with Elmire in the too-public space of the traditional *salle basse*, especially after Damis's violent interruption of act 3. Therefore he suggests that a setting be designed to create a more intimate space so that the audience can accept Tartuffe's belief in a possible intimacy between himself and Elmire. The absence of such a suitably intimate setting would, in his opinion, prompt the audience to be skeptical of Tartuffe's acceptance of the possibility of "real" intimacy with Elmire. Arnavon's desire to help his audience learn the lessons of Molière's *morale* by providing appropriate visual images seems to have something in common with Elmire's conviction that her husband needs to see Tartuffe's improper behavior with his own eyes in order to be convinced. Arnavon, too, wants to convince his audience, but he is not satisfied with a mere acceptance of the "truth" of the dramatic fable; he wants his audience to appreciate the moral lesson represented in that fable. It is worth recalling here Arnavon's contention that a "rational" mise en scène will help the uneducated spectator enter imaginatively into the historical situation of the dramatic action, a notion that appears to echo the view of the theater as a "paupers' bible" that Strindberg expressed in his preface to *Miss Julie.*

Arnavon's second kind of realism springs from his belief in the influence of prevailing cultural norms on the formation of the spectator's sense of the real. According to Arnavon, an audience cannot be expected to take seriously a representation of erotic behavior that is obviously "artificial" or "fake" when compared with contemporary representations of similar behavior. Thus, when staging a love scene from a classic text, the director must, in Arnavon's view, employ contemporary aesthetic conventions if the scene is to be convincing. The argument that Arnavon made in 1909 has, in the course of the intervening decades, become an axiom of twentieth-century stage directing. In response to shifts in their own cultural environments, directors have provided audiences with more and more realistic representations of erotic behavior. While we are now accustomed to explicit representations of sexual behavior by partially unclothed and even naked actors, dramatists in Molière's time observed the *bienséances,* a kind of self-imposed set of standards that guided what could and could not be represented decently on the public stage. Although these standards were not observed in every case (some of Molière's plays, for instance, display a certain interest in the excretory functions), they would have cautioned Molière against staging an explicitly sexual encounter between Elmire and Tartuffe. Arnavon suggests that a contemporary mise en scène should adopt contemporary, not seventeenth-century, norms of stage behavior. In the 1970s, both Roger Planchon and Antoine Vitez accepted Arnavon's advice and staged frankly erotic encounters between Elmire and Tartuffe. Indeed, in Planchon's production the act 4 seduction took place in a decidedly inappropriate place, whereas Antoine Vitez deliberately situated the entire action of the play on a stage. Neither director, however, attempted to foreground the scene's erotic potential by setting it in a traditionally eroticized setting, although one could argue that, particularly in the case of Vitez's tetralogy, the stage itself is treated as if it were an already eroticized space.

The relationship between *vraisemblance* and the *bienséances* in Molière's time was (and to a certain extent still is) complicated by the issue of genre. Since the birth of Western drama in Greece, comedy and tragedy have been understood to be engaged in the discussion of different topics. From a doctrinaire seventeenth-century, neoclassical perspective, Molière's plays, by virtue of their subject matter, and not simply by virtue of the treatment of that subject matter, belong to the genre of comedy. The question of genre has, however, always been an unusually complex one, and playwrights have, even from the earliest days of the theater (e.g., Euripides), manipulated recognized genre boundaries for dramatic effect. French neoclassical theorists and playwrights quite self-consciously attempted to reinvent for their own culture the dramatic forms of ancient Greece and Rome. Quite quickly, however, they found themselves reenacting the very conflicts between theory and practice that seem to overshadow Aristotle's *Poetics*. Like Corneille before him, Molière found himself embroiled in conflicts between theory and practice that often focused on Molière's inclusion of improper subject matter in a serious comedy, such as the controversy that surrounded certain scenes in *The School for Wives*. What is pertinent in that controversy to the present discussion is not, however, the charge of obscenity that Molière successfully defended himself against but, rather, the fact that the controversy was to a very large extent the result of Molière inserting farce into a comedy. In other words, Molière offended some contemporary sensibilities and was accused of ignoring the *bienséances* because he used two different genres in the same play, a practice that contemporary theorists immediately declared to be nonrealistic.

For Jacques Arnavon, Molière is the author of serious, humanist comedies, and he repeatedly rejects any attempt to introduce elements of farce into modern productions of the plays. His understanding of Molière's realism cannot be separated from his sense of the genre in which he locates the play. Arnavon's staging of the erotic scenes in *Tartuffe* results from two inextricably related influences. The first of these is the influence he readily identifies—namely, the staging of such scenes in late nineteenth-century theaters. The second influence is the more subtle of the two and is generic in nature. In Arnavon's mind, Molière's *grande comédie* has been transmuted into its late nineteenth-century generic equivalent, a kind of hybrid mixture of romantic comedy and problem play. Seen from such a perspective, the relationship between Tartuffe and Elmire must appear ridiculous if presented in the farcical manner preserved in the traditional mises en scène at the Comédie-Française that Arnavon finds so implausible.

The third kind of realism mentioned by Arnavon relates to the existence of a believable moral dimension in the world created onstage that corresponds to the moral dimension identified by the humanist tradition.

He believes that because the humanist tradition has located a moral and philosophical component in the play, and because that *morale* has become an integral part of the play's very identity within the national culture, no performance can be called realistic if it fails to reflect this pedagogic content. Thus, Arnavon suggests that the audience must believe in the risk taken by Elmire: if there is no risk of her being sexually abused by Tartuffe, the play becomes less of a serious analysis of the human condition and more of a theatrical entertainment. If it offers only entertainment, Arnavon argues, the mise en scène has failed in one of its principal goals, which is to embody the script's identity as a classic.

All three "realisms" require a scene with a convincing erotic potential if the play's important values (i.e., the values that are important to Arnavon) are to emerge:

> If one imagines the inhospitable setting in which that scene is played today, with nothing but a table and two chairs, one might perhaps be persuaded that Elmire was more apprehensive than necessary and that her virtue was hardly at risk in such a frugal setting. Since the scene is unquestionably realistic in a truly graphic manner, one must be able to see more than a chair and a table. Modern drama has so frequently . . . put the unimpeachable evidence of everyday adultery on display for us that we do not hesitate to present it for public viewing now, when the circumstances call for it. . . . If one has decided to stage the play as it is and not as one might have preferred it to be, it seems to me difficult to omit the elements of furniture that the entire text imperiously demands. . . . One can only distort the conversation by transforming it into a banal and cold flirtation. (*Tartuffe* 109–10)

By shifting the encounter between Elmire and Tartuffe from its usual abstract setting, Arnavon presents a familiar event (Molière's scene) in an unfamiliar setting (a realistic stage setting). In 1907–9, such a setting was unfamiliar only in the context of a production of *Tartuffe;* realistic scenery was absolutely familiar to the members of Arnavon's audience because they encountered it as a matter of course while attending performances of contemporary plays. Arnavon thus makes the personalities and issues of Molière's play more immediately relevant to his contemporaries by translating Molière's dramatic ideas and motifs into their equivalents in the vocabulary of early twentieth-century theatrical realism.

Jacques Guicharnaud (541, 543) and others usually describe Arnavon's aesthetic as naturalistic because they associate him with the theories of André Antoine. Although Antoine was willing to borrow Arnavon's ideas for a production of *Tartuffe* and Arnavon was equally willing to associate himself with Antoine's production, the mere fact of their association does not in itself substantiate the designation "naturalistic." Arnavon's sensibility is very far from that of Zola or the other Naturalists: he has no interest in the lower classes, the demimonde, or the "raw-meat" subject matter that is typically associated with Naturalism. Indeed, despite his insistence on scenographic realism, Arnavon never actually analyzes the formative pressure of milieu on Molière's characters. There is nothing naturalistic in Arnavon's treatment of Elmire's pretended seduction of Tartuffe. What concerns Arnavon most is the need to show very real erotic possibilities while at the same time avoiding the potentially sensationalist aspects of such a scene. Such niceness of taste seems to have little in common with the Naturalists that Guicharnaud clearly has in mind. Arnavon knows that his public is "hungry for emotion," and he wants to give them opportunities to empathize rather than to analyze (*Tartuffe* 227).

Arnavon's realism is the strategy of a conservative; he wants to preserve the "old" values in a world that is increasingly ignoring them. And yet, paradoxically, he is also a revolutionary, a man who challenges the outmoded practices of one of his country's central cultural institutions. After all, the Comédie-Française is familiarly known as the Théâtre-Français, a name that identifies it more closely with what is most essential in the French cultural sphere than the theaters that have sprung up in this century under the banner of the Théâtre National Populaire (TNP).[12] At the same time, Arnavon is more of a Modernist than he might like to acknowledge. While his taste is reactionary, his intellectual attitude is not, and his skepticism in the face of a long-established and venerable tradition remains a recognizably Modernist critical posture even today.

Evolutions in Realism: Changing Conventions

Scenic realism in Molière's time can scarcely be compared to the modes of scenic realism in the early years of this century. Indeed, our notions of scenic realism have very little in common with the practices of the seventeenth century. Arnavon reminds us of the limited nature of scenic *vraisemblance* that was available in Molière's time, a kind of empty-stage mode of performance that provided Copeau with an important model for his *tréteau nu* aesthetic:

> On his stage, encumbered by privileged spectators on reserved bench seats on the left and on the right, and enclosed upstage by a simple drop unfurled in haste (the room, the forest, the countryside, or the *palais à volonté,* as Laurent and Mahelot used to say), Molière was obliged to have his characters make their entrances upstage from one side or the other of that good-for-any-location cloth, bring them down to the candles [footlights], underneath the chandeliers, then, once they had delivered their last lines, have them make their exits the same way they had come in. A total, and obvious, absence of frame. In any case, nobody felt a need for one. There is no shortage of examples. . . . An engraving by Le Pautre [shows us] *The Imaginary Invalid* performed in a sort of vast park with bushes, groups of trees, grottoes, statues, fountains, basins, etc. An armchair is brought out, placed in the center of this open-air scene design, Argan takes his seat, and the public—and what a public! the elite of the kingdom!—is content. (*Notes* 166–67)

If the king and his court, which Arnavon somewhat disingenuously suggests formed the cultural elite of the period, were not troubled by the obvious lack of "realism" involved in juxtaposing the essentially bourgeois world of *The Imaginary Invalid* with such an ostentatiously aristocratic garden, it seems reasonable to conclude that the mimetic adequacy of the scenic backdrop was hardly a criterion for truth in neoclassical theatrical representation.

Arnavon is undoubtedly correct in viewing the presence of a portion of the audience onstage as evidence of the relative unimportance of the backdrop in Molière's time. From many of the seats on stage the backdrop would simply have been invisible. In the Parisian theater of the seventeenth century, the backdrop functioned only as the sign of a location, as an aid to the imagination. The images of locations featured on the backdrop were both idealized and generic—a "street," a "room," or a "garden," not a particular street, room, or garden. Instead of "transporting" the spectator to an imagined other location, the backdrop, because of its illustrative function, actually reinforced the spectator's sense of being in a theater watching a performance.

If the backdrop in Molière's time marked the scenic space as a place of performance by referring to one or more absent locations while, at the same time, asserting the presence of the stage itself as the only real focus of attention, the wings (when there were wings) also functioned as part of an illustrative frame that focused attention on the stage rather than on an offstage space. Like the backdrop, they did not suggest the presence of an offstage world contiguous with the onstage space. With a wing and drop setting, there were no doors or windows to move through, no possibility of suggesting other adjacent interiors; characters could not exit into the visible offstage rooms or closets familiar from more recent drama, nor could they exit from an interior into a visible exterior or vice versa. The scenic conventions of the period allowed only for onstage or offstage space, and with a substantial number of spectators onstage, no illusionist treatment of the offstage space was possible. Nor, indeed, was there any illusionist manipulation of the onstage space for the same reason: no illusion is possible when the stage is shared by both actors and audience in close proximity to each other. Whatever illusion existed was confined to the scenic elements that framed the onstage space, and the mimetic relationship between actor and frame was self-consciously artificial and conventional.

Seventeenth-century illusionism did not entail the production of illusions of the real as we understand the term. Where we expect to see the photographically accurate replication of details observed in the real world, Molière's spectators expected an iconography that was explicitly generic and idealized, a symbolization of the real. The popularity of the *pièce à machines* was due to their spectacular appeal, an appeal similar to that of the extravagant "special effects" of contemporary cinema. Although he showed relatively little interest in experimenting with stage machinery, Molière's interest in the visual aspects of performance grew throughout his career as he became more and more interested in the aesthetic possibilities of the *comédie-ballet,* a form he virtually invented.

Jacques Scherer's reconstruction of Molière's staging in his *Structures de Tartuffe* emphasizes the anti-illusory quality of the scenic treatment while pointing out that the script's suggestions of location (*lieu*) do not coincide with the customary single set:

The fact that there is only one setting does not, strictly speaking, mean that there is only one location: the setting represents the location, it makes allusion to it, it keeps reminding us of where we are, but the problems of staging the action are not always resolved in an absolutely satisfactory manner by certain settings. The setting can adroitly circumvent problems posed by the location. (173)

Like Arnavon before him, Scherer focuses on the pronounced level of movement in the play as the source of the tension between the setting and the demands of the action. In short, both of them find the set "too small" for the play.

In about 1678, Mahelot described the set and its contents in his *Mémoire:* "The stage represents a room. . . . Two armchairs, a table with a covering, two torches, and a slapstick are required" (qtd. in Scherer, *Structures* 174). The chairs were needed only in the third scene of act 3 during Tartuffe's conversation with Elmire and were employed in a celebrated bit of stage business; the table and its covering were used to make a hiding place for Orgon on an otherwise open and unencumbered stage.

Scherer doubts that the table was visible to the audience before it was required by the action, reasoning that if Elmire had to suggest moving the table ("Bring that table over here and get under it" [Approchez cette table et vous mettez dessous]), it was because the table was not yet in the acting area (*Structures* 217–18). What is significant is that the table is moved to the center of the stage to play its role and removed once it is no longer needed. It is not put onstage to reinforce the "roomness" of the place being represented but, instead, to participate in the playing of the dramatic action. (Similarly, Roger Planchon and Antoine Vitez use simple chairs and a table as props to support the dramatic action rather than as furniture to situate the action in a specific kind of room.) In the same manner, the chairs used in act 3 do not dress the set or signify "room"; instead, they are brought onstage for one scene alone (219–20).

In Scherer's reconstruction, the room is represented exclusively by the backdrop, or rather, the backdrop announces that the stage represents a room. At no time is the scenic space defined as a room; there are no walls, doors, or windows to mark the extent of the room, nor do the actors "play" that they are in a room. The "room" is wherever the actors are, and the actors are always self-consciously "onstage." Both table and chairs are moved into position by the actors who use them, a movement of furniture that is itself incorporated in the scripted events of the play. Unlike in Arnavon's version of the scene, neither the movement nor the use of the furniture is in any way illusory (Tartuffe may be fooled by the covered table, but the audience is not); their dramatic necessity is plainly acknowledged. In keeping with Molière's use of the self-consciously theatrical motif of spectating and his emphasis on the actor/audience relationship as a central theme of the play (with Tartuffe as the actor and the rest of the cast as the spectators), the table and chairs do not represent the furniture of Orgon's household but, instead, serve as necessary adjuncts to the dramatization of a sequence of interactions between characters. They do not participate in an illusion of reality, only in the performance of a play. Whereas Molière's "set designers" were content to indicate a generalized location, Arnavon wanted to recreate a room or house of the period in which every detail told the audience more than was contained in the dialogue or scripted events.

The difference between these two modes of scenic treatment represents a fundamental difference between two models of theatrical performance. Arnavon's spectators stand, like voyeurs, outside the world of the play and look into that world through a privileged peephole (the proscenium arch), whereas Molière's spectators stand inside the world of the play (literally onstage at times) and participate in what is going on around them. Arnavon's spectators require a certain quality (and quantity) of illusion in performance for their characteristic mode of theatrical pleasure taking to become possible; the actor must be "over there" in a world that seems as "real" and as self-contained as the audience's own world. Thus, Arnavon's reading of the play takes pains to remove anything that might signal the play's theatricality: he calls for a scenography in the modern natural style as well as for a modern and natural kind of acting that employs a natural mode of speech and a natural style of movement (*Tartuffe* 15–16, 34, 37). Molière's spectators, on the other hand, take their pleasure from precisely the "other world's" proximity and its simultaneous lack of "reality."

Despite all his efforts to create a perfect and convincing illusion of the real, Arnavon remains blind to the conventional nature of his adopted aesthetic; he seems to believe that realism tricks the eye and ear and convinces its readers and spectators that they are in the presence of life itself. He never entertains the possibility that his chosen aesthetic might itself be seen as artificial or even traditional (in Arnavon's own pejorative sense of that term). After all, 1909 hardly marks the high point of realism in any of the arts: indeed, in 1907, the same year in which Antoine produced his realist *Tartuffe*, Picasso unveiled his *Demoiselles d'Avignon*. Arnavon insists that Molière himself would adopt Antoine's realist techniques if he were alive in 1909, but who is to say that Molière would not have followed the example of Alfred Jarry instead?

Seventeenth- versus Twentieth-Century
Theatrical "Illusion"

Arnavon's aesthetic is grounded in the belief that the most powerfully seductive and effective theatrical performances take place when nothing causes the spectators to question the actuality of what they have been allowed to overhear and observe through the fourth wall of the proscenium. In the presence of such performances, Arnavon believes, the spectators remain unaware of any distinctions between actor and character and do not consciously recognize that they are not observing human behavior but, instead, a theatricalization of human behavior. Arnavon's aesthetic is, of course, equally grounded in his appreciation of Antoine's technical achievements, and Arnavon's sense of the kinds of illusion that are possible onstage emerge from his experience of Antoine's productions.

Many of Antoine's most successful productions employed little-known actors. All of the actors at the Théâtre Libre, for instance, were amateurs and completely unknown to the spectators. Even at the Odéon, Antoine employed relatively few star actors and preferred to work with an ensemble of actors willing to subordinate themselves to the demands of the play and the director. The presence of star actors in a cast, however, especially individuals who insist on giving "star performances" and treating the play as a vehicle for those performances, seriously compromises the kind of illusion that Antoine worked to achieve and Arnavon never ceased to advocate.

In Molière's time, however, the situation was quite different, and nobody can have believed for a second that he or she was watching anyone other than Molière or a member of his company onstage. The actors were obviously playing characters, not becoming them. Each actor presented the character by displaying him or her in action, by marshaling a complex sequence of dramatic signs to create the illusion of a personality involved in the illusion of a situation. Neither the personality nor the situation need have corresponded to their "normal" counterparts in the historical, material world, although those embroiled in the *Tartuffe* controversy had a difficult time remembering that Tartuffe was just as much a creation of the theater as Sganarelle. Both the illusion of a personality and the illusion of a situation resulted from an active, imaginative participation on the part of the spectators, a participation grounded in an understanding of the conventions of both the dramatic form and the mode of performance.

Molière's audience's active participation was further encouraged by the absence of the separation between stage and auditorium that we, in the twentieth century, take for granted. As we read or watch one of Molière's plays today, it is almost impossible for us to acknowledge or comprehend the degree to which the presence of spectators onstage contributed to the audience's perception of scenic space. Although we rarely see spectators sitting on a proscenium stage today, it is not unusual (at least outside the commercial theater) to find productions or even entire theaters in which the architecture or set design have partially eliminated the binary spatial separation that is so characteristic of proscenium theater.[13] It is, however, very unlikely that contemporary spectators will attend a production for which the stage lighting does not establish a marked separation between stage and auditorium. In productions staged in arena, environmental, or thrust configurations, lighting defines the area that is the stage and separates it from the area occupied by the audience. Thus, scenic alternatives that were in many cases designed specifically to eliminate the distance between actor and spectator continue, as a result of prevailing modern lighting conventions, to do precisely what they were invented to avoid.

In Molière's time, indoor theaters were illuminated by candles hung over both the stage and the auditorium. The actors constantly saw their spectators looking at them, and spectators watched one another looking at the actors. We know that the spectators who sat or stood onstage frequently considered themselves part of the show and dressed in their most "theatrical" clothes to go to the theater; we can also infer that those in the cheaper seats took a similar pleasure in seeing and being seen. We, in the late twentieth century, sit in the dark, unaware of all but the most overt of the other spectators' reactions, whereas Molière's viewers and listeners sat or stood in full light, completely aware of the reactions of other members of the audience. Agreement, disagreement, pleasure, and displeasure were mutually and instantaneously known to both actors and spectators alike. To the extent that all were illuminated by the same light, all shared the same space. Clear visibility, of course, was something that some members of the audience were prepared to pay well for, and the clearest view was to be had from the onstage seats. The onstage seats were, therefore, doubly valuable: they afforded the best view of the actors as well as the best opportunity of parading oneself and one's finery in public.

Décor was, in Molière's time, a conventional sign for the presence of the theatrical; thus, the spectators could be satisfied merely by the token presence of a scenic object rather than a fully elaborated scenic illusion, as Arnavon understands it. The desire for scenery that articulated a specific vision of a single play was simply unknown in French neoclassical theater and did not become an accepted aesthetic principle until the nineteenth century.

For Jacques Arnavon, and for the innovative director who adopted his ideas about staging the classic repertoire, décor is more than mere *décoration* of the scenic space. Arnavon's desire for a perfect illusion of the real stems from his interest in seeing the playwright's ideas fully embodied in a context that makes them appear concrete; that is, he wants to frame the ideas with a convincing simulacrum of human behavior of three centuries ago to help his audience respond to these ideas as lived by Molière's "historically real" characters. The images of that world of three centuries ago onstage, as recreated through the conventions of a certain kind of late nineteenth-century pictorial realism, are, for Jacques Arnavon, the indispensable correlative of the values implicit in Molière's script. For Arnavon, it is the very materiality of that recreated world that gives body to Molière's humanism.

Chapter 3

Roger Planchon: Reconstructing/ Deconstructing the Grand Siècle

I like to show a world in the process of change—the end of an era, the beginning of something else. There is something unstable at such times.

—Roger Planchon

Mise en Scène as Critique

Roger Planchon's 1973 production of *Tartuffe,* his second mise en scène of the play, marks one of the high points of his career.[1] Indeed, Planchon's reputation as a first-rate director of classic plays rests on his stagings of this play, along with his productions of other plays by Molière, Racine, and Shakespeare. His first production of *Tartuffe* opened in November of 1962 at the Théâtre de la Cité in Villeurbanne, near Lyon. It was revived seven times between 1963 and 1971 and toured extensively in Europe, the former Soviet Union, and the United States. In 1973, Planchon prepared a new mise en scène to mark the celebration of Molière's tercentenary. This second version of *Tartuffe* was performed for the first time in Buenos Aires and also toured extensively between 1973 and 1977. Both versions are unusually well documented.[2] Planchon has acknowledged his obsessive relationship with *Le Tartuffe:* "It's a play that I can reread every year, that I can rework every year. . . . For me, it's an inspirational work. . . . I have never made a definitive mise en scène of it. . . . My relationship to this play is one of fascination" (qtd. in Kowzan 284). Planchon's mises en scène of *Tartuffe* represent one of the most far-reaching reinterpretations of a classical text in French theater history; indeed, his stagings can best be understood as a complex critique of *Tartuffe*'s cultural and theatrical history.

Planchon explained his dissatisfaction with traditional stagings of the play by pointing out the degree to which that tradition existed in name only:

When I decided to stage *Tartuffe* I studied all the previous productions. That's when I realized that there is no such thing as tradition. You know how much trouble Molière had from the Church. . . . Well, in 1850, at the Comédie-Française, the director did show that Tartuffe was a mean, nasty atheist. Fifty years later, at the same Comédie-Française, there is no question of Tartuffe being an atheist. What has happened? The Comédie has become violently anti-clerical. . . . [Tartuffe is] a villain because he's a Catholic; all Catholics are scoundrels. Another fifty years elapse and Jouvet stages his *Tartuffe*. Now he does this in the style of the great Christian novelists of his time: Mauriac, Bernanos. . . . Twenty years later I decide to stage *Tartuffe*. I've read Marx and Freud and so of course my staging of the play will reflect this new knowledge. (104–5)

His research taught him that previous mises en scène were shaped in part by the director's own cultural milieu, an influence that Planchon believes also shaped Molière's play itself. For Planchon, *Tartuffe* is not a "moralizing" comedy about Tartuffe's criminal behavior but, rather, a political play about Orgon and his family, a drama about the inner turmoils of a wealthy bourgeois family on the fringes of the Court of Louis XIV. André Merle quotes Planchon as saying that *Tartuffe* is "the first comedy of bourgeois life in which one sees an important servant of the State experience an uncommon passion and give over the control of his private life to a crook who can deftly exploit religious sentiment" (41).[3]

Planchon's two productions of *Tartuffe* can be seen as a return to the questions of the play's milieu first explored at the beginning of this century. Although Jacques Arnavon and André Antoine did not think of *Tartuffe* as a political play, they were, like Planchon, interested in the bourgeois milieu of the play and believed that Orgon's house, as a concretization of the characters' milieu, should be a central element of the play's mise en scène. In 1907, however, Antoine and Arnavon were interested in recreating the physical environment that a family such as Orgon's would have lived in as a means of intensifying the illusion of the reality of the events enacted onstage. They did not seek to provoke their audiences to reflect on the ways in which such an environment might have influenced the actions of Molière's characters in the manner of the naturalist dramatists. Instead, they presented the milieu of the play as neutral—neither a positive nor a negative determining influence on character. As I indicated in the previous chapter, neither Antoine nor Arnavon was interested in (or did not even consider the possibility of) exploring the ways in which Louis XIV's politics might have determined the actions of Molière's characters. Planchon, on the other hand, is interested in the relationship between character and action, culture and politics. In Planchon's productions, the scenic environment explicitly evokes the architectural, cultural, political, socioeconomic, and other environments of 1660s Paris. No longer a neutral background against which actors play out the classic drama of Molière's timeless characters, Planchon's scenography seeks to inform the spectator about the ways in which the environments of the 1660s might have acted on Molière's contemporaries.

Planchon's productions are remarkable for the wealth of scenic imagery he uses to investigate the relationship between *Tartuffe* and the political and cultural forces that operated on Molière (and his characters) at the moment of the play's creation. Planchon's two mises en scène of *Tartuffe* (the second is both an extension and a critique of the first) offer unusually complex montages of scenic images: every encounter between characters competes for the audience's attention with an almost surreal *écriture scénique* as Molière's script is reinterpreted from the triple perspective of Marxist political theory, post-Freudian psychology, and neo-Brechtian scenography.[4]

Planchon is generally considered the preeminent French disciple of Bertolt Brecht. Like Brecht, his work is intellectual, analytical, political, and complex: his productions reflect his thoughts on the playscript, the theater, and their possible interrelationships within the culture, both past and present. With Planchon, the mise en scène of a well-known classic is not only a performance but also a critique of the play. As Yvette Daoust remarks, Planchon has a "Brechtian respect for the spectator's intelligence" (22). Like Brecht, he wants to provoke as well as entertain; he simultaneously seeks emotional, intellectual, and political engagement. Whether or not he intended to produce Brecht's mythical *verfremdungseffekt*, Planchon's mise en scène of *Tartuffe* succeeded in defamiliarizing a very well-known play and in recreating the "shock of the new" that attended the play's several premieres in the 1660s.

Redecorating chez Orgon

Planchon's *écriture scénique* for the 1970s production seeks to reveal Orgon's world as both a physical environment and a site of cultural textuality. Planchon presents a series of domestic spaces—it is difficult to see them as ordinary rooms—in which the very fabric of "established" French culture is being dismantled to make way for the "new" ascendant culture of Louis XIV's monarchy. In Planchon's scenic text, the focal metaphor is that of writing. Figuratively speaking, Orgon is shown in the process of rewriting the text that is his house, erasing one set of signifiers and replacing them with another. On a more literal level, with his 1970s mise en scène, Planchon himself is rewriting the scenic text of his 1960s staging, replacing one narrative of Orgon's seventeenth-century milieu with another.

René Allio, Planchon's favored designer during his early years in Lyon, designed the 1962 production. Allio's scenography offered an ingenious variant on the traditional single-room setting that was still in use half a century after Antoine's and Arnavon's experiment.[5] Allio designed a box set that represented an elegantly appointed salon with as much attention to realistic detail as Antoine or Arnavon could have desired. The box set, however, had a series of false back walls, and the entire salon was revealed only during the fifth act. At the beginning of the play, the first back wall was close to the forestage, creating an extremely shallow playing area. At the end of each act, the back wall was raised to reveal another back wall bordering a now enlarged playing area. Each successively enlarged playing area, however, appeared to represent a complete room. Allio never offered visual clues to the fact that the room was much deeper than it appeared; there were no obvious gaps where the side walls joined with the back wall, and the back wall itself, with its functional doors, seemed every bit as solid as the two side walls. Yet, despite this apparent solidity, each raising of the back wall challenged the spectator's acceptance of the very scenic illusion the wall in question had been constructed to produce. Allio thus called attention to the illusory power of trompe l'oeil scenery by repeatedly unmaking the image of a coherent, domestic space that his box set seemed to represent. But almost as soon as the spectators saw one illusion broken, Allio was fashioning yet another illusion, the newly revealed back wall and furniture blending seamlessly with everything already revealed. Raising four back walls thus became a metaphor for the play's and seventeenth-century society's shifting and illusory surfaces.

Hubert Montloup based his 1973 design on Allio's spatial conceit for the first mise en scène; the theater program acknowledged that the décors were "inspired by a scenographic idea of René Allio's" (qtd. in Kowzan 289). Montloup retained the idea of raising a series of scenic facades to reveal more and more of Orgon's house. Although he treated it quite differently, Montloup also retained the image of Christ being taken down from the cross that Allio had used as a stage curtain, as well as Allio's strategy of using seventeenth-century art objects as self-conscious citations of Molière's period. But instead of situating the entire play in the same constantly expanding room, Montloup located each act in a different part of the house.

Montloup's scenic imagery differed significantly from Allio's in other respects. In place of the perfectly polished surfaces of Allio's elegant salon, Montloup fashioned a scenic world of undecorated spaces in which bits and pieces of architecture, furniture, and artwork had not yet been assembled into a coherent visual statement. Instead of basing his design on the fully developed style we know as "Louis XIV," he arranged each of the five spaces in Orgon's house (corresponding to Molière's five acts) so as to focus the spectator's concentration on the confrontation between the old and the new. He envisioned Orgon's house as a building site where a solidly built, older house was being transformed into a showpiece of the latest domestic architectural and decorative fashions.

Both designs reflect different approaches to the representation of the past. Allio's design functioned, for the most part, like a conventional box set and placed the spectator in the position of a voyeur watching the action through a fourth wall. Although the scenographic motif of the receding back wall repeatedly challenged the apparent realism of the room, the spectator's own voyeuristic relationship to the action of the play was allowed to remain largely unproblematic. The mise en scène as a whole was presented as a realistic narrative, and Allio's scenography provided an apparently natural environment for the story that Planchon wanted to present. Although some features of Allio's scenography (such as the black-and-white photographs of period paintings) cannot be reconciled with the demands of scenic realism as practiced by Antoine, Allio's representation of the past clearly owes a great deal to the conventions that Antoine did so much to develop. With its attention to the detailed re-creation of a "real" seventeenth-century room, Allio's carefully displayed interior design elements from the reign of Louis XIII created the impression that the spectator was being allowed to witness a series of events taking place in the meticulously maintained private salon of a wealthy bourgeois family. The impression of looking into the private space of an individual family at a specific moment in history is clearly one that Antoine and Arnavon were equally committed to creating. It is important to

remember, however, that Allio was not attempting to create the kind of illusion that Antoine and Arnavon sought to achieve: his rather obvious borrowings from Brechtian scenography (such as exposed lighting instruments) clearly signaled to the spectator that this version of Orgon's house should not be read as a recreation of an actual seventeenth-century dwelling but, rather, as the carefully constructed frame for a theatrical fiction.

Allio's recreation of Orgon's salon in the 1660s is historically accurate and, like Antoine's, is derived from research into the architecture and interior design of the period. As Daoust points out, Allio's design was grounded in the decorative taste of Louis XIII's reign and thus accurately reflected the fact that, in the 1660s, only the most lavishly appointed and most recently redecorated châteaux would have contained what we now recognize as "early Louis XIV" pieces (90). Arnavon, too, used Louis XIII furniture for the same reason. When Molière wrote the different versions of *Tartuffe* in the 1660s, Louis was a young monarch, and the artistic style we associate with his reign had not yet been fully developed. Certainly, the Louis XIV style represented by Versailles was by no means "mature" in 1669, when Molière was finally permitted to give public performances of the third and final version of the play. Although the Palais de Versailles has served in modern culture as a familiar emblem of the opulence of the Sun King's reign, and a source for innumerable productions of Molière's plays, the completed palace as we know it today is by no means the product of Louis XIV's reign. Louis enjoyed one of the longest reigns in French history, and as he grew older, his taste changed considerably. Artists and artisans, the majority of whom owed their livelihood to royal and aristocratic patronage, adjusted their aesthetics accordingly. Molière died in 1673, before the exuberant classicism of the early years of the reign gave way to the austere aesthetic that characterizes Louis's later years.

Allio's design for the first mise en scène conveys the impression that the events of the play take place in an essentially unchanging environment, an elegant home that is maintained in its present spotless and polished condition by what we must assume is a significant number of servants. (Planchon's productions frequently feature large numbers of anonymous servants engaged in menial tasks.) In such an unchanging environment, the events of Molière's play might appear as nothing more than a transitory disturbance, however emotionally unsettling, in a stable domestic world.

It is precisely Planchon's decision to highlight the process of change as a determining element of the play's dramatic structure that distinguishes his second mise en scène from the first. In his second mise en scène, Planchon wishes to emphasize the fact that a number of profound changes transformed French society in the early years of Louis XIV's reign. Montloup's scenography offers a different kind of historical accuracy from Allio's in that it provides a representation of some aspects of the process of that change. It reflects Planchon's interest in Orgon as a man who lived through the troubles of the Fronde (while maintaining his ties to members of both factions) and who survived to amass a considerable personal fortune.

Despite the significant differences between the two productions, both designers create complex *écritures scéniques* that reflect and comment on (rather than merely illustrate) the play's thematic concerns. Allio's furnishings suggest wealth and power, two of Tartuffe's three objects of desire (Elmire is the third). The numerous paintings on the walls (they were, in fact, photographs) feature large-scale religious images in black and white in which Christ appears both tortured and ecstatic. Together with the other elements of Allio's décor, the photo-paintings evoke an eroticized atmosphere in which luxury, pain, and ecstasy accompany every daily incident. Allio's black-and-white photographs function both as citations from seventeenth-century culture (a visual equivalent of the period's pervasive religious rhetoric) and as images of images. By removing color from these images, Allio makes them comment on the play as it is performed in the present of 1962–63 rather than function as part of an illusionist recreation of a past era.

The black-and-white reproductions of seventeenth-century religious motifs also serve to remind the audience that the entire décor is a reproduction of a seventeenth-century interior, a twentieth-century scenic recreation of seventeenth-century architectural and interior decorating motifs.[6] The paintings stand for their historical counterparts in much the same way that the backdrops and other stage fixtures stand for a historical model of bourgeois, domestic space. As a result, the theatricality of the set design is emphasized as the primary focus of the design's metaphoric statement: theatrical illusion is part of the play's thematic structure and not simply a metatheatrical gesture. Planchon and Allio are not simply saying, "You are in the theater watching a play"; instead (following Brecht), they are saying, "You are in the theater watching a play that explores the persuasive power of theatrical representation in the world beyond the stage."

Because Planchon and Allio can assume on the part of their audiences a modern interest in "reading" the scenic text, they are able to exploit the theater's ability to juxtapose a series of visual and dramatic elements that possess no preestablished coherence. Where Arnavon sought a seamlessly realistic treatment of *Tartuffe* in which visual signs and dramatic structures blend to form an aesthetic continuity, Planchon and Allio introduce a series of discontinuities between the familiar script and its mise en scène; they do not attempt to make their aesthetic merge with Molière's by presenting Molière's script as if he had written it for the twentieth century. The black-and-white pictures and the rising backdrops disrupt the "classically" seamless blending of actor and setting, form and content, that is the norm of "organically" unified mise en scène. In this trompe l'oeil design that paradoxically never attempts to deceive the spectator's eyes, the actor's display of personality immediately presents itself as a consciously manipulated persona—the actor is playing a role, not creating the illusion of an autonomous individual—just as the setting presents itself as a consciously selected series of scenic motifs. In short, nothing occurs by accident; nothing is "natural." The mise en scène frankly declares its analytic and intellectual purposes and invites spectators to interrogate each and every event as something that is consciously presented. As Judd Hubert and others have pointed out, Tartuffe is always "onstage," always presenting himself to others. Planchon thus frames his mise en scène as a theatrical event in which a seventeenth-century cultural product is recreated and reinterpreted in the context of a self-consciously contemporary performance.

Reframing the Familiar

Although Planchon has usually been classified as a Marxist director/playwright working in a more or less orthodox Brechtian mode, such a classification privileges the apparent "political" content of his plays and mises en scène over their complex poetics. More than any other factor, perhaps, this pigeonholing of Planchon as a doctrinaire Brechtian, an identity that Planchon himself explicitly rejected, has influenced the reception of Planchon's work.[7] It is useful to remember that Planchon has devoted considerable time and energy in the course of his career to the work of playwrights whose politics and poetics are quite different from Brecht's. Planchon has, for example, worked frequently with texts by

Eugène Ionesco, whose antipathy to Brecht is well known. While Planchon's stagings of classic texts are obviously influenced by Brecht, they are not all equally "Brechtian." Indeed, the first mise en scène of *Tartuffe* in the 1960s represents a break with the Brechtian scenography that Planchon employed in his productions of *George Dandin* and Shakespeare's *Henry IV*. The scenography of the second version of *Tartuffe* from the 1970s owes little to the visual ideas developed by Brecht and his designers.

Like Brecht, Planchon is interested in the politics of the society from which Molière's play emerged, and he finds numerous ways to inscribe those politics in his mises en scène, explicitly thematizing them in the second mise en scène, invoking them more obliquely in the first. But Planchon's *écriture scénique* stages more than the ideology (or a critique of the ideology) of the 1660s. It also calls our attention to the problem of representation itself. In both productions of *Tartuffe,* but especially in the second, Planchon seems to be embracing a poststructuralist problematics of the real: that there is no reality as such, but only different ways of constructing the real; that our realities are the products of a variety of representations. Thus, his aesthetic strategy is to call attention to the ways in which "framing devices" (such as the director's choice of performance aesthetic) alter the very subject under investigation. Since a subject is always already determined by the "frame" used to isolate it, Planchon can easily manipulate our understanding of *Tartuffe* simply by manipulating its frame in order to bring his own point of view into sharper focus: his belief that the play's historical moment plays a crucial role in his own interpretation.

Planchon does not perceive Molière's sociocultural milieu as the stable entity suggested (if not created) by the phrase Grand Siècle (thus he does not share Arnavon's nostalgia for "presence"); instead, rather than attempt to recreate a lost moment of glory (Molière's so-called timeless truths), Planchon chooses, in his second *Tartuffe,* to focus the spectator's attention on the political and cultural interventions on the part of Louis, his administration, and his wealthy subjects that fashioned the period's characteristic identity. Planchon is not content, however, with persuading the spectator to acknowledge that Louis imposed a certain identity on France and his subjects; he also wants the spectator to recognize the extent to which the very notion of a Grand Siècle imposes a false view of the cultural if not the political stability of Louis's reign. Planchon's *écriture scénique* can be read as both a representation of a society that is being torn apart and a representation of a society that is being built. In this scenic world, Planchon reinscribes the histories of Orgon and his family as individuals who barely escape destruction in the midst of pervasive change.

The recurring images of redecorating Orgon's home constitute the most important scenic metaphor for the changes that Planchon wants the spectator to consider. In itself, this metaphor of redecoration serves to historicize the action of the play by supplying an unconventional and unfamiliar context for the all-too-familiar events of Molière's drama. Planchon historicizes further by framing Molière's dramatic action with a mixture of graphic, textual, and musical documents from Molière's period that serve to historicize *Tartuffe* and Molière himself, and not just the onstage events. The second group of frames includes: a poster, a montage of architectural documents attached to the proscenium arch, a large painting that functions as a stage curtain, a montage of seventeenth-century music, and the opening and concluding passages from the *Introduction to the Devout Life* by Saint Francis de Sales.

These citations from seventeenth-century culture are not designed to be seen as representative icons of the same culture from which the play originally emerged, as is the case in conventional realist mises en scène of period plays. In Planchon's production, they do not function to bolster the illusion that the characters of Molière's drama and the spectator are both "present" in the same fictive place and time—Orgon's house on a given date in the mid-1660s. Indeed, Planchon appears to have abandoned Allio's recreation of a luxurious seventeenth-century interior precisely because it resembled too closely the traditional décors associated with modern productions of seventeenth-century plays (undoubtedly, he also abandoned it because it did not explore sufficiently his own principal thematic interest, the often violent transformation of French society in the early years of Louis's reign). Planchon was not satisfied with a décor that might be seen as a natural or realistic setting for the action of *Tartuffe;* he wanted no superficial scenic *vraisemblance.* Instead, he and his designer, Montloup, developed a number of ways of reinserting Molière's play in the unstable cultural context within which it was created while, at the same time, reminding spectators that they were witnessing a contemporary re-presentation and an analytical reexamination of a well-known play.

The Poster

The Théâtre National Populaire poster that advertises Planchon's mise en scène features a reproduction of Simon Vouet's *Sainte Véronique,* in which Christ's face has been replaced by a portrait of Molière wearing a crown of thorns; the shroud also bears a reproduction of Molière's signature. Kowzan has found three levels of signification in this image: a reference to the religious painting of Molière's time, a disrespectful reference to the Christian tradition, and the presentation of the author as a martyr (292). The poster invites the spectator to analyze and appreciate the way in which the three levels of reference that Kowzan identifies are juxtaposed rather than focus, as he suggests, on the somewhat banal content of each separate signifier. At the same time as it advertises the production, the poster suggests that the technique of montage informs the aesthetic of the mise en scène itself.

Kowzan's reading of the image, however, remains bound by traditional readings of the play and the events surrounding the productions of its three different versions in the 1660s. To read the poster as pointing to Molière as a victim of religious persecution, for instance, recalls the familiar history of Molière's struggles with the *dévot* faction. Similarly, the irreverent presentation of Molière's portrait as a religious icon reflects received opinion on Molière's satiric intention in *Tartuffe.* But Kowzan fails to consider the possibility that the potential spectator looking at the poster may pay more attention to the manipulation of the relationships between the images than to the images themselves. It is unlikely that the spectator will "read" the poster solely as a straightforward representation of Molière's personal history as it relates to this play; instead, he or she is just as likely to focus on the poster as an example of contemporary poster art and enjoy its clever manipulation of familiar icons.

The poster is eloquent evidence of the fact that appearances can be manipulated: if Molière's face can be made to replace Christ's face so "naturally," the poster seems to suggest, the entire Christian iconography can be manipulated to an almost infinite degree. Certainly, the poster helps draw our attention to the extent to which the placement and displacement of religious iconography features prominently in Planchon's scenic text. Perhaps most important, the poster draws the spectator's attention to the play's much discussed appearance/reality thematics in an unusual way. Most commentators confine their discussions of this aspect of the play to the character of Tartuffe. Will Moore's presentation of the play's dramatic action in terms of the "unmasking" of Tartuffe provides a good example of the traditional treatment of this thematic idea. The poster, on the other hand, like the mise en scène it serves to introduce, invites us to consider the appearance/reality issue, not in the rather abstract thematic terms of humanist commentators, but in the context of the cultural discourses that support and enable representations such as those made and manipulated by Tartuffe and his acolyte, Laurent. In a similar manner, it encourages us to look at the different ways in which Orgon and the members of his household interpret those representations.

The Montage of Architectural Documents

Montloup attached a series of panels, covered with reproductions of details from seventeenth-century architectural drawings, to the exposed surfaces of the proscenium arch that remain visible throughout the performance. The panels emphasize the presence of the proscenium arch as the stage's architectural frame and serve as a constant reminder to the spectator of the fictitiousness of the images presented onstage. These fragments of architectural drawings extend the metaphor of the redecoration of Orgon's house; at the same time, they suggest that the destruction and reconstruction of Orgon's house should not be read as a metaphor that Planchon has arbitrarily imposed on the play. Planchon's spectators were certainly aware of the unprecedented scale of construction during Louis's reign, as Louis's architectural achievements are a core component of Grand Siècle mythology. The enormous scale of the disruption of Orgon's household as represented by Planchon in his mise en scène merely serves to remind the audience of the extent to which Louis's architectural ambitions entailed the demolition, either total or partial, of what already existed.

While the architectural motifs of the proscenium panels echo the images of destruction and reconstruction that make up the successive décors, they also call attention to the constructed nature of the aesthetic object that comes into being in the course of the performance.[8] Whereas Antoine worked to make the audience forget that they were watching a man-made performance, these fragments of drawings make it impossible for the audience to forget that they are watching a purposefully arranged sequence of events. Although the fragments stand for a type of historical document and thus have a historical significance, they call attention to the present of the performance and to its assembled character: the performance is made up of a number of carefully selected segments, just as the panels themselves are made up of a number of carefully selected fragments of architectural drawings. The panels invite the audience to observe the manner of presentation—the way in which the segments are assembled—while reminding them that their perceptions are being manipulated at all times.

The Stage Curtain

The mise en scène is also framed by a stage "curtain" that features an enormous painting of the dead Christ taken down from the cross, a reproduction of an anonymous work in a Dijon museum. The curtain is made up of fourteen panels, seven wide and two high, and frames the production in the sense that it fills the proscenium before the performance begins, during the intermission (taken between acts 3 and 4), and at the end of the performance (a single panel version of the same image was used as a stage curtain in the first mise en scène). Dividing the image into fourteen sections emphasizes the stage curtain's status as a theatrical construct, a scenic reproduction of a painting that reproduces the iconographic content of the image but not its single painterly surface. In addition to emphasizing the extent to which the theater has appropriated the image of Christ for its own ends, the division of the image into segments also seems designed to interrupt the spectator's conventional response to a pictorial work of art in the realist tradition; the rhetorical impact of the painted image itself is delayed, if only for a moment, by the introduction of the fourteen-frame analytical grid. The segmenting seeks to remind us that the painting is, first and foremost, an artifact that may seduce us to accept its truthfulness as a representation by virtue of its successful deployment of a range of pictorial conventions.

Planchon's spectators sit in the auditorium, waiting for the houselights to dim and the performance to begin. This waiting time gives them the opportunity to examine the stage curtain and speculate about the significance of the segmented image. The first entrance of a character (Flipote), however, only adds another level of complexity to the "Christ curtain," as she enters through a hidden door in the curtain panel that represents Christ's sexual organs covered by a cloth.[9] The opening of the door thus disrupts the integrity of the Christ curtain as a decorative barrier between stage and auditorium. The revelation of the existence of a door in the curtain suggests that we should remain skeptical no matter how smooth and seamless the surface of an object or an image might appear to be.

This warning about the deceptive integrity of constructed surfaces is further complicated by the existence of the image of Christ quite clearly broken up into fourteen separate panels. Flipote's entrance causes us to reassess yet again our relationship to the painting, for she enters through a seam that was hidden from us by the very same people (Planchon and his scenographer) who revealed the artificiality of the image of Christ in the first place. With Flipote's entrance, the curtain now cautions us to beware of trusting images, even when we think we understand the ways in which they have been manipulated to seduce or persuade us. Furthermore, the location of the door in the very section of the image that contains a conventional sign of concealment (the loincloth) mocks both the function of concealment and what is concealed: Christ's genitalia.[10] The religio-erotic motif of the painting and Planchon's burlesque of the sacred iconography echo the black-and-white treatment of seventeenth-century religious iconography of the earlier mise en scène. Taken together, the stage curtain and Flipote's entrance introduce the focal scenic motif of the mise en scène: the deceptive potential of architectural and decorative surfaces.

The Music

The music played over the loudspeakers at the beginning and end of each act (Planchon's two acts, not Molière's five) provides a fourth frame for the production. Planchon chooses a montage of music by De Lalande, Praetorius, Monteverdi, Corelli, Telemann, and Bernier. Like the painting/stage curtain, the music is distorted: Planchon uses only short excerpts from the works of each composer, offering a montage of seventeenth-century music similar to Hubert Montloup's montage of the period's architectural graphics and the reproduction of the dead Christ, assembled in fourteen sections. Like the graphics that emphasize the presence of the proscenium and the artificiality of the performance, the electronically reproduced music works against any sense of illusion by highlighting the means by which the sound is reproduced.

The Language of Devotion

For his fifth frame, Planchon uses sections from Saint Francis de Sales's *Introduction to the Devout Life,* which was first published in 1609 and reprinted several times throughout the seventeenth century. After forty-five seconds of music, the opening words of de Sales's book are relayed by loudspeakers throughout the auditorium:

> You aspire to be devout . . . because, as a Christian, you know that this is a virtue His Divine Majesty finds extremely pleasing. But first you must learn what the virtue of devotion consists of, for just as there is but one true kind, and a large number of false and vain kinds, if you are only familiar with that which is the true, you run the risk of falling into error and distraction by following some upstart and superstitious devotion. . . . Every individual paints devotion according to his or her fantasy.

At the end of the play, as the actors stand in a final *tableau* and before the final dimming of the stage lights, the last words of the same book are spoken:

> And when the burdens of devout life seem heavy, sing along with Saint Francis:
>
> > Because a just reward is my anticipation
> > My labors seem like recreation.
>
> Long live Jesus. May He, along with the Father and the Holy Spirit, be honored and glorified now and forever, throughout the ages. Amen. (Qtd. in Kowzan 292, 328)

As many commentators on the play have pointed out, Tartuffe's language uncannily replicates the seventeenth-century language of the *dévots,* a perception that Planchon's mise en scène seems, at first sight, designed to support. Gaston Hall, for instance, has argued that Planchon "used Salesian texts as if they were the straightforward context of the extravagant devoutness of Orgon and his mother," whereas, in fact, de Sales's book strongly condemns the extreme behavior of individuals such as Orgon and Mme Pernelle (148). But Hall has failed to grasp Planchon's irony. Just as the Christ curtain suggests that the image of Christ himself can be manipulated, Planchon's use of the words of de Sales as a frame for the play's events reminds us that there is nothing inherently trustworthy about devout language in itself. By citing Francis de Sales, Planchon echoes Molière's proposition that nothing distinguishes the language of Tartuffe from that of a genuinely devout individual.

Rethinking Unity of Place: Metaphors of Transformation

Arnavon's conviction remains unshaken throughout his many books that Molière's plays should not be made to suffer in performance from being confined to a strictly (and, in his view, erroneously) interpreted unity of place. Accordingly, he tries to find a way in which to situate each act of a play in the most plausible location. He then seeks a solution that allows him to present as many locations as are necessary without blatantly flouting the principle of unity. In the case of *Tartuffe,* as we have seen, the organizing principle is supplied by the concept of "Orgon's house," and different acts are played in and around Orgon's house. The set design of each act is carefully worked out in order to make clear which portion of the house each act is played in and how that portion relates architecturally to the rest of the house.

Planchon's second mise en scène seems to be based on a similarly flexible interpretation of the unity of place rule. He, too, places each act of Molière's script in a different part of Orgon's house, but unlike Arnavon, he makes no effort to relate the different locations to one another, with the result that the audience is given no clear indication about where in the house any particular event is situated. While each backdrop suggests a distinct location, the side walls suggest (subsequent to the first act) that the audience is being offered a sequence of three-dimensional cross-sections of Orgon's house, none of which constitutes a separate room.

Planchon's scenic text shows the transformation of Orgon's house into the dwelling of a wealthy bourgeois who is in step with his times, a devoted believer, and a loyal subject (e.g., an immediately recognizable miniature of the well-known equestrian statue of Louis XIV by Bernini provides the centerpiece of the act 3 décor). Planchon displays the process of renovating Orgon's home, drawing the spectator's attention to certain architectural elements and free-standing objects that once represented Orgon's personal status and beliefs and, by implication, the status and beliefs of the socioeconomic class to which he belongs. These elements are now in the process of being dismantled and removed. At the same time, Planchon invites the spectator to examine the new decorative elements that will eventually take their place, elements that express Orgon's new sense of his social and personal identity. Orgon's house thus represents, in microcosm, the kind of "world in the process of change" with its inherent lack of stability that Planchon refers to in the epigraph to this chapter.

With the raising of each backdrop, a new space is created. Each new backdrop blends only with those portions of the side walls to which it is immediately adjacent. The newly revealed portions of the side walls do not continually reconstitute a coherent decorative facade as they did in the first mise en scène of the 1960s. The parts of the side walls associated with each of the first three acts do not, for instance, blend with the backdrop of the fourth act but, rather, stand in opposition to any pretense at a spatial or decorative coherence. Thus, as the succession of backdrops of the first four acts continues to reflect an ongoing redecorative and reconstructive project that is taking place simultaneously in different parts of Orgon's house, the side walls suggest, with their mismatched and patchy treatment, that a unifying aesthetic for the entire project has not yet been, and may never be, articulated.

At first glance, Planchon appears to respect the rule of unity of place in the same fashion as Arnavon: Montloup, his designer, seems to provide a suitable space for each major sequence in the play and to link these different spaces by a single frame of reference—the concept of Orgon's house. Montloup's scenography, however, both rewards and frustrates this realist assumption. The patchwork side walls offer the audience a valuable clue with regard to how to "read" Montloup's scenic treatment. While each new backdrop suggests a different space in Orgon's house, the patchwork walls prevent the spectator from accepting the décors for acts 2 through 5 as realistic representations of single rooms. Indeed, Montloup's scenography seems designed to prevent the spectator from thinking in terms of a set of actual rooms. Perhaps Montloup's single most important revision of Allio's 1960s design is his decision to abandon the box set. Instead of the "permanent" walls of the box set, Montloup offers a set of spaces in which the walls are no more permanent than what decorates their surfaces. As a result, the spectator cannot integrate the five different spaces to form a coherent mental image of Orgon's home.

Act 1 takes place in an unidentifiable section of the house under construction. A voluminous hanging cloth that partially covers wooden scaffolding serves as a backdrop for this act. Side walls are revealed on both sides of the cloth; above the partially concealed rear wall we see more scaffolding, the wheel of a large pulley, and high above stage right, the statue of an angel in flight with sword outstretched suspended by a rope from the flies. Above and behind the scaffolding and pulley hangs what appears to be a painted skycloth.[11] The floor is covered with tiles and remains unchanged throughout the performance. At ground level in front of the backdrop is a gangplank that holds two large sacks, some tools, and, sitting at its stage left end, a statue of Christ wearing a crown of thorns. Like the angel, the gangplank is suspended from the flies.

The angel remains stationary throughout the performance and thus acquires a special prominence as the only scenic element (with the obvious exception of floor and skycloth) that does not move.[12] The statue of Christ will be raised with the gangplank at the end of act 1 and will remain suspended for the rest of the performance. The flying angel is a decorative element that has either not yet been moved into its destined position or not yet fully removed from its accustomed position. The angel's status as a decorative image "in transit" emphasizes its identity as an icon, just as the black-and-white reproductions of religious paintings in the earlier mise en scène pointed to the iconicity of these images. Suspended high above the stage, this object, which was crafted as a static representation of flight, is thus presented in a manner that literalizes its central metaphor and, at the same time, mocks its religious significance. But the angel is more than simply one piece of sculpture that has been displaced by Orgon's redecoration. From a mimetic perspective, the angel belongs to the story of Orgon's project; from a scenographic perspective, it can be read as a scenic object that can be displaced at will by the members of the stage crew. Like the fourteen-panel curtain, it reminds us that we are less engaged in observing Orgon making images than we are in watching Planchon's images of Orgon making images. Planchon's suspended angel thus functions in a manner similar to the exposed lighting instruments that Allio employed in the 1963 production.

Planchon continues to focus on the making and unmaking of images by introducing the members of Orgon's family in their underwear. As Martine Millon has observed, "From the beginning, the spectators are placed in the position of a voyeur: they are going to see an aspect of this family that is not supposed to be shown to the eyes of 'society'—that which is private" (46). As the play progresses, family members appear in full costume. In act 2, Mariane even dresses in full view of the audience. In the final act, the family again appears in their underwear. Showing family members in their underwear represents a radical break with the traditions of staging the play. By breaking with the neoclassical tradition of decorum and the bourgeois good taste of the previous century, Planchon suggests that he is interested in probing both the public and private aspects of these characters. Showing Molière's characters in their under-wear also marks a departure from the traditional representation of neoclassical character as a fixed essence, a *nature* (and its corollary in theatrical production, the character type—usually a stereotype—wearing an appropriately "typical" costume). Instead, Planchon views character in terms of a series of interactions between an individual and his or her physical and cultural environment. Planchon's affinities with Antoine on this point are obvious, although Planchon's mise en scène is clearly more committed to revealing the pressure of environment on Orgon and his family.

Mme Pernelle is the only principal character who appears fully dressed during the whole of Molière's first act; Orgon's first activity upon entering is to remove his street clothes, thus dismantling his public image as a rich, successful businessman. Throughout the act the family eats breakfast holding their plates in their hands while Orgon uses a stack of building materials as a makeshift table. Ordinary amenities such as a table and some chairs have not yet been installed. The family has either not yet moved into the house or has been completely discomfited by the inordinate scale of the reconstruction. We might conclude that a man who reduces his family to such discomfort in order to satisfy his desire for a home that reflects his new image of himself is a man in the grip of an obsession that takes precedence over any concerns for his loved ones. The sheer scale of Orgon's reconstruction thus reflects the degree of change that Tartuffe's presence has wrought in Orgon.

At the end of act 1, the back cloth and gangplank are raised to reveal a space that more closely resembles a Surrealist stage design than a room. The raising of the backdrop allows Planchon to change the framing of the action by adding a new set of images to the pair that remain from the first act: the angel and the statue of Christ. Act 2 takes place in the laundry room, or rather, the activity of washing the family's dirty linen appears now to dominate a space that was once used for other things. Three oversized sheets are suspended stage right just below the gangplank and immediately above what remains of an enormous trompe l'oeil shell. A large wooden tub rests on the floor in front of the shell; the wooden gutter that supplies the tub with water is also large. Indeed, all of the scenic objects shown in act 2 are unusually large. Stage left of the tub is a trestle table covered with another sheet, and above the table is a lion's head that is not obviously attached to any architectural fixture. Scattered downstage are a number of straight-backed chairs.

For the first time, sheets (or other large pieces of fabric) are added to the play's inventory of signs, where they remain prominent until the end of the play. The sheets, like most of the elements of the décor, are "in transit"; we see them at various stages in the process between dirty and clean (throughout the act Dorine works with the sheets).[13] Like the exposed underwear of the family members in the preceding act, we are invited to look at the sheets not just as ordinary household objects but also as representing aspects of seventeenth-century life suppressed by the *bienséances*. Their presence on stage signals the breaking of a taboo: they immerse us in the everyday banalities of dirt and laundry, realities that normally have nothing to do with the *vraisemblance* of a *grande comédie*.[14] The sheer size of the sheets, however, serves to distance the spectator somewhat from the action, so that the spectator sees the activity of doing the laundry and hanging the sheets up to dry as both a representation of a hitherto never-staged moment in the life of a wealthy bourgeois family (i.e., a disruption of the usual norms of representation) and as a metaphor for the actions of the play.

Act 1 takes place in an ambiguous space that might be either an interior or an exterior; act 2 takes place in an interior, although the space is otherwise indeterminate. Intense shafts of light from both the wings and the flies create a division between upstage and downstage. The space is also divided by the large wooden gutter that supplies water to the tub (the source of the water is a mystery, as the upper end of the gutter does not seem to be connected to anything). All of the nonfunctional scenographic elements—that is, those elements that are not used by the actors—are placed upstage of this barrier of light, while all of the functional scenic elements (the trestle table, the tub, and the chairs) remain on the downstage side. Upstage thus becomes the domain of the director's *écriture scénique*, while downstage becomes the domain of the actors.

The upstage images are further separated from the downstage events by their sheer scale. Their large contours stand out against the surrounding darkness; like the angel, they seem to float in space. These upstage images serve to define a location insofar as they are identifiable as objects plausibly belonging in a laundry room; on the other hand, they do not define a location in that they clash with what remains of the old décor. The upstage images identify the upstage area as a kind of three-dimensional image screen, a three-dimensional theatrical backdrop that suggests the director's perspective on the downstage action. These directorial images are rendered significant by virtue of their lack of obvious relationship to the events of the play as they are traditionally understood (e.g., nothing in

Molière's script suggests that act 2 takes place in Orgon's laundry room). Indeed, they are recognizable as belonging to the director's *écriture scénique* precisely because they do not provide a natural context for the action of the play in the manner of a conventional realist mise en scène. They constitute, in effect, a poetic discourse parallel to the well-known play and assist the director in defamiliarizing the play to the extent that they avoid replicating the visual images traditionally associated with the play's already familiar dramatic events. (Planchon, of course, also reinterprets these "well-known" events, particularly the relationship between Orgon and Tartuffe, Orgon's reaction to Tartuffe's sexual advances toward Elmire, and the King's intervention.)

Although Planchon's use of different locations for the various acts of the play as well as his deployment of seventeenth-century images (if not simulacra of period artifacts) owes much to the example of Antoine, he does not adopt all of Antoine's methods. Planchon's splitting of the stage into what are, in effect, two different areas with two corresponding modes of signification represents the most telling difference between the two aesthetics. Antoine, as we have seen, seeks to show the characters *in* their environment as it might have appeared to an observer at the time; his is a kind of "photographic," or conventionally unmediated, realism. Planchon, on the other hand, prefers not to offer his spectators a facsimile of an actual period dwelling. Instead, he seeks to stimulate a kind of dialectical remembering in his spectators. He invites the members of his audience to recognize that he is showing them an "unvarnished," critical version of seventeenth-century domestic life (he achieves the unvarnished quality by rejecting the demands of the *bienséances*—a time-honored realist strategy) that is quite different from the more or less idealized and romanticized versions offered by previous directors. Whereas Antoine offers a seamless illusion of reality viewed in its "natural state," Planchon reminds his spectators that there is nothing natural about the images that he is presenting to them. In place of a seamless illusion, Planchon offers explicitly disconnected images. By presenting recognizable Grand Siècle images in such a disconnected manner, he suggests that the images themselves can be connected and disconnected in whatever configurations an individual might find pleasurable and/or productive. At the same time, he offers his spectators a representation of reality that is radically different from that offered by Antoine and Arnavon. For Antoine and Arnavon, reality is unified and whole and can be represented accurately only by images that contain appropriate signifiers of unity and wholeness. For Planchon, on the other hand, these notions of "wholeness" and "unity" reflect an ideology that he wishes to challenge, a desire that accounts for the interest in showing "a world in the process of change" that Planchon refers to.

The Royal Perspective: Political Realism and Classical Comedy

At the end of act 2 the backdrop is raised to reveal yet another space under construction. This room's decorative future is more apparent, however, than its past. The back wall contains two enormous murals, *The Massacre of the Innocents* and *The Sacrifice of Isaac,* flanking a marble-enclosed niche that contains a scaled-down copy of the familiar equestrian statue of Louis XIV. The statue and the marble pillars that flank it are almost totally covered by thick cloth wrappings. The area behind the statue is also obscured by a heavy cloth, a variant of the cloth motif introduced in act 2. The same simple chairs occupy the playing space in front of this facade, accompanied by what appears to be one of the trestles that supported the laundry table. There is also a small basket of laundry (which will feature prominently in act 4) left over from the previous act.

Unlike in act 2, where the enigmatic combination of scenic images teases the spectator's imagination, the flanking murals of act 3 offer an obvious, even banal, comment on the principal events of the act. The *Sacrifice of Isaac* offers an ironic comment on Orgon's "sacrifice" of Damis and Mariane; the *Massacre of the Innocents* foreshadows what may happen to the entire family. What is most surprising, however, is that the backdrop forms a triptych in which the central element seems out of place. Although the décor appears to be a great deal more finished than that of the preceding act, its final effect is disturbing because, at first sight, the three images simply do not belong together.

The central image of the veiled horseman challenges the spectator by presenting a familiar icon in a somewhat puzzling manner. The spectator, of course, immediately recognizes the outline of the statue and understands that the new décor of Orgon's house celebrates the king's importance by giving his statue the privileged central position. The centrality of the royal image is, moreover, heavily emphasized by the architectural frame that encompasses it: the statue stands in a niche, surrounded by black marble, backed by a blacked-out window, and flanked by two ceiling-high murals. While the two painted images propose an ironic commentary on the central events of act 3, the wrapped statue invites another reading. As with many of the other decorative elements, the statue is wrapped because it has not yet been unwrapped; it is in transit between an earlier setting (the sculptor's workshop, or the factory—Louis XIV was the first monarch to order the mass production of cultural artifacts as part of a program to promote French culture and his own importance) and its destined location in Orgon's newly decorated home.

Planchon made some changes in this image during tours of the production after 1973 that help clarify his intentions with regard to the statue's significance. By October 1975, the wrapping on both the statue and its framing marble columns has been removed. The large drape that obscured the window behind the statue has also been taken away. Backlighting through the window gives the statue a sharply defined silhouette; the statue is also spotlit in the manner of a museum display, which further emphasizes Orgon's worship of the monarchy.[15] As a result, the statue appears more strongly framed than ever before and emerges as an even more "central" visual focus. One piece of fabric remains, covering only the head and torso of the king's statue. The cloth now draws attention to the part of the statue that it covers rather than to the parts of the statue that are revealed. Because the king's eyes are covered, the statue can be read as a metaphor for the monarch's (apparent) ignorance of the events transpiring in Orgon's household. The king's statue may be compared to the two statues that are suspended above it—the flying angel and the seated Christ. Like them, it is one of a number of significant images chosen by Orgon to represent his personal values (and, of course, his ability to pay for their representation). More significant, the king, like the angel and the Christ figure, does not appear to watch the events unfolding downstage. Although the king's statue is blinded by the cloth (a sign of Orgon's unconscious desire that the king not see what transpires in the household), we know that he is aware of what is happening because we *do* know how this play ends.

For the same reason that we understand the image of the blind king, we understand why Planchon directs his actors to frame certain moments by pausing before speaking any lines connected with the play's overtly political elements. For instance, he inserts a long, silent pause during the Exempt's long *tirade* in act 5, a part of the text that most directors (and critics) have found embarrassing.[16] The pause indicates both the importance of what the character will say and the importance of the utterance in question in the larger context of the play. By directing his actors to foreground the political themes of the play, Planchon implicitly criticizes the tradition of glossing over these lines in performance. Planchon emphasizes lines that relate to the Fronde and treats the political refugee's papers in Orgon's safekeeping with unprecedented gravity. He asserts the importance of plot in what both the theatrical and scholarly traditions have seen as a comedy of character. At the same time, he locates a principle of coherence in Molière's plot that had remained unexplored throughout the play's history. Because Planchon is particularly interested in the political dimensions of the play, he is able to see Molière's resolution as something other than the contrived, comic resolution that directors loyal to traditional readings of the play have felt compelled to provide.

The king replicated in the equestrian statue is the same king who, on different occasions, upheld and dismissed the interdiction against public performances of *Tartuffe*. In the first years of his reign, after assuming his full powers, Louis found himself in the midst of a variety of powerful political lobbies, each of which sought decisions in its favor. Molière's play and Molière himself were a source of irritation to one of these lobbies, the *dévots*. Many of his plays attacked (or at least the *dévot* faction felt that they attacked) their habits of mind and their un-Christian intolerance. With the possible exception of *Dom Juan*, no play of Molière's infuriated them more than *Tartuffe*, in which they saw some of their number blatantly lampooned.

Planchon's version of the play asks us to forgo the pleasures of farce and lampoon and instead take Molière's characters and their situations seriously. Planchon resembles Arnavon in his insistence on interpreting the characters realistically, but the two men do not mean the same thing by the term *realistic*. Arnavon felt that he was presenting a historical reality, that Molière's play depicted a family in 1664 engaged in important domestic disputes. The realism of such a representation was grounded in what Arnavon took to be Molière's ability to understand the changeless nature of human behavior and to dramatize an ethics of human conduct.[17] For Arnavon, Molière's play was contemporary because the insight it offered into the human condition was "timeless"; this timeless truth was to be staged in a realistic representation of a seventeenth-century milieu because the characters, events, and language were of that period and would seem false and artificial in any other context. Planchon differs radically from Arnavon in his conception of the real; he sees the real as the matrix of economic, societal, and political forces that formed Orgon as a member of the rich bourgeoisie during the period after the Fronde. Character, for Planchon, is not a product of timeless human nature but, rather, of a specific historical moment, which must be as fully represented as possible onstage. Throughout his *Tartuffe,* therefore, Planchon's contribution takes the form of a series of juxtapositions of visual signs representing the political and aesthetic tumult of the period of the play on and within the walls of a single family's home. Planchon seizes on the historically specific post-Frondist context of the play to provide his imagery of destruction/reconstruction, while Arnavon employs Versailles and its architecture as somewhat abstract emblems of the lasting achievements of the Grand Siècle.

Orgon's personal involvement in the rebellion of the Fronde is only hinted at in Molière's script. He knows people who were directly involved and that knowledge itself is dangerous in a time when all memory and trace of the Fronde is being systematically obliterated (Louis XIV's manipulation of history may rival Stalin's in its obsession with the control of documentation).[18] Orgon's redecorating project, like those of his king, seems designed to remove all traces of the old order and replace them with those of the new.

Reframing the "Table Scene"

The set for act 4 retains the side walls from the previous acts and adds, as usual, a new backdrop. The downstage area contains two trestles (the laundry table from act 2 is reassembled to provide a hiding place for Orgon), the two draped high-backed chairs from act 3, the by now familiar simple chairs, and the basket of laundry. The backdrop consists of a cutaway wall, pierced by a small window high in the upper stage right corner through which we can see a ladder. Thanks to the removal of the lower stage left portion of the wall, we can see that it is, or was, a false wall. In the space between the false wall and the real wall (although, this being act 4, we suspect that this wall, too, will later be raised to reveal yet another wall), we see the other end of the ladder. In front of the broken-away wall stands a statue amidst a pile of old bricks, remnants of the room's earlier décor. Above the statue we see suspended another shell, a smaller version of the one in act 2, this time without a crumbling ornate frame. Suspended beneath the shell is an artificial egg.

The shell repeats an important scenic image and invites a reconsideration of those scenic elements that are, in a sense, the "leftovers" of previous acts. The simple chairs, the draped high-backed chairs, and the trestles share the playing area with the actors. Indeed, because they are so inextricably connected to the moment-to-moment dramatic action of the play, they tend to become neutralized through constant manipulation by the actors; we no longer see them as signifying anything other than the class of banal domestic objects to which they belong. They are further neutralized by their presence in the downstage section of the stage, a location that sets them in opposition to the upstage objects/images. Planchon consistently calls our attention to two classes of objects in his mise en scène of *Tartuffe:* the banalized, everyday object that is a theatrical signifier for its counterpart in the ordinary, everyday world; and the carefully framed object that performs a range of symbolic functions.

It is important to remember that both sets of objects are treated as scenic objects, that is, as objects whose range of possible signification, by virtue of their presence within an aesthetically manipulated frame, exceeds that of such objects in the world outside the theater. If some of Planchon's objects can be seen as banal or natural, that is only because the mise en scène has been articulated so as to identify them in that way. The simple downstage chairs that remain onstage even though the décors represent a variety of different locations have been as carefully selected as any of the more obviously symbolic elements of Planchon's scenic text. Indeed, the opposition between the banal world of everyday work and the "exotic," aristocratic, or, in the case of *Tartuffe,* bourgeois worlds of Molière's characters is one of the most readily identifiable motifs of Planchon's mises en scène of classic texts.

The fourth act is especially important in Molière's dramatic structure because it presents the events leading to a radical break in the established continuity of Orgon's relationship with Tartuffe and, indeed, with his whole family. Molière ordered the events of this act to emphasize the supreme importance of convincing Orgon by the evidence of his own eyes: Elmire stages a play-within-a-play, offering herself as bait, for an audience of one person: her husband. By recapitulating significant visual motifs (his own, not Molière's) from the three preceding acts, Planchon seems to echo Molière's metatheatrical strategy. The introduction of variants of images from earlier acts allows Planchon to refer the spectator back to earlier events by suggesting a kind of poetic resonance in which two sets of scenic images echo each other back and forth and, in the process, suggest a parallel between the dramatic images of the past and the present. The smaller shell of act 4, for example, echoes the large shell of act 2. Similarly, the sheet that covers the table and hides Orgon (and which Elmire subsequently drags to the floor—a literal soiling that suggests a range of symbolic soilings) echoes the sheets suspended above the shell as well as the sheet that covered the table in act 2. It also recalls the sheets that drape the two high-backed chairs, cover the statue of the monarch and the architectural frame that surrounds it, and lie in the laundry basket, waiting to be attended to from the very beginning of act 2.

The return of the shell in act 4 is no mere repetition, however, as the shell now appears in a smaller version, in a different part of the stage, without its previous frame, and linked with a new image, a white egg, suspended beneath the shell but above the head of the mutilated statue. The egg attracts attention as a new addition to the shell image, but it is included in the composition as a means of reactivating interest in the more familiar image. While the egg hangs lower than the shell and comes more readily into the spectator's line of vision by virtue of its greater proximity to the actors, its direct connection to the shell above it leads the spectator's gaze upward toward the shell and beyond. The shell itself hangs in front of and at the level of the highest point of the breach in the wall, a composition that further draws attention to the shell. As a result, while it is the egg that appears, at first sight, to be the new element in the scenic text for act 4, it is the shell that is the compositional focus of the décor, and the shell recalls the events of the second act. Parallels between the events of the second and fourth acts are easily located: both are structured around a significant exchange between Orgon and a female member of his family—his daughter in act 2 and his wife in act 4. The shell and the sheets unmistakably echo their related images in a previous moment of the mise en scène while, at the same time, drawing attention to their status as images, as elements of parts of Planchon's *écriture scénique*.

Planchon's images remain, however, decidedly enigmatic; their general range of reference is more readily discerned than any precise significance. They remain, in effect, intellectual and aesthetic puzzles that Planchon has inscribed within the world of the play, puzzles that substitute for the element of the unknown that is usually absent from an encounter with a well-known classic text. Planchon's mise en scène provides a new way of experiencing an old play: he provides a parallel text of images for the spectators to read simultaneously with the playing of the familiar text. Molière's text is thus rendered at once both familiar and strange: the spectator sees and hears the familiar characters, words, and events of Molière's script (to the extent that Planchon subscribes to conventional modes of their presentation) now embedded in an original, contemporary, theatrical event. Planchon's scenic text thus addresses the spectator's need to be surprised, a need that is difficult to satisfy when the play is so very well known. Indeed, the enormous influence of this mise en scène stems precisely from Planchon's ability to find a new story in Molière's familiar plot. Planchon's new story is nowhere more striking than in his treatment of Orgon.

Planchon takes advantage of the fresh perspective on the play's events created by his rich scenic text to propose an innovative interpretation of Orgon. Planchon gives us an Orgon who is not only subject to the violent outbursts of emotion that have traditionally been associated with the character but who is also given to self-deprecating laughter. Planchon directs Orgon to give a nervous, self-conscious laugh whenever Tartuffe is criticized. He laughs, for instance, when Dorine mocks Tartuffe's table manners, with the result that he appears to understand her point of view while not agreeing with her conclusions. Orgon's laughter is at once the most surprising and the most important feature of Planchon's conception of the character. It is surprising because it undermines the usual interpretation of Orgon's character as being almost farcically blind and uncomprehending. Not only does his laugh imply an understanding of the criticisms leveled at Tartuffe, it is an indulgent laughter (e.g., he finds Tartuffe's enormous appetite very amusing) that suggests that Orgon knows what he is doing, that he has not been taken in by Tartuffe. Instead of a foolish Orgon who falls for Tartuffe's theatrics, Planchon gives us an Orgon who falls for Tartuffe himself despite his behavior. Planchon thus addresses a question that most productions have ignored: why would a successful, mature man like Orgon (a man who has maintained his social position through a turbulent period in French history by shrewdly assessing his environment and acting accordingly) fail to see through Tartuffe?

Planchon's interest in this question leads him to see Dorine's portrait of Tartuffe as a malicious exaggeration rather than an objective description, since he believes that Orgon could not have been attracted to a man such as Dorine describes. Planchon, who played the part of Tartuffe, is himself neither *gros* nor *gras*, although he did endow the character with a certain reptilian grace. His Tartuffe moved noiselessly and with great ease, creating an image of the *faux dévot* as a dangerous reptile in place of the Rabelaisian boor suggested by certain details in Molière's script. Planchon considerably amplified the role of Laurent (an innovation later adopted by Vitez and other directors) by showing him constantly flitting through the shadows, eavesdropping on conversations, behaving in a manner that explicitly manifested his conspiratorial intentions as well as his lack of his master's polished social graces. Planchon thus substituted Laurent's behavior for the traditional corpulent, boorish Tartuffe as a visible sign of Tartuffe's nefarious intentions.

Although Planchon's Tartuffe was neither as young nor as physically attractive as that of Michel Auclair, who played Tartuffe in the first mise en scène, he was nevertheless far from being unattractive.[19] Indeed, as Bermel reminds us, the "magnetic" and "virile" presence of Planchon's Tartuffe greatly influenced the staging of a number of key moments (167). In act 2, for instance, Valère seems genuinely to fear that Mariane might indeed be considering a marriage with this magnetic Tartuffe. Furthermore, Elmire may not find the advances of an attractive Tartuffe entirely welcome in the face of her husband's apparent indifference. Finally, in one of his most famous innovations, Planchon presents an attractive Tartuffe that even Orgon himself appears to find appealing. It is useful to remember that although this production is discussed by reviewers and historians as if it actually presented an explicitly sexual attraction between Orgon and Tartuffe, Planchon's mise en scène contains no overt homoerotic behavior. In every case, Planchon maintains an ambiguity with respect to the degree of sexual fascination that Tartuffe might provoke in Mariane, Dorine, Elmire, or Orgon. Planchon exploits this ambiguity frequently throughout the play and makes it the dramatic motor of a number of celebrated sequences, such as Mariane's and Valère's quarrel of act 2, Orgon's rejection of Damis and decision to make Tartuffe his heir at the end of act 3, and the so-called table scene in act 4.

Planchon's ideas about why Orgon welcomes Tartuffe into his home and continues to support him in the face of the energetic opposition of the members of his family result in a decidedly unconventional staging of the famous table scene of act 4. Planchon shows Orgon rendered impotent by the sight of Tartuffe making love to his wife, a radical departure from the tradition that shows Orgon reacting violently to the discovery of Tartuffe's duplicity.[20] In Planchon's mise en scène, Orgon is incapable of getting out from under the table and is dragged to his feet by Elmire, only to collapse immediately into a nearby chair. When Tartuffe returns from checking to see that the coast is clear, Elmire is lying on the floor on the sheet that she has pulled from the table. Orgon sits and watches, inert and without a trace of emotion, as Tartuffe sinks to the floor to resume his lovemaking with Elmire.[21] Orgon's presence as an onstage spectator is thus literalized by Planchon, encouraging the audience to reflect on his reasons for maintaining silence. When he finally speaks, it is in a weak, almost inaudible voice that prefigures his slide into despair and depression throughout the rest of the play. Planchon's mise en scène focuses the spectator's attention on this moment, when Orgon impotently beholds his wife's seduction by the man he has welcomed into his home and heart, as the climax of a play that details the emotional and spiritual destruction of a representative member of a certain class of individuals in the 1660s.

Reconstructing the Grand Siècle

Whereas the first of Planchon's mises en scène presented Molière's script in a recognizably coherent interior space that recalled the fully developed style of Louis XIII's mature years, his second mise en scène presents *Tartuffe* in a construction site, a place where all the emergent fashions of the new monarchy clamor for equal attention. Instead of the monolithic culture that has been seen from the vantage of later periods as the Grand Siècle, Planchon offers a kind of theatrical montage of the competing elements that eventually coalesced to form, retrospectively, that famous culture. By refusing to settle for an abstraction of the period's style, Planchon shows us the process of events becoming history.

Planchon's view of *Tartuffe* has, then, evolved from a position not unlike Arnavon's, who sees it as a still-living part of a great culture, to one not far from that of Antoine Vitez, for whom the text has a mainly historical significance as a representative of the discourses of its time. Each in his own way decided to present *Tartuffe* as a document that relates directly to both the author himself and his immediate circumstances. Vitez's tetralogy is a barely veiled theatrical biography; Planchon's method is more directly dialectical. He presents a highly self-conscious figure (Orgon), endowed with a number of appetites and possibilities, both emotional and economic, in a sequence of scenic environments that comment on (or look like they are commenting on) his responses. Where Arnavon offers the audience a sequence of realistically recreated locations in and around Orgon's house, Planchon offers only a sequence of symbolically dense spaces whose form and function remain vague from a realist point of view. Planchon's theater, like Louis Jouvet's, is a symbol-making machine, an innately poetic medium that freely confesses its artifice in order to tell significant stories.

Planchon's radical difference from Arnavon and Jouvet is perhaps nowhere more apparent than in his staging of the long *tirade* spoken by the Exempt in Molière's fifth act. Planchon presents the Exempt and his men as agents of Louis's secret police, sent to terrorize Tartuffe, Laurent, and all the members of Orgon's family. After breaking down the door, the Exempt's men open trapdoors in the floor and thrust Orgon and his son into them. Orgon's house thus becomes a kind of dungeon. The image of a prison is further enhanced by the high stone walls that surround the space, as well as by the large wheel (a part of the construction project) that pierces the upstage left wall, from which Laurent is suspended. In this setting, it is difficult to see the final scene as a contrived comic resolution. Instead, it appears as the final expression of a royal power that has been pervasive from the beginning.

Jouvet was embarrassed by the *tirade* and invented a staging that he hoped would serve as a solution: instead of having one character speak the entire speech, he raised the back wall of the set to reveal a panel of magistrates, among whom the Exempt's lines were divided.[22] While Jouvet appreciated that Molière's Exempt was the dramatic vehicle by which the action of the play was concluded, he did not find Molière's resolution satisfying. (His resolution of *The School for Wives*—the ballet of American Indians—betrays a similar unease with Molière's resolution of that play.) Jouvet's rejection of Molière's ending reflects the traditional view of the play's resolution as dramaturgically deficient.

Arnavon was almost as disturbed by the Exempt's role as Jouvet but tried to work on the hypothesis that Molière knew what he was doing. In general, Arnavon's credo has much in common with that of the New Critics: he takes it as axiomatic that the text "contains" all the answers. Arnavon's notion of the "text," however, is a limited one; for him the text is nothing more than the words on the page, the published text of *Tartuffe*. Consequently, his projected mise en scène gives the Exempt's words due weight as having serious consequences for the world of the play; unlike Jouvet, he does not reject Molière's resolution on the ground that the Exempt's only function is to mollify Louis. Arnavon, then, accepts that the Exempt has a dramatic function of some consequence and, accordingly, makes an effort to accommodate his mise en scène to that position.

Planchon not only takes the Exempt's dramatic function seriously, he presents his intervention as one of the high points of Molière's drama in a mise en scène that positions Molière's text within a critically viewed historical context:

> A squad of armed militia . . . burst through the walls and drove the
> terrorized family into a dungeon before turning to arrest and gag
> Tartuffe. Planchon implied that Tartuffe was to be executed: not for
> his treatment of Orgon or his alleged criminal past, but because
> absolutism required the elimination of a disruptive anarchist. Orgon,
> as the Royal emissary says, had been saved because he was a loyal
> supporter of the King in the civil war. But the Officer's manner as
> he said this—deliberate and menacing—made this seem less an act
> of magnanimity than a warning against future disobedience. Where
> Orgon's pardon had previously been seen as the far-sighted wisdom
> of a divine monarch, Planchon presented it as a calculated political
> act by the head of an efficient police state. (Whitton 254)

The Exempt is important to Planchon because he personifies the contextual world that is Planchon's principal area of interest.[23] *Text* means something quite different to Planchon. It is no longer the document published under Molière's name, which Arnavon takes as his sole frame of reference, but a fragment of a much larger discourse that includes Molière's personal history, the histories of his characters, and the history of France during the period of the play. Planchon conceives his mise en scène of *Tartuffe* as a metaphoric representation of those three histories as histories-in-progress.

Unlike Arnavon's consistent efforts to present a coherent real stage world throughout *Tartuffe*, Planchon takes pains to signal his own interventions by introducing a series of disruptions of and deviations from the norm of mid-twentieth-century performances of Molière. Planchon's *écriture scénique* proclaims its presence at every moment of the mise en scène, from a spectator's first encounter with the poster to the final fall of the enormous image that Planchon substitutes for the curtain. But his ubiquitous signature need not be seen as proof of Planchon's appropriation of Molière's script for his own purposes as an *auteur*. What the volume of scenic writing proclaims is nothing more (or less) than the presence of an interpretation. Planchon does nothing to hide his presence as the director, the guiding critical and imaginative intelligence behind the large collective project that is a mise en scène. His impressive montage of signs reminds the audience that Molière's script is itself also a montage of signs that can, indeed can only, be interpreted.

Unlike Arnavon, Planchon wants the audience to reflect both on the play itself and on the historical period from which it came. Thus, Planchon offers a world in transition, full of turmoil and radical unease, whereas Arnavon offers an image of seventeenth-century Paris as a place essentially at peace with itself, in which the social forms are coherent and stable. The most significant difference of all, however, is that Arnavon seeks only to stage a great text of humanism, a text that needs no historical context to be understood clearly and appreciated (for him, the text is its own context), whereas Planchon is concerned with the text's historical moment, how the text comes to be seen as we see it, and what we might learn from exploring it as a historically circumscribed part of our culture in the context of our own times.

Chapter 4

Jacques Arnavon: Romantic Realism, Nostalgia, and the Grand Siècle

A "Flawed" Masterpiece?

Literary historians agree that *The School for Wives* marked a significant turning point in Molière's development as a playwright because it represented a movement away from farce toward a comedy grounded in neoclassical principles of style and dramatic structure. Writing in the new and officially approved neoclassical style (i.e., approved by the Académie Française), Molière eventually created, according to these same literary historians, the "masterpiece" of neoclassical comedy, *The Misanthrope.* It is worth remembering, though, that despite the admiration of those with orthodox neoclassical tastes, *The Misanthrope* was not one of Molière's most popular plays in the 1660s, whereas both *Tartuffe* and *The School for Wives* were enormously successful at the box office. While *The Misanthrope* is unquestionably a major achievement and has established itself over time as one of Molière's most popular plays, its status as "Molière's finest play" has, unfortunately, resulted in a skewed vision of the majority of his creative output. The critical tradition has, for example, consistently underrated or ignored the *comédies-ballets,* which make up almost half of the Molière canon, in favor of the so-called *grandes comédies* (i.e., the five-act comedies written in verse that mimic what Molière's contemporaries took to be the form of classical comic drama) because it could not see them, to paraphrase Boileau, as the work of the artist who wrote *The Misanthrope.*[1]

These five-act comedies are indeed formidable works; it is also important to bear in mind, however, that they are far more readily appreciated as dramatic literature than the *comédies-ballets,* which by comparison have little or no "life" on the page. Although the *comédies-ballets* represent an important formal innovation on Molière's part, that innovation is not principally a literary one. Literary historians have undoubtedly ignored these strange mixtures of drama, dance, and song because they did not feel adequately prepared to deal with their purely theatrical aspects. When they have dealt with these plays, they have usually discussed them as if the nonverbal elements did not exist.

Molière criticism habitually approaches the playwright's work with an array of analytic tools derived from neoclassical dramatic aesthetics. Since the playwright is presumed to be writing a certain kind of play for a certain kind of theater, which is assumed to be best exemplified in *The Misanthrope*, each play is read in the context of the neoclassical ideal as a conscious attempt to create drama according to a set of rules, the *règles* and *bienséances* that are invoked in almost every theater-related document in seventeenth-century France. Paradoxically, however, it is a commonplace in Molière criticism that his plays reveal a consistent disregard for the rules of neoclassical dramaturgy. And Molière is by no means alone in this respect: Jacques Scherer's *La Dramaturgie classique en France* has persuasively demonstrated that these rules were broken or disregarded as a matter of course by almost every playwright of the period, both major and minor. Indeed, breaking the rules was such a common practice that Scherer adopted the methodology of inferring neoclassical dramatic practice from a correlation of all the known departures from the norm. Before the publication of Scherer's important research, scholars as well as theater artists tended to assume a more widespread observance of the rules on the part of seventeenth-century artists.

From the somewhat restricted perspective of the neoclassical ideal, *The Misanthrope* represents Molière's greatest achievement: its dramatic structure, its characters, and the poetic subtlety of its language all qualify it as a *grande comédie*. But the neoclassical perspective is not particularly appropriate to either *Le Bourgeois gentilhomme* or *Les Fourberies de Scapin* or, indeed, to *The School for Wives, Tartuffe,* or *Dom Juan.*[2] While few critics would be tempted to see either *Le Bourgeois gentilhomme* or *Les Fourberies de Scapin* as attempts at neoclassical comedy, they have taken for granted that both *The School for Wives* and *Tartuffe* are comedies in the neoclassical mold, although neither play fits the mold particularly well. Indeed, Molière spent a large portion of his professional life defending both plays against attacks from the literary establishment, attacks that condemned him for his failure to "adhere" to the rules. The literary establishment and, in the case of *Tartuffe* and *Dom Juan,* the political and religious establishments attacked Molière for his lack of seriousness or, to put it differently, for treating "important" subjects in a farcical manner. The battles over *The School for Wives, Tartuffe,* and *Dom Juan* were, in part, battles over Molière's use of farce in otherwise "classical," and therefore "serious," comedies. Three hundred years after the first productions of these plays, many critics and theater artists remain uncomfortable with Molière's characteristic mixture of styles and tones in the *grandes comédies.*[3]

Molière criticism continues to focus on the variety of ethical, philosophical, or sociopolitical themes that have been identified in the playwright's writings or as important elements of the context of the writings. Because Molière's perspectives on life in general and life in seventeenth-century Paris in particular are held to be the true guarantors of his "classic" status, critics have usually preferred to analyze his *morale* or the sociohistorical context of the plays rather than investigate his poetics. As a result, Molière scholarship is not troubled by the paradox of acclaiming *The School for Wives* a major neoclassical comedy while simultaneously enumerating its many dramaturgical deficiencies.

Although Will Moore and René Bray performed an indispensable service in reminding us that Molière was above all else a man of the theater and that the theater ought to provide the context for all future discussions of the playwright's work, they did not warn future generations of critics against taking Molière too seriously. Molière continues to be seen as a serious, gloomy, even tragic figure, and commentators make very few concessions to the spirit of farce that pervades his theater, despite Gustave Lanson's much quoted arguments to the contrary in his essay "Molière and Farce," which appeared at the beginning of the present century. Critics appear reluctant to recognize the presence of farce in all of his "great" comedies (it is present even in *The Misanthrope*), perhaps because such a recognition might lead to a radical rethinking of the nature of French neoclassical comedy. If Tartuffe is perceived as a coarse buffoon and Orgon as a gullible fool (well-established interpretations in both the theatrical and scholarly traditions), it makes little sense to claim that Molière was engaged in a systematic consideration of subtle religious and ethical questions in *Tartuffe.* Nevertheless, most of the criticism written about this play assumes that Molière was indeed engaged in just such a project.

Along with a number of other departures from the accepted ideals of neoclassical dramatic structure, Molière's recurrent use of farce matters far more as a factor in the interpretation of his work than most Molière scholarship has usually been willing to concede. Indeed, Molière's dramaturgy is more complex and "irregular" than any traditional notion of neoclassical dramatic structure allows. Scholars have, for example, tended to see *Dom Juan* as deviating from the norm of Molière's practice, which in the standard reading is represented by *The Misanthrope*. This view, however, gives too little weight to the fact that Molière wrote *The School for Wives*, *Tartuffe* (in its several versions), *Dom Juan*, and other more "frivolous" plays during the same time that he was working on *The Misanthrope*. As the mises en scène of *The School for Wives* studied in the following pages suggest, directors have struggled with a *Misanthrope*-centered understanding of the playwright's aesthetic, attempting to observe the niceties of neoclassical dramaturgy and scenography in the belief that they were respecting the author's intentions.

Although the critical literature on *The School for Wives* reveals an unquestioned agreement that it is Molière's first major play, there is little or no agreement on why it is a good play. There exists, on the other hand, a substantial consensus on the identity of the play's "faults." Both theater artists and literary scholars point out that the play contains too many speeches reporting what has happened offstage as well as too many soliloquies. The result of this preponderance of narrative and monologue, they suggest, is an essentially undramatic play. They also complain about the play's implausible resolution, a complaint that has often been made with reference to *Tartuffe* and other plays by Molière. They further argue that the play is also rendered implausible by what they see as Molière's scandalous disregard for the unity of place. Finally, they accuse Molière of failing to maintain the integrity of the play's genre by introducing elements of farce into what (they assume) is supposed to be a classical comedy. To all of these dramaturgical "flaws" must be added the charge of obscenity, a charge that makes sense only in the context of serious comedy. If the play had been composed in the genre of farce and presented to the public as a farce, the issue of obscenity would either not have arisen at all or arisen in a significantly attenuated manner.

The catalog of complaints about the play's construction has remained almost unchanged since 1663, despite a long history of successful production both in France and abroad. The play is accused of being undramatic, unrealistic, irregular, obscene, and confused about its own generic identity. But how, we might ask, can a play continue to appeal to theater artists, audiences, and scholars for more than three centuries, with the degree of change in dramatic practice and popular taste that such a span of time necessarily implies, and still be considered a collection of dramaturgic faux pas? It is surely something of a paradox that *The School for Wives* can command so much respect and still be considered seriously flawed.

Only a study that considers how a play's dramatic structure has been articulated in performance can provide insights into how a play works as a dramatic whole. Such a study seems particularly crucial in the case of a classic play such as *The School for Wives* because the script has already been incorporated in a long series of very different mises en scène, just as it has been subjected to a wide variety of analytical and critical methodologies. While the script of *The School for Wives* has remained largely unchanged (apart from translations into other languages, which are constantly revised), its dramatic identity has not.[4] The Romantic mises en scène of Arnolphe's "tragedy," for example, seem not to be discussing the same play that was almost universally recognized as an uproarious comedy (or farcical comedy) by Molière's contemporaries in the 1660s (Loret records the side-splitting laughter of the members of the royal family).[5] Molière scholars have not, however, traditionally understood such differences of interpretation as evidence that *The School for Wives* might be two radically different plays in the eyes of two different groups of readers. Since Molière's published text remains relatively constant, they have preferred to read both the "tragic" and the "farcical-comic" interpretations as reflecting two equally valid interpretive responses to the same printed text without taking into account the theatrical and cultural contexts of each reading. This misperception can be avoided only by discussing *The School for Wives* in terms of the relationship between script and performance. Such a discussion might also shed light on the discrepancies between reading the script through a critical screen derived from accepted notions of neoclassical orthodoxy and the experience of the play in the theater, and between a neoclassically based analysis that argues that such a play can work only imperfectly and a mise en scène that attests to its force in performance.

Unfortunately, many aspects of past productions are not completely recoverable for scholarly examination. Such things as an actor's tone of voice, the inflection of a line reading, or the pacing of a particular gesture or movement can, at best, be partially reconstructed on the basis of first-hand accounts of specific performances. More significant, perhaps, we have no way of experiencing at first hand the personalities of the actors in past productions. Although Roger Herzel's *Original Casting of Molière's Plays* has provided us with some very valuable insights into the professional attributes of the members of Molière's company, we are not in a position to reconstruct Molière's own mises en scène. It is possible, however, to describe the treatment of scenic space in considerable detail because such descriptions need rely only on comparatively few pieces of concrete information. On the basis of a reconstruction of an individual scenography, it is possible, I believe, to come to some understanding of how, in a given historically circumscribed moment, the complex of relationships between script and performance, actor and character, was articulated. The following discussion of *The School for Wives* examines that complex in three representative twentieth-century articulations, by Jacques Arnavon and Louis Jouvet in 1936 and by Antoine Vitez in 1978.

"Outdated" Stagecraft and Modern Mise en Scène

Arnavon's edition of *The School for Wives* appeared in 1936 and, like his earlier book on *Tartuffe,* takes the form of a notebook mise en scène. Like all his books on Molière, *L'Ecole des femmes de Molière* rests on the premise that a successful modern mise en scène will, indeed must, ignore traditions of staging, however venerable, in favor of presenting the classic script as clearly and as convincingly as possible to a contemporary audience: "Our task consists . . . of composing and describing the décor, and subsequently of directing the movement of the actors in such a fashion that the illusion of life as it is lived is achieved to the maximum degree possible" (16). Arnavon believed that a mise en scène could be both clear and convincing only if it succeeded in leading the spectators to believe that they were witnessing a real event. For Arnavon, a compelling realism in mise en scène could be achieved only through the reenactment of psychologically and sociologically realistic behavior in an illusionist, realist setting. (Paradoxically, however, Arnavon seems to have had little interest in the disciplines of either psychology or sociology.)

Arnavon's approach to the staging of Molière varied little from his first collaboration with Antoine in 1907 to his last book on Molière, a notebook mise en scène of *Dom Juan,* which was published two years before his death in 1949. Although he was familiar with the productions of the French and European theatrical avant-garde from the early years of the century on, he never deviated from his conviction that Molière's was a quintessentially realist dramaturgy, almost in the modern sense of the term.[6] He was particularly opposed to the kind of staging that Jacques Copeau had developed at the Vieux-Colombier and was no doubt disturbed by the increasingly widespread influence of Copeau's antirealist aesthetic. Copeau, for his part, believed that realist mise en scène presented a distorted view of classic plays: "To do realism in the classic is to betray it" (qtd. in Descôtes, *Molière et sa fortune littéraire* 106).

Beginning with *Notes sur l'interprétation de Molière* in 1923, Arnavon devoted considerable energy to challenging what he saw as the negative cultural side effects of Copeau's practice of mise en scène. In his 1929 book, *Molière, notre contemporain*, for instance, Arnavon argues that Copeau's stylization is inappropriate because of its "artificiality":

> With their bare stage and their set designs made of light on floating folds of material, men of taste have managed to obtain results that are curious, compelling, perhaps even beautiful, or beautiful in a particular kind of way. But . . . one is obliged to note that we are dealing here with artifice and nothing but artifice—a kind of artifice that is quite different from the time-honored tricks of the trade. . . . Only a violent act of will, which inevitably turns into an assault on the masterpiece, makes it possible to rip human beings out of the normal world in which they go about their business in order to relocate them in an empty space, which we might as well call "the ether." (175)

Arnavon here echoes E. H. Gombrich's well-known thesis that we "see" only what we have been taught to see, when he argues that the *vraisemblable* is inextricably related to the already known, that what appears to be true is the *déjà lu*, the *déjà vu*, and the *déjà entendu*. Arnavon assumes, however, that the *vraisemblable* is a constant, stable category, located in a specific aesthetic and immune to displacement. But the history of art is the history of just such a series of displacements. Paradoxically, Arnavon's own project is itself one of displacement in that he seeks to undermine the older *vraisemblance* embodied in the traditional stagings at the Comédie-Française, which were still in the repertory in 1936.

For Arnavon, the most important goal in the staging of a classic text is maintaining the intelligibility of the author's ideas. He advocates scenic realism as opposed to the "artificiality" of Copeau precisely because, in his opinion, scenic realism allows the spectator a more direct access to Molière's *morale*. In Arnavon's mind, Copeau's propensity toward abstraction presents much the same problems of intelligibility as the superannuated, conventional theatricality of the classic style of the Comédie-Française:

> The director can create the décor either by using the time-honored methods (*la formule ancienne*), which seek to achieve the illusion of reality by careful attention to detail, or by adopting the modern principles of simplification and stylization. The author of the present volume does not conceal his own preference for the first of these methods. (*L'Ecole des femmes* 57)

It is important to note that Arnavon is not simply referring to the work of Antoine and other scenic realists of that generation when he uses the phrase "*la formule ancienne.*" What he has in mind is the function of detail in the entire tradition of *vraisemblance*. Consequently, he sees modern scenic realism as it was developed by Antoine and others as engaged in pursuing solutions to the very same problematic of realist representation that was formulated by the neo-Aristotelian theorists of the French classical period, the same problematic that Molière himself grappled with. Arnavon sees the work of the nonrealists, on the other hand, and in particular the "stylization" of Copeau, as introducing issues of representation into the mise en scène of texts from the French classical period that are quite foreign to the aesthetics of that time.

When Arnavon rejects Copeau's aesthetic in favor of already familiar modes of realist performance, he is making a statement that reflects his own relationship to his culture: he is proposing a model of truth and beauty that has the advantage of being fully developed and completely familiar, he believes, to the members of his cultural peer group. Arnavon's critique of Copeau's more abstracted representations of the world of Molière's play is not only the reaction of a man who does not appreciate the aesthetics of the "new" nonrealist mise en scène; it is also the reaction of a man who cannot see or understand the humanistic aspects of *The School for Wives* or any other classic in the absence of a representation of a material, historic context:

> If one situates the characters and the action in a completely imaginary atmosphere that is absolutely unknown in the world in which we live our lives, if one situates them on a denuded stage, in front of some more or less stylized and schematized composition of beams of light

and drapery, one removes them from humanity, one takes away from the work a portion of its spiritual value and its significance, one disfigures it, and its powerful, heart-rending, inner meaning dissipates and is lost, despite the laughter that lights up faces and convulses bodies. One might as well quit the theater and, in solitude, take up the text and read. (*Molière, notre contemporain* 174–75)

Convinced that Molière was a realist who achieved an exemplary understanding of the human condition, Arnavon grappled with the problem of presenting *The School for Wives* in a manner that communicated the play's moral vision to a contemporary audience. Molière's script, however, was not written for early twentieth-century theater artists; it addresses itself to a theater praxis that was exclusively of Molière's own time. Arnavon was disturbed, for instance, by the number of asides in Molière's script: "Some asides are barely tolerable for a modern public, notably those in the notary scene" (*L'Ecole des femmes* 54). He believed that a modern audience would perceive a large number of asides as an affront to "common sense." At the same time, curiously enough, he felt no anxiety about the modern spectator's ability to tolerate the alexandrine. Both the aside and the alexandrine are dramatic conventions that have fallen into disuse in the present century. What distinguishes them in Arnavon's mind, however, is that while the alexandrine passes unnoticed as the traditional and therefore natural medium of French poetic drama, the aside can only call attention to itself as an outdated convention of performance that is, by virtue of its having fallen into disuse, "unnatural." (On the other hand, Antoine Vitez's postrealist work is remarkable for its insistence on presenting the alexandrine as a self-consciously unnatural, intensely manipulated dramatic technique.) The aside causes problems for Arnavon because it calls attention to itself as an outdated, unrealistic stage convention that can only serve to undermine the illusion of the real that he takes to be the goal of mise en scène.

As in his book on *Tartuffe,* Arnavon devotes a large portion of his analysis to developing a modern scenography for *The School for Wives.* In the case of this play, however, Arnavon suggests that a modern stage design might do more than provide a convincingly realistic frame for the familiar events of Molière's classic drama. He suggests that a persuasively articulated realist mise en scène will provide a solution to the structural problems that have been identified in *The School for Wives:*

> Chrysalde, who appears and disappears, holding forth in amusing monologues having little to do with the action, . . . numerous conversations between Arnolphe and Horace. . . . That charming story made up of nothing but reports . . . loses its sparkle if one fails to find some staging device that will introduce some variety into these meetings. . . . The design should, therefore, be conceived in such a fashion that these oddities, and quite a few others, will barely be noticed. (30–31)

From his point of view, these "oddities" constitute obstacles between the play and its audience; they obscure Molière's message just as they inhibit the play from realizing its full aesthetic potential.[7] These oddities are, of course, problematic only to the extent that they do not conform to either Arnavon's or the traditional critics' sense of what a *grande comédie* ought to be; they certainly did not prevent Molière from staging a powerful and successful theatrical event in 1662–63, and they were successfully "overcome" by Arnavon himself as well as by Louis Jouvet and Antoine Vitez, to name only the directors under discussion here. Rather than regard them as oddities, however, which implies that these elements are peripheral to the main thrust of Molière's dramaturgy, it may be more helpful to recognize that the so-called problems frequently involve the most theatrically complex scenes in Molière's play, scenes that are, in fact, the key scenes in the play. I would also argue that the directors under consideration found their most striking and influential staging ideas, ideas that gave each mise en scène its characteristic profile, in their solutions to the problems presented by Molière's irregular dramaturgy.

The problems that Arnavon encounters in Molière's script call attention to the presence of the actor as actor onstage and, by so doing, disrupt the illusion of the real that he wants to create. These problems are not, however, confined to dramatic conventions such as the asides and soliloquies; Arnavon is also disturbed by traditional mises en scène that fail to communicate what he takes to be the essential "simplicity" of the play:

> The interpretation will give full measure to this admirable simplicity by refraining from emphasizing numerous bits of staging that have, until now, provoked fairly vulgar and notoriously superfluous hilarity. Under the pretext of remaining faithful to the ancient ways . . . many artists, even some among the most renowned, have turned classical comedies into buffooneries ([ils] ont "bouffonné" la

comédie classique). Great masterpieces have, by this process, been transformed into farces. (*L'Ecole des femmes* 41)

Arnavon uses the term *simplicity* interchangeably with *clarity* in this and other books to invoke Molière's status as a classic author. The kind of simplicity that Arnavon has in mind, however, is not the opposite of "complexity." Arnavon himself, after all, is proposing a mise en scène that is considerably more complex than the traditional model in a variety of ways. What Arnavon seeks to achieve with his rhetoric of simplicity and clarity is to undermine the apparently natural linkage between the conventional mises en scène that were still in the repertory of the Comédie-Française in 1936 and Molière's meaning. His proposed mise en scène will be "simple," he suggests, because it will refrain from introducing a layer of overt theatricality between Molière's message and Arnavon's intended audience. All aspects of the ideal mise en scène, according to Arnavon, will serve a precise function in the most economical manner, just as the great classic achieves its aesthetic effect with the utmost economy of means; no masterpiece includes unessential comic sequences.

Given Arnavon's faith in the classic's potential to delight and instruct, it is not surprising that he should condemn what he sees as the tendency to introduce buffoonery into these plays, which results, he seems to imply, in mocking the plays themselves (*bouffonner* may also be translated as "to make fun of" or "to ridicule"). Arnavon might, therefore, be understood to imply that by showing a proper degree of respect for the classic text, the mise en scène teaches, by example, respect for the playwright's moral vision embodied in the work of art as well as respect for the canon of great works that make up, in Arnavon's view, the foundation of the national culture. Arnavon's belief that Molière's *morale* has an enduring pedagogic value has its roots in the nineteenth century. In his well-documented article, "The Molière Myth in Nineteenth-Century France," Ralph Albanese, Jr., traces the growth of a "strong . . . confusion between nationalism and Moliérism" that endeavored to "make of Molière an *instituteur national,* to extract from his works the constitutive elements of an inalterable morality capable of preserving national cohesion" (244–45).

Arnavon does not argue that traditional comic stage business fails to provoke laughter or provide a specifically theatrical pleasure; rather, he insists that such laughter, along with the comic routines that provoke it, prevents the audience from appreciating what he takes to be the play's more important qualities: "We must admit that our classic theater has moved further and further away from all reality and has turned into a kind of exercise, almost like being in school—a spectacle in which the effort of composition is too obvious" (*L'Ecole des femmes* 16). Arnavon is more interested in "how the classics ought to be used," as Bernard Dort puts it, than in remaining faithful to the traditions of performance, and he is concerned that *The School for Wives* not be perceived as merely a "bit of theater" (*morceau de théâtre*) (*L'Ecole des femmes* 41).

Arnavon believes that classic comedy is fundamentally serious both in substance and tone, and that farcical routines and other kinds of clowning about onstage are, consequently, totally inappropriate to the contemporary reenactment of a classic drama and the contemporary enjoyment of a classic text. They are inappropriate, however, only to the extent that the classic text is itself perceived as incapable of including "superfluous" elements. Arnavon is careful, however, to distinguish between the superfluous stage business that he finds adorning traditional mises en scène and the nonrealistic facets of Molière's script. The former may be simply ignored (because it no longer calls attention to itself), whereas the latter cannot. As a result, even Arnavon incorporates some carefully controlled farcical elements, usually involving Alain and Georgette, in his own mise en scène.

Scenic Realism and the *Place de Ville*

Arnavon's décor is designed to provide a realistically justified location for each event in the play, whether it be physical or verbal, as well as a psychologically sympathetic environment for the humanist concerns that he locates in Molière's text. Arnavon conceives his décor as a response to a perceived cleavage between the twentieth-century perception of the play and the seventeenth-century theatrical practice that provided the context for its initial creation. Broadly speaking, Arnavon seeks to stage what he sees as the eternal truths of the play—namely, its insights into human behavior and an attendant moral commentary (from the perspective of a twentieth-century understanding) on these truths and their potential place on the contemporary stage. In his opinion, Molière's characters promise to satisfy a contemporary audience because their psychological depth and complexity continue to afford matter for thought, whereas the staging derived from the seventeenth century (or its corrupted twentieth-century equivalent as it is enshrined at the Comédie-Française) would only bury the substantive issues in the plays beneath layers of self-conscious theatricality.

Each element of Arnavon's mise en scène is calculated to impress upon the spectator the enduring validity of Molière's moral vision. Given Arnavon's unwavering conviction that Molière's vision could be effectively communicated only through the medium of a realistic mise en scène, he seeks to deemphasize those aspects of *The School for Wives* that have most frequently provoked accusations of implausibility. The most important of these aspects, in Arnavon's mind, is Molière's decision to set the action of the play in a *place de ville* (town square), the most open of all urban spaces. Arnavon encounters problems with Molière's chosen setting as early as the play's opening dialogue. For Arnavon, the problem arises because Molière's setting of the *place de ville* seems to provide a highly implausible frame for Chrysalde's remark to Arnolphe, that they can now converse "without fear of being overheard" (*sans crainte d'être ouïs*). Schooled in the realist aesthetic that dictates that the scenery and the script should not openly contradict each other (unless an obvious dramatic irony requires they do so), Arnavon comments: "Hearing these words, the listener wants to see the characters have their conversation in complete privacy" (*L'Ecole des femmes* 45). Such an irony, however, was indeed what Molière may have had in mind, for when Arnolphe (played by Molière) and Chrysalde first had this conversation in 1662, they were standing on a stage that was already populated by spectators. Molière's *place de ville* refers both to the fictitious urban area for which the scenic space metaphorically substitutes as well as to the public arena that is the stage itself. Ironically, Arnavon's misplaced confidence in the self-sufficiency of Molière's printed text (the very principle that provides the foundation for his attack on the stage tradition) leads him to an interpretation of Chrysalde's line that undermines the essential dramatic irony that structures Molière's script. Arnolphe's desire to pursue his pedagogic and matrimonial designs in secret are progressively exposed and deflected in the course of the play (a dramatic action, moreover, that Arnavon himself consistently emphasizes), and the obviously public setting for this supposedly private conversation marks the beginning of the dramatic process of exposure.

Arnavon's staging of the opening conversation of *The School for Wives* is unavoidably influenced by his own experience of the actor/spectator relationship. His aesthetic is grounded in a rigorous separation of stage and auditorium that has provided the basis for theatrical realism since the nineteenth century but which was quite unimaginable in the seventeenth century. For the modern spectator, the stage is a brightly lit space adjacent to a darkened room; for his or her seventeenth-century counterpart, the stage is merely a platform erected at one end of a dimly lit room. The seventeenth-century actor is in the same room as the spectators; both the stage and the auditorium constitute one and the same large public space. As with many of Molière's major roles, Arnolphe's character appears to have been created to exploit the proximity between actor and spectator that characterized the seventeenth-century stage.

Arnavon is not, of course, the first commentator to find the town square an inappropriate setting for the apparently domestic events of the play, nor is his suggested staging an original response to the problem. In her article, "La Scène est dans une place de ville," Roselyne Laplace reproduces brief descriptions of a number of scenographic treatments of *The School for Wives*. These descriptions range from Mahelot's terse description of the first production ("There are two houses downstage and the rest represents a town square") to Michel Cournot's review in *Le Monde* of Claude Lemaire's design for the Vitez tetralogy. Laplace also includes an excerpt from Francisque Sarcey's review of a production that was staged by Montigny at the Théâtre du Gymnase in 1873:

> To frame the action, Montigny has given us a *place* which doubles as a public garden, what we today would call a square. It strikes me as a useful innovation. It justifies those long outdoor conversations, not to mention the armchair that is brought out for Arnolphe to sit on when the urge to deliver a sermon takes hold. (41)

Montigny was one of the most innovative French directors of the nineteenth century, and his experiments with furniture and realistic blocking paved the way for Antoine's mode of mise en scène.[8] Montigny's "garden" was subsequently adopted by André Antoine at the Théâtre de l'Odéon in 1908, by Lucien Guitry at the Théâtre Edouard VII in 1924, and at the Comédie-Française in 1924. Arnavon used it as the basis for his notebook mise en scène in 1936.

Arnavon considered the garden an ideal solution to the problem of where to stage scenes that realistically could not be staged in the town square, such as the promenade, the reading of the "Maxims for Marriage" (Maximes du Mariage), or the private conversation between Chrysalde and Arnolphe that opens the play. In the case of each of these sequences, Arnavon felt that the twentieth-century spectator would be taken aback by the obvious disparity between what was said by the character and the visual image presented to the spectator. He has this to say, for example, about the promenade: "The cold town square of the tradition obviously did not provide a very attractive setting in which to take a stroll. Seeing Arnolphe and Agnès going around in circles on the bare stage, the spectator was taken aback to hear, at line 459: 'This a nice place for a stroll'" (*L'Ecole des femmes* 48). The garden setting "justified" the line in the sense that it seems realistic to take a stroll in such a setting. (Arnavon found justification for the garden setting itself at l. 1149.)

The garden solved more, however, than the problem of providing a realistic justification for certain lines; it also provided a means of exploring scenographically the inside/outside dynamic that gives the dramatic structure of *The School for Wives* its characteristic contour. Indeed, the garden proved to be such a productive innovation that it was adopted, although never with as much attention to realistic detail as Jacques Arnavon's, in all major French productions, including those of Louis Jouvet and Jean Vilar, until Antoine Vitez addressed the problem of the *place de ville* in a radically new fashion in 1978.

A detailed study of Molière's script reveals, according to Arnavon, the need for twelve different locations. Arnavon was convinced that his audience would not tolerate so many scene changes, even if stage machinery were used to effect these changes as rapidly as possible. Instead of designing twelve different locations, he opted for a single setting that incorporated the twelve different locations.[9] Arnavon's single setting included an architectural unit with functional doors, windows, and a balcony; a tree-lined lane; a garden; a suburban roadway substituting for the town square; and a collection of trees, shrubs, and outdoor furniture indicating the presence of an outdoor café (*guinguette*) opposite the private entry to the house. The tall brick wall that separates the garden from the roadway divides the scenic space between the private space of Arnolphe's hideaway for Agnès (stage left) and the public space of the country lane and the café (stage right). The public nature of the space outside the walls of Arnolphe's property is indicated by the presence of a modern institution, the outdoor café, which can hardly have been a fixture of life in seventeenth-century suburban Paris but which became a ubiquitous feature of French life in the nineteenth century. This obvious anachronism reveals Arnavon's desire to create a mise en scène that communicates directly to his own contemporaries; what matters in the café scenes is the perceived realism of the social transaction between the two characters, rather than the historical accuracy of the setting itself.

Conversations in the Town Square

For Arnavon, and for all who share the traditional view of Molière as a *moraliste,* Molière's characters are the locus of his genius as a playwright. For those who share this opinion, Molière's great characters—Arnolphe, Alceste, Tartuffe—are the reason why his plays have achieved such lasting renown and continue to be studied and performed. Arnavon's mise en scène of *The School for Wives* reflects his preoccupation with Arnolphe in that each critical choice revolves around the question of the correct, "clear" presentation of the central character. Indeed, with a separate area of the stage allocated to each of Arnolphe's important experiences, the scenic space is designed to facilitate the actor's creation of a "three-dimensional," "true-to-life" character. An Arnolphe presented in such a fashion will strike the spectator as real, Arnavon believes, because the different physical environments will enable the actor to employ a much richer range of everyday movements and postures than a flat, bare stage floor. This richer range of everyday physicalization, which complements the apparent ordinariness of the setting (i.e., it looks like an ordinary house of the period), allows the actor to present Arnolphe as a man who moves like you and me rather than like an actor in a classical play.

A series of five conversations between Arnolphe and Horace serves both to frame the action of the play and to drive it forward. Each meeting between these two competitors for Agnès's affections marks a decisive turning point in the play's development while providing the actor playing Arnolphe with a series of superb opportunities for demonstrating his comic skills. Each conversation includes a lengthy narrative by Horace of his latest offstage exploits, narratives that provoke Arnolphe to increasing degrees of panic and rage. The repeated encounters between Arnolphe and Horace present a real difficulty for directors concerned with realism. Realism normally cannot accommodate the kind of dramatic structure that Molière employs in *The School for Wives,* a structure that blatantly calls attention to its own artificiality. Consequently, since Arnavon is attempting to create a realist mise en scène, he is obliged to mitigate the anti-illusionist effects of Molière's decision to build the play around five conversations between Arnolphe and Horace:

These five "accidental" (!) meetings . . . in the same location obviously annoy the audience by making too many demands on their willingness to suspend disbelief. In order to recover a semblance of reality and to remain within the bounds of plausibility, the décor should be sufficiently complex that some surprising and unexpected detail can be introduced into the scene on each occasion. (*L'Ecole des femmes* 50–51)

Molière's dramatic strategy, however, relies on the spectator's ability to accept and even anticipate with pleasure the frequency of these meetings. Indeed, Molière's dramatic structure depends on the spectator's appreciation of the fundamental *implausibility* of the recurrent meetings between Arnolphe and Horace. Much of the comedy of these meetings stems from the purely theatrical logic that determines their frequency: they are creations of the stage, not copies from "life" (a fact that Louis Jouvet and Antoine Vitez emphasized in their mises en scène). *Vraisemblance* may require that Molière refrain from "making too many demands on [the spectators'] willingness to suspend disbelief," to use Arnavon's terms, but comedy, especially when it borders on farce, seduces the spectator with an entirely different kind of realism. The kind of realism that Arnavon seeks, however, must suppress anything that might remind the spectator that *The School for Wives* is a dramatic fiction and not a representation of the behavior of autonomous individuals in 1662.

Whereas in Molière's time the stage was both literally and figuratively a public space (in which the wealthiest patrons displayed themselves by taking seats on stage), the stage in Arnavon's time was an essentially private, metaphoric space open to the public only through the "fourth wall" of the proscenium arch. The actors in that private space were aware that they were being watched but did not allow that awareness to show through their performances. Molière's *School for Wives,* however, demands that the actor acknowledge the presence of the spectator, something he or she could not have avoided doing in the seventeenth century, when the playing area was surrounded by spectators who remained fully visible to both the actors and each other. *The School for Wives* exploits the spectators' proximity by allowing Arnolphe (and the actor playing Arnolphe—Molière himself in 1662) to communicate directly with the spectators by means of a large number of asides and frequent soliloquies. Arnolphe thus becomes a special kind of onstage spectator, a character who both participates in and observes the action in which he himself is a principal actor.

Although Arnavon's realistic aesthetic cannot accommodate Molière's onstage spectator (indeed, individuals devoted to such an aesthetic may be incapable of perceiving Molière's use of such a dramatic device), it does allow him to create what he considers plausible stagings for many of the crucial scenes in the play, notably the conversations between Arnolphe and Horace and Arnolphe and Agnès. The phrase "plausible stagings" has, of course, several ramifications: it refers to the plausibility of the location of the scene, of the characters' behavior in the scene, of the interrelationship between character and scene, and of the relationship between dialogue and scene (the ability of the décor to illustrate or to assist the spectator in imagining what is referred to by the characters, principally the events recounted by Horace).

At their first meeting in act 1, scene 4, Arnolphe directs Horace to a table in the outdoor café and buys him some wine, a generous gesture that echoes his later offer of financial support to his friend's son (*L'Ecole des femmes* 105). The café table provides a distinct location for a scene that might otherwise be identified as taking place, from Arnavon's point of view, nowhere. Since he cannot accept the *place de ville* as a realistic location for this conversation, any décor that merely represents a nonspecific, abstract public place can never satisfy Arnavon's realism-inspired concerns about precise location.

In addition to providing a specific location, the scenic image of the café establishes a frame of reference for the conversation—a conversation between two men in a café—with which spectators are bound to be familiar. The familiar parameters of café behavior provide a specific frame of cultural reference for the scene, an identity and style that Arnavon prefers to the kind of overtly "theatrical" acting that a staging devoid of realistic location tends to impose on the performers. Such overtly theatrical acting may succeed in diverting the spectator's attention away from what Arnavon perceives as the fundamental implausibility of such a performance, but Arnavon insists that something essential is lost in the process:

> In order to conceal the lack of realism, the actor pushes his performance to the extent that it becomes an exhibition of virtuosity. . . . Technical skill and dexterity end up taking the place of sincerity, without which the actor's art no longer possesses genuine beauty or grandeur. (*L'Ecole des femmes* 17)

Familiar, everyday settings, such as the sidewalk café, are more suited to the realistic mode of acting that seeks to offer representations of recognizably "ordinary" behavior. Unlike the rhetorical mode of classical acting that Arnavon rejects, the realistic mode presents behavior that might, plausibly, be found outside the theater. Because realistic acting reflects contemporary behavior (i.e., the behavior of the actor's contemporaries), Arnavon believes that it permits the spectator to appreciate the gradual revelation of Molière's characters.

As we have seen, Arnavon's reading of Molière's characters derives from his own conviction that Molière's is a realist dramaturgy. The complex, realistic characterizations that Arnavon seeks to present in his realist mise en scène are, to his way of thinking, more fully representative of the ideological complexity of Molière's play than what he sees as the caricatures of traditional mises en scène. When the actors no longer seek to demonstrate their virtuosity, Arnavon believes, Molière's characters emerge as individuals sincerely embroiled in an emotionally charged sequence of events. Rejecting the traditional interpretation of Molière's characters, which are based on the belief that Molière's script is intended principally as a vehicle for virtuoso acting, Arnavon arrives at a revisionist understanding of the characters' identities. His description of Horace, for instance, rejects the traditional reading in favor of a more sympathetic perspective on the young man's behavior: "Horace is not a rake who boasts of his conquests. On the contrary, he is honest, loyal, truly in love with Agnès; he respects her and dreams only of marrying her" (*L'Ecole des femmes* 113).

Arnavon effectively uses his realistic scenography to justify realistic blocking in which each movement is designed either to illustrate an emotional reaction or to represent ordinary behavior that is not apparently emotionally charged. (We are now accustomed to seeing such realistic blocking in otherwise nonrealistic mises en scène.) From time to time, the blocking achieves both ends simultaneously, as in the encounters between Arnolphe and Horace and Arnolphe and Agnès. In act 3, scene 4, for instance, Arnavon uses the downstage right bench to create a staging that departs in significant ways from the established tradition:

> Traditionally, the actors play the entire scene on their feet with much crossing back and forth and with Horace making a display of exuberance, petulance, wit. . . . On the other hand, one could show, in the first half of the scene, . . . a Horace who is demoralized, downtrod-

> den, who . . . throws his hat on the bench and flops down beside it,
> lost in thought, and . . . with a sad and vacant look in his eyes, re-
> counts all his setbacks in a disturbed tone of voice. . . . While Horace
> unburdens himself . . . Arnolphe moves about the stage, striking a
> variety of poses, offering Horace a hypocritical sympathy that is
> moderately amusing while he reveals to the audience a delight that
> is no less comic. (198–99)

By rejecting the frenetically paced, highly physicalized traditional presentation of the scene in favor of representing what is almost banal behavior,
Arnavon succeeds in creating a fresh perspective on Horace's situation at
this moment in the play. Rather than using Horace's frustrations as the
vehicle for a set piece of bravura acting, he invites us to take Horace's
problems as seriously as Horace himself does. Of course, the actor playing
Horace is still acting, but he is no longer calling attention to the fact;
instead, he is subtly representing his character's emotions in as lifelike a
manner as possible. He is behaving more like a member of his public than
like an actor; his performance, Arnavon believes, is therefore more likely
to be judged for its sincerity than for its technical dexterity and theatrical
flair. While Horace sits on the bench, letting his facial expression and
posture convey his (temporary) sense of defeat, Arnolphe strolls back and
forth along the country lane that runs parallel to the downstage edge of the
stage, an activity that allows him to display his sympathies to Horace
while savoring his own (again temporary) victory.

Conversations in the Edenic Garden

Throughout the course of the play, Arnavon uses movement to reflect
Arnolphe's inner agitations so that each movement around the garden or
up and down the country lane comes to suggest the passing of a new
thought through the character's mind. Arnavon uses the realistic garden
to support a leisurely and halting performance of the promenade in act 2,
scene 5. Arnolphe guides Agnès slowly around the garden, making almost
a complete circuit before the first word of the scene is spoken; when the
characters finally speak (underneath the cedar tree, stage left), the conversation proceeds haltingly: "The tone is hesitant, as when a person ventures
to speak in the midst of a silence" (*L'Ecole des femmes* 140–41). This
awkward silence remains the salient feature of the scene, suggesting that
Arnolphe and Agnès have little to say to each other. Indeed, throughout

Arnavon's mise en scène, Arnolphe remains relatively inarticulate in Agnès's presence, breaking into fluent speech only when he makes his final and desperate declaration of love. The garden setting allows Arnavon to suggest the twists and turns of Arnolphe's mental landscape as he parades Agnès around the various pleasing features of the garden's design; later in the scene, when Agnès recounts her meeting with Horace, Arnolphe staggers around the garden in a subtle parody of his earlier more graceful passage.

Later, in act 3, scene 2, Arnavon places Arnolphe in an armchair underneath the cedar tree, while Agnès reads the "Maximes du Mariage" (*L'Ecole des femmes* 179). Arnavon instructs the actor playing Arnolphe to react "discretely" in order not to distract attention from Agnès (190). Although this direction suggests that Agnès is the focus of the scene, the scenic composition is designed to focus our attention on what Arnolphe himself sees. Sitting in the chair, watching and listening, Arnolphe becomes an onstage spectator, a self-appointed tutor and confessor observing his favorite pupil read her lesson. The lesson, however, is not going well, and Agnès begins to cry as she senses the future her teacher has in store for her (191).[10] The tranquil garden setting appears sharply at odds with the emotional turbulence manifested in this scene, just as Arnolphe's staggering around in the previous act seemed comically at variance with the well-groomed landscape. Watching the scene through Arnolphe's eyes, we might well see the garden as a kind of Paradise before the Fall in which the innocent Agnès substitutes for Eve. Unfortunately for Arnolphe, however, he has not assigned himself a role in this Eden. He has not cast himself as Adam; instead, he has chosen to play a divine role and remain at a distance from the arena in which his project has developed through many years. Arnolphe has been and will remain a visitor to this house. When he declares his intentions, even obliquely, Arnolphe is obliged to relinquish the role of observer and adopt the role of participant; he must become a principal player in the drama that he has scripted and so carefully prepared. Unfortunately, he is ill equipped for the role and seems unable to escape the language of the instructor. As Barbara Johnson has pointed out, he cannot teach Agnès to behave as a wife without first teaching her the very things that he has labored to keep her ignorant of for so many years, and he can "maintain his smug spectator status as long as he is his pupil's only teacher," which both he and we know is already no longer the case (167).

As Agnès begins to weep and becomes more and more emotionally distressed, the garden's Edenic identity begins to shift to a darker image. Arnavon's décor serves to identify the reading of the "Maximes du Mariage" as the turning point in the play's action. At the same time, the realistic garden that he designed as a support for the text takes on a metaphoric significance and suggests a more symbolic reading of the proposed scenography. Arnolphe's fantasy of connubial bliss starts to fade at the very moment in which he first reveals the hidden purposes of his many years of expensive pedagogy. The Romantic autumnal palette of Arnavon's imagined landscape provides an ironic comment on the development of the dramatic action as the rich, warm colors of the leaves already signal the decay of Arnolphe's dream of "life in the garden with Agnès" and suggest that the energies of the young Horace and Agnès will triumph over the guile of the older Arnolphe.

Chapter 5

Louis Jouvet: Inside and Outside
The School for Wives

The School for Wives is a vaudeville. It's different from . . . *The Misanthrope;* it's a
vaudeville.

—Louis Jouvet

A Different Approach to History

In 1936, the same year that Jacques Arnavon published his *L'Ecole des
femmes de Molière,* Louis Jouvet presented his mise en scène of *The
School for Wives* at the Théâtre de l'Athénée in Paris. With sets and
costumes by the painter Christian Bérard, the Jouvet mise en scène has
become one of the most influential Molière productions of the twentieth
century (Dort, "Un Age d'or" 1003). Indeed, Jouvet's *School for Wives*
maintains a special position among twentieth-century productions as the
production that rehabilitated the play's reputation after a long period of
relative neglect.[1] As a testimony to the influence of Jouvet's mise en
scène, Lipnitzki's photographs of Bérard's scenic designs have been
widely reproduced and are still included in school editions such as those
published by Bordas and by Larousse. Indeed, the Bérard/Jouvet
scenography continues to influence productions whose directors interpret
The School for Wives in a manner quite different from Jouvet's. For
example, Jacques Le Marquet's décor for Jean-Paul Roussillon's noteworthy 1973 production at the Comédie-Française clearly derives, in many
important respects, from Bérard's.

As usual with productions that challenge orthodox interpretations and
stagings sanctioned by tradition, the critical response was mixed. Some
critics welcomed Jouvet's innovations; others rejected them. In short,
Jouvet's mise en scène was received by the critics in exactly the same
fashion as Antoine's revolutionary *Tartuffe* in 1907. The public, on the
other hand, responded with enthusiasm, and Jouvet's production enjoyed

111

an unprecedented long and profitable run. The production's success was all the more remarkable as the Théâtre de l'Athénée was not, at that time, a subsidized state theater whose audience had developed a taste for the classical repertory.[2] On the contrary, the theater was almost exclusively associated with the presentation of new plays, among which were the plays of Jean Giraudoux in productions directed by Jouvet. The popular acclaim that greeted this production attests to Jouvet's success in finding a way of making a compelling piece of contemporary theater with Molière's script.

As we have seen, the realist theater of the late nineteenth and early twentieth centuries provided Arnavon with a model of a theater that spoke to his contemporaries with an urgent and compelling voice. This theater explored many of the most disturbing issues of the period in a fashion that struck Arnavon as analogous to the ways in which Molière's theater must have struck his seventeenth-century contemporaries. Arnavon believed that, if he were alive, Molière would embrace the realist aesthetic and take on the important political and social questions of the modern era. Ultimately, for Arnavon, Molière's theater was a realist theater—that is, a theater that represented life as seen by the human eye and heard by the human ear, a theater devoted to representing the offstage world by replicating it in an immediately accessible fashion, however coded. From Arnavon's perspective, theater history could be seen as a process of refining the codes of representation to the point that the need for codes all but disappeared, and "life" itself, in its innumerable physical details, could be figured onstage. Life, for Arnavon, meant social life, the life of men and women in the everyday world.

Arnavon's work, then, can be viewed as an effort to make Molière's dramaturgy and moral philosophy intelligible to his contemporaries. This goal could best be achieved, Arnavon decided, by showing the extent to which Molière was already a realist playwright as well as by showing how readily his scripts could be accommodated to the practices of the modern realist stage. In order to carry out this task, Arnavon was compelled, as we have seen, almost page by page, to suppress or compensate for what he saw as the outdated aspects of Molière's dramatic structure. Ultimately, Arnavon was both helped and hindered by his own understanding of realist dramaturgy and scenography. His familiarity with the realist creative process as it had been developed in the nineteenth century enabled him to apply that process in a detailed fashion to the rereading of Molière. At the same time, however, his immersion in the realist aesthetic made it literally impossible for him to appreciate a dramatic structure that exploited discontinuity and improbability. Arnavon's techniques permitted him to construct an image of the seventeenth century that was convincing from the rational, positivist perspective of late nineteenth-century historiography; that is, they allowed him to create a "historically accurate" scenography that framed those events in such a manner that his contemporaries would, Arnavon believed, be able to comprehend their emotional, psychological, and moral resonances. Those same techniques even made it possible for Arnavon to "correct" some of the problems that commentators have repeatedly identified in the structure of the play. To the extent that he and directors like him succeed in suppressing the obviously outdated aspects of the classic text (directors continue to use the very techniques that Arnavon and Antoine pioneered), they make it seem as if the years that separate Molière from us hardly matter. If only we can rethink Molière's dramatic ideas in terms of contemporary practice, Arnavon's example implies, Molière can remain our contemporary forever.

Like Arnavon, Jouvet found a way to reread Molière's text in the light of contemporary theatrical practice; the difference, however, lies in the nature of that practice. In order to understand the ways in which Jouvet differs from Arnavon, we need to examine the factors that shaped Jouvet's aesthetic. As we have seen, Arnavon's aesthetic is grounded in the post-Naturalist phase of André Antoine's realist aesthetic—that is, in Antoine's mises en scène of the 1890s and the early 1900s. Jouvet's work, on the other hand, is rooted in the antirealist theater of the late nineteenth and early twentieth centuries and, more specifically, in the bare stage (*tréteau nu*) aesthetic of Jacques Copeau.

In the early years of his career, Jouvet was one of the core members of Jacques Copeau's company at the Théâtre du Vieux Colombier.[3] At the Théâtre du Vieux Colombier, Jouvet worked, at one time or another, in almost every position usually found in a theater: actor, stage designer, lighting designer, stage manager, carpenter, electrician, and others. In short, he began his career as a true *homme de théâtre*, interested in exploring every aspect of the art. The only field in which he did not make a significant contribution was playwriting. His years with Copeau gave Jouvet an opportunity to develop his art in an arena removed from the economical constraints of the mainstream professional theater. When he left Copeau, he went on to become one of the most powerful and influential personalities in French theater, as one of the four members of the Cartel. In addition to his influence as an artistic director, he achieved considerable fame as an actor and as a teacher of acting at the Conservatoire. Although he spent only a small part of his long career with Copeau, and although much of his work is quite different from (if not a rejection of) the kind of work advocated by Copeau, most historians have seen Jouvet's work as an extension of Copeau's.

Copeau is usually seen as one of those artists whose aesthetic is rooted in the antirealist, symbolist theater, in the broadest sense of that term, of the late nineteenth century. This was a theater that proclaimed itself devoted to the representation of those subjective experiences and intuitively apprehended phenomena (emotional, psychological, and spiritual) that the realist theater, with its professed devotion to the presentation of objective, observable, and quantifiable data, was content to relegate to painting, poetry, and music. On a purely technical level, the symbolist theater reintroduced painting, poetry, and music at the same time as it banished what it saw as the prosaic elements of realist writing and realist mise en scène: the preoccupation with events and objects of everyday life. In this sense, the anti-realists might be understood to be echoing Aristotle's conviction that poetry was superior to history:

> Poetry is a more philosophical and serious business than history; for poetry speaks more of universals, history of particulars. "Universal" in this case is what kind of person is likely to do or say certain kinds of things, according to probability or necessity; that is what poetry aims at, although it gives its persons particular names afterward; while the "particular" is what Alcibiades did or what happened to him. (33)

In Aristotelian terms, Arnavon and the realists he sought to emulate were concerned with history, with the life of individual men and women in a specific culture and at a given moment in time. Copeau and Jouvet, on the other hand, were more interested in those aspects of the human experience that transcended space and time. (I do not mean to imply by this that Arnavon saw Molière as a "historian" and that, as a consequence, he did not think Molière's characters universal. On the contrary, he did see them as universals. For Arnavon, both Molière's characters and Molière's *morale* transcended space and time; only his stagecraft did not.)

Copeau's work at the Vieux-Colombier represents a rejection of the realist aspects of nineteenth- and twentieth-century theater, with its pseudoscientific emphasis on observable, quantifiable phenomena in favor of an older and more poetic, more metaphysical mimesis. Jouvet expressed his own devotion to a metaphysical theater in words that might well have been written by Copeau:

> In the theater, the performance, the playing is a verification of the discovery of meaning. . . . The playing . . . must be spiritual, abstract, artificial, without affect. . . . It is a demonstration in the abstract, with no more grounding in fact than is strictly necessary, with a quick dip into the carnal, just enough to make it perceptible, to make it work on the senses. . . . What we need is a theater of abstraction. We need the great theater, the classic theater. (Qtd. in Dhomme 166)

In an effort to create a metaphysical theater, Copeau rejected the realist preoccupation with replicating the appearance of life outside the theater. He rejected even more firmly the realist project of persuading spectators to "forget" that they were in a theater along with all of the techniques of acting and mise en scène that made such persuasion possible. He rejected the realist box set filled with everyday furniture and objects in favor of a bare stage with no proscenium, backed by an abstract composition of arches, platforms, ramps, and steps, which Jouvet played a major role in designing (indeed, the architectural drawings for the renovation of the Théâtre du Vieux-Colombier are by Jouvet). This bare stage was, in Copeau's opinion, the scenic environment best suited to the universals of poetry. He enthusiastically embraced the ideas of thinkers such as Jacques Rouché, Gordon Craig, and Adolphe Appia and devoted himself to developing a language of the stage. He also attempted to reintroduce the commedia dell'arte, which he used as a reference point in developing a new system for training actors, one of whom was Jouvet. In short, Copeau preferred a blatantly theatrical style of performance and privileged an exuberant theatricality over all other values. If Arnavon used the phrase *morceau de théâtre* (a slice of theater) to condemn a performance of little or no value, Copeau could have used the same phrase to express high praise.

At Copeau's theater, all plays were staged on the same basic set. While the architecture remained constant, drapes and panels of different colors were added to create an appropriate atmosphere for each play. In addition, each production employed costume, lighting, and sound designs that were specific to the play in question. More often than not, Jouvet was

responsible for the lighting design. Copeau followed the practice of the Elizabethan theater when it came to identifying a change of location in the course of performance: he relied on his spectators to follow references to location in the dialogue. In addition, he used lighting and sound to create images of different locations.

As we have seen, Arnavon criticized Copeau's bare stage precisely because it refused to indicate, in a manner that Arnavon found legible, where a given event was taking place. Jouvet's own practice in the years following his departure from Copeau's company suggests that he may have agreed with Arnavon to a certain extent. Away from the Vieux-Colombier, Jouvet never sought to repeat Copeau's experiment with the permanent set. Instead, like the realists, he prepared a scenography for each production that was designed to complement each play's salient features. After he left Copeau, he devoted his energies almost exclusively to the discovery and production of new plays. His decision to undertake a mise en scène of *The School for Wives,* then, represents a return to the classics after almost twenty years of working with living playwrights such as Jules Romains and Jean Giraudoux.[4]

Jouvet's experience as a director of new plays significantly influenced his approach to *The School for Wives.* Although he acknowledged the difficulties presented by Molière's dramaturgy, he refused, unlike Arnavon, to accept the notion that the play's structure was flawed. Instead, he preferred to approach the play as a piece of new writing whose structure had yet to be investigated. His response to the ambiguities of character and the discontinuities of style was to design a mise en scène that would take advantage of those qualities and even present them as the most interesting features of Molière's play. Dort suggests that it is precisely this approach that separates Jouvet from his contemporaries, Jean-Louis Barrault and Jean Vilar, as well as from his mentor, Jacques Copeau:

> In the majority of his stagings of the classics, Barrault did nothing more than develop Copeau's ideas about stylization as well as his conception of an acting style that is both realistic and poetic.... Where Jouvet brought contradictions to light, Barrault fabricated unity.... One could say as much about certain Vilar productions. ("Un Age d'or" 1010–11)[5]

Barrault's and Vilar's a priori presumption of aesthetic unity (a central precept of neoclassical theater aesthetics that was further reinforced by the

Romantic theory of organic unity) places them in the same tradition of classical interpretation as Arnavon. Jouvet's willingness, however, to accept the possibility that Molière's script might contain unresolved contradictions (or that the script might even invite the exploitation of certain structural or stylistic discontinuities) associates Jouvet with a more modern attitude to the classic text.

In his article, "Un Age d'or ou: sur la mise en scène des classiques en France entre 1945 et 1960," Bernard Dort names Jouvet's productions of *The School for Wives, Tartuffe,* and *Dom Juan* "the most expansive and the most fecund work on the classics" during what he calls a "golden age" (1009). Dort attributes the exemplary achievement of Jouvet's work on Molière to his refusal to treat the apparent difficulties and contradictions of Molière's script as faults that needed to be covered over:

> What makes this trilogy so rich is precisely the sum of all the contradictions that are at its foundation. Certainly Jouvet claimed that he was being scrupulously faithful to Molière . . . but that fidelity was not a fidelity to a certain preconceived idea about the text: it was a fidelity to the text in all of its complexity—whence all of those contradictions that, rather than masking, Jouvet exposed on stage and literally turned into the engine that powered the performance. (1009)

Like Arnavon and his own mentor, Copeau, Jouvet set aside conventional professional notions of how the play should be staged and grounded his mise en scène in a detailed reading of Molière's text. In fact, Jouvet's statement, "I don't believe in mise en scène because I don't believe in having 'ideas' about plays," could have been spoken with the same conviction by Antoine, Arnavon, or Copeau (Jouvet and Pignarre 379). In Jouvet's case, however, the statement had somewhat different ramifications. Each in his own way, Arnavon and Copeau attempted to reduce the impact of, if not eliminate entirely, any element of Molière's dramaturgy, such as the town square setting, that might remind the spectators that they were watching an old play. Jouvet, on the other hand, decided to approach the problem from a different perspective. Rather than try to compensate for what the stage and literary traditions identified as Molière's "inadequacies," Jouvet chose to make those inadequacies the key elements of his production. As a result, Jouvet's *School for Wives* presented a scenographic solution to the town square problem that succeeded in completely reframing the issue. What Jouvet's mise en scène suggests is that Molière's "irregular" dramaturgy flouts the rules deliberately in order to direct the spectator's attention toward the actor playing Arnolphe (i.e., Molière himself) as the focal point of the performance. *The School for Wives* is not, Jouvet's production suggests, an objective representation of a certain society but, rather, a theatrical fable that allows Molière/Arnolphe (or in this case, as I hope to show, Jouvet/Molière/Arnolphe) to share his subjective experience with an audience.

Jouvet's mise en scène finds a solution to the problem of the town square by accepting its unreality as a setting for the play. This general acceptance of the play's fundamental antirealism also removes the issue of what realist critics and artists have considered the excessively lengthy monologues and too-frequent soliloquies. Although Jouvet's *School for Wives* succeeds because it embraces the illogical, irrational, and irregular aspects of Molière's fable, it is important to recognize that the Jouvet/Bérard scenography owes as much to the realism of Arnavon and Antoine as it does to the bare-stage poetics of Copeau. From Copeau and other nonrealists, Jouvet derives elements of an acting technique grounded in a modernized commedia dell'arte as well as a scenographic aesthetic that privileges the text and the actor over all other elements of mise en scène. From Antoine, he derives a vision of scenography that grounds characterization in a specific physical environment. In his greatest divergence from Copeau, he accepts the realist principle that a dramatic action must be located in a specific place and time. Having decided to retain Molière's designated setting for the dramatic action—a town square in seventeenth-century France—he and his scenographer visualize the Grand Siècle as the historical context of Molière's play in a way that is, as we shall see, radically different from the essentially Romantic images of that period, which had prevailed since the publication of the novels of Alexandre Dumas and the histories of Jules Michelet, images that Arnavon, along with his contemporaries, accepted without question.[6] Jouvet's mise en scène of *The School for Wives* is significant, then, for the way in which it approaches the representation of Molière's historical context, a dramatic subject that Antoine had already shown was worth exploring in its own right.

In his production of *The School for Wives*, Jouvet departs from the classic practice of mise en scène in which the director seeks to illustrate, realize, or translate (to use Marvin Carlson's terms) the classic text while making every effort to conceal his own interpretative interventions. Unlike Arnavon, Jouvet makes no effort to present his mise en scène as a natural, historically accurate representation of either seventeenth- or twentieth-century human behavior; unlike Copeau and Barrault, he makes no effort to make a specific stylistic choice (such as a twentieth-century recreation of commedia dell'arte) appear as the natural or historically accurate performance vehicle for a classic text. Arnavon's, Barrault's, and Copeau's strategies ultimately seek to make the mise en scène of the classic text appear as organically unified and homogeneous as possible; they propose a unified performance aesthetic as the naturally appropriate correlative of the "unified" classic text. Jouvet's mise en scène of *The School for Wives* represents a significant shift of directorial perspective: instead of presenting his mise en scène as yet another naturalized recreation of a familiar play, he presents a familiar play in a conspicuously theatricalized manner that calls attention to its unnatural, outdated, artificial aspects.

Jouvet does not seek to authenticate his mise en scène by suggesting either that "this is how Molière and his contemporaries looked and behaved" or that "this is how Molière and his fellow actors performed this play." Both of these modes of authentication have the unfortunate potential of inviting the spectator to draw the conclusion that he or she is attending a piece of museum theater—that is, a performance whose interest derives from its success in recreating the past. Jouvet's mise en scène of *The School for Wives* marks a significant turning point in the stage history of the play because it is the first modern production to call into question the value of reconstructing the past, whether in the manner of Antoine or in the manner of Copeau. Rather than suggest that Molière might have played Arnolphe in this fashion or that Agnès's house might have looked like this, Jouvet offers a resolutely modern version of the play that is neither modernized nor naturalized. He does not present the play as if it were the work of a modern playwright or as if its characters were real, historically contingent subjects. Instead, he takes advantage of what he saw as Molière's timeless dramaturgy to present a dramatic fable in a mise en scène that employs an acting style that blends moments of farce, realism, and romance. Jouvet's mise en scène couples this acting style with a scenography that juxtaposes a realist treatment of space with an almost surreal montage of seventeenth-century domestic, urban, and theatrical architectural details. Rather than frame the play as a historically significant product of the Grand Siècle, as earlier directors had done, Jouvet historicizes the play and, as a result, calls into question for the first time the relationship between the Grand Siècle and the modern era.

Bérard's Fairy-Tale Scenography

Today, more than fifty years after the Athénée production, Christian Bérard's scenography is still ranked among the most respected French scenic designs of this century.[7] It not only solves many of the staging problems posed by Molière's script with considerable ingenuity but also proposes a new approach to the twentieth-century scenography of plays from the classical period. In the jacket notes to a 1955 Pathé recording of Jouvet's *School for Wives* (the production became a signature piece for Jouvet, which he periodically revived whenever he needed money until the end of his career), Jouvet credits Bérard with renovating the treatment of neoclassical scenic space for both comedy and tragedy: "He is the one who rid us of the generic anteroom and those godforsaken settings with improbable architecture. . . . "

In making this claim for Bérard, Jouvet seems to ignore the work of Arnavon and Antoine, whose achievements represent a crucial stage in the development of a realist critique of "generic anteroom" scenography.[8] Similarly, and perhaps more surprisingly, Jouvet also seems to ignore Copeau's equally powerful challenge to the same kind of scenography from a nonrealist point of view. Instead of claiming that Bérard alone struck the crucial blow in the battle, it would be more accurate to say that Bérard's décor challenged the same tradition that Arnavon, Antoine, and Copeau challenged, not to mention Jouvet's own colleagues in the Cartel. On the other hand, although he ignores the tradition of revolt against the outdated norms of Molière mise en scène within which it is possible to locate Bérard's work, Jouvet is nevertheless correct in seeing Bérard's scenic designs as representing a decisive shift in Molière mise en scène as well as a decisive shift in the scenographic representation of the Grand Siècle itself. Indeed, it is possible to see Bérard's scenography as an early instance of what Planchon later called *écriture scénique.*

In the remainder of this chapter, I will be considering Bérard's scenic ideas in two ways: first, as a traditionally understood décor that seeks to provide a mimetically intelligible location for the specific sequence of dramatic events suggested by an essentially realist reading of *The School for Wives;* second, as a collection of visual references to an offstage reality (French History, French Culture, the Grand Siècle) that, when taken together, makes up an *écriture scénique* that is more concerned with Molière's play as an intersection of cultural and historical ideas and significations than as a realistic portrayal (either in seventeenth- or twenti-eth-century terms) of a group of individuals.

Christian Bérard rejected the essentially painterly aesthetic of An-toine and Arnavon in favor of neoclassical architectural forms that he abstracted and manipulated (in what might today be called a postmodernist manner) to serve Jouvet's reading of the play. Departing from the scenographic techniques derived from Renaissance perspective painting, Bérard used a free-standing three dimensional unit to represent Agnès's house. This unit stood in the center of the stage and was surrounded on three sides by an arcade. Agnès's house, with its walls and garden, was thus located in the very center of the town square.

By placing Agnès's house in the center of the stage and by making no attempt to replicate the scale of an actual dwelling, Bérard does not offer the kind of specific information about the milieu of Arnolphe's hideaway that characterized Arnavon's naturalism-inspired approach. As a result, Bérard's version of the house does not supply a realistic socioeco-nomic identity for Monsieur de la Souche's suburban property; nor does it undermine one of the play's fundamental premises—that Horace first caught sight of Agnès while wandering through a town square.

It is difficult to imagine this very first meeting in Arnavon's décor; indeed, as the play progresses, Arnavon encounters more and more difficulties in justifying his chosen location. Arnavon's décor adroitly solves the problem of finding a realistically plausible alternative to the blatant falsity of the performance tradition, in which no attempt was made to compensate for the implausibility of the repetitive meetings between the two men. Paradoxically, however, because Arnavon's realist mise en scène can never obscure the fact that Arnolphe and Horace meet more often and in a fashion that no realist dramaturgy could ever justify, it eventually draws the spectator's attention back to the very problem of implausibility that it was created to solve. Although Arnavon's mise en scène makes a strong argument for a realistic reading of the play, its power to persuade us (as a realistic drama) is finally compromised by the play's own dramatic structure.

Bérard's décor, on the other hand, eschews the kind of decorative surface detail that is typical of the realist aesthetic, freeing the spectator from questioning whether such a meeting could occur in such a location. Bérard's solution is to locate Agnès's house unequivocally *on the stage* and nowhere else. His décor suggests that the spectator might find houses somewhat like this as well as characters and events somewhat like these outside the theater but that no house exactly like this and no characters and events exactly like these could ever be found anywhere but on this stage. Bérard thus refuses to offer the illusion of a one-to-one correspondence between the stage and the world that nineteenth-century realist mise en scène was developed to create.

With its swinging walls, obviously fake shrubbery, chandeliers floating over a garden, and its "unreal" scale, Bérard's set was decidedly anti-illusionist. The spectators were never invited to forget that they were in a theater: everything onstage was presented as being of the stage—scenery, not reality. Where Arnavon felt that he had to remove all possible obstacles between stage and audience in order to make the world of the play as close as possible to that of the audience, Jouvet opted for emphasizing the theatricality of the experience in order to reveal the truths hidden in the interstices of this make-believe world on stage. The realism that interested Jouvet had nothing to do with superficially true-to-life representation; as the passage quoted earlier attests, he preferred the metaphysical to the physical.

Instead of copying historical patterns for the house and garden as Arnavon did, Bérard chose to present an abstract vision of the seventeenth century; instead of adopting a documentary approach and showing the spectator what a suburban dwelling looked like at a chosen moment in the seventeenth century, Bérard offered a stylized recreation of the dominant architectural forms of the reign of Louis XIV as they are remembered from the perspective of the twentieth century.[9] Bérard's house makes no pretense at actual scale, and his miniature neoclassical garden emphasizes the geometric ideal at the expense of the natural beauty of the vegetation. At all times, the theatricality of Bérard's décor (theatrical because it is explicitly and self-consciously of the theater) dominates, allowing it to support and supplement the play's action. In Arnavon's design architectural and landscaping elements are always in danger of being understood merely as copies of their counterparts in the real world, as scenic elements that exist merely to provide the illusion of a real place. Bérard's blatantly theatrical scenery, however, cannot be read as a set of signs referring to the real physical world, although his scenic elements clearly address the generalized notions of Grand Siècle architecture and *décoration* that exist in the minds of his spectators.

Pierre Brisson, a leading theater critic of the time, gives the following evocative description of the décor:

[The] décor [is] harsh and raw, a great deal of white, a few splashes of red; a town square surrounded by covered arcades; upstage, a tall house built like a pigeon coop, a large window with a balcony on the second floor and, in front of the house, a garden enclosed by two walls meeting at an acute angle like the prow of a ship. These walls open for certain scenes like the outside sticks of a fan, revealing squares of grass lawn, some roses, some attractive fruit growing on a trellis, the yellow stool upon which Agnès comes to get some fresh air. Four chandeliers with candles suspended between earth and sky are there to remind us—as if there were any need—that we are dealing with a piece of theater. With the clear hues and somewhat brittle allure of a colored engraving, the whole thing looks partially like a toy, partially like a décor for a carnival. (43–44)

Interestingly enough, Brisson remarks on what he sees as a similarity between Bérard's scenographic idiom and the visual vocabulary of an engraving. There is, of course, nothing remarkable in itself about his perceiving the scenic image in terms of painting or related media; the stage has been seen as a three-dimensional painting or as a kind of *tableau vivant* for centuries, and the techniques for representing the visual world onstage have usually evolved in tandem with their counterparts in the graphic arts. Indeed, visual ideas of the real have always been borrowed by the theater from the other arts, just as the other arts have borrowed ideas about the "dramatic" and the "theatrical" from the theater. What is worth remarking in the present context, however, is that Brisson's attention is caught by those elements of Bérard's visual composition that tend to question any realist or illusionist reading of the image. By invoking the medium of engraving, Brisson suggests that Bérard is attempting to create a self-consciously artificial illusion, a visual image that calls attention to itself as a coded image, an abstracted and therefore avowedly partial, even distorted, image of reality. At the same time as Bérard foregrounds the artificiality of the world he represents onstage, he is equally careful to draw our attention to the ways in which he presents this world as being closely related to the kind of reality that a scenography such as Arnavon's represents. With garden walls that converge at a preposterously acute angle at a point slightly downstage of centerstage, Bérard seems to be inverting the convention of single-vanishing-point perspective that has stood as a sign of the objectivity and truthfulness of scenic design since the Renaissance. In addition to this citation of perspective scenery and the complex of codes of representation that it calls to mind, Bérard's scenic image is entirely composed of familiar icons from French cultural history. In fact, the entire scenography is grounded in the spectator's cultural "memory" of the Grand Siècle.

Bérard's set is a montage of imaginatively transformed period details, designed to provide an environment for a comic action. Each element of this montage seems to be a comic extension or diminution of its referent in the real world of French cultural history in much the same way that items from our own everyday culture are distorted by cartoonists. Bérard offers a comic distortion of the Grand Siècle aesthetic; with their excessive regularity, his flowers and gardens mock the rational bias of Molière's period, just as the ornate chandeliers suspended over the set mock the period's taste for excessive decoration. Whereas Arnavon idealized the seventeenth century as a great flowering of humanism, Bérard and Jouvet gently mocked its worship of reason; Arnavon's Romantic décor best suited his vision of the play as a great moment in French cultural history, whereas Bérard's satirical scenic statement seems more appropriate to the farce that Molière wrote.

Brisson complimented Jouvet for incorporating farce in his mise en scène:

> While highlighting that energetic physicality that sparks the play (*pace* Brunetière and the "naturists" of the previous century), Monsieur Jouvet has managed to retain the rational tone of the dialogue. What he offers us, consequently, is purely French, which is to say, Moliéresque: a perfect balance of farce and classical drama. (44)

Like many critics, Brisson did not perceive décor as an integral part of the mise en scène: for him, scenic design was not yet scenography. As a result, he does not appreciate the extent to which Bérard's design participates in creating what he calls the "Moliéresque" tone of the production. Indeed, Bérard provides much more than just a plausible location for the events of the play; he also creates a visual environment that complements the many different tones that make up the play's "Moliéresque" quality.

Bérard's scenography succeeds in complementing the play's structure by reminding the spectator of the technical realities of seventeenth-century theatrical performance. For instance, the chandeliers that Bérard suspended over the stage recall the stage lighting that Molière himself used and provide a stark contrast with the stage lighting of Jouvet's production.

Molière's candles can never have approached the sheer intensity of the light that Jouvet's electrical floodlights and spotlights direct toward the stage. Molière and his actors performed under the same candlelight that illuminated their audience; to the extent that Jouvet's spectators were illuminated at all, they were lit only by the light reflected by the white walls of Bérard's set. The chandeliers thus economically historicize both Molière's play and Jouvet's mise en scène, reminding the members of the audience of the years that separate Jouvet from Molière by calling attention to the significant technological developments that have been introduced during the intervening time span. In addition, the chandeliers lend a surreal, fairy-tale aspect to Jouvet's mise en scène that reminds the spectator, perhaps subconsciously, that traditional notions of realism might not be relevant to *The School for Wives* at all.

Inside and Outside Arnolphe's Schoolhouse

Disturbed by the "irrationality" of showing Arnolphe conducting his private relationship with Agnès in the town square indicated in Molière's script, Arnavon developed a scenic treatment for *The School for Wives* that distinguished clearly between events on the basis of where they took place. Arnavon's most important distinction was between those events that occurred on Arnolphe's property—that is, inside the house or garden—and those that took place outside Arnolphe's walls, whether in the country lane or the roadside café. Because he was more interested in the events that transpired inside the walls of Arnolphe's property, Arnavon devoted the greater part of the stage to the scenic representation of Arnolphe's house and garden. Although his décor suggested the importance of the inside/outside dynamic in the world of *The School for Wives,* his division of the stage into two areas separated by a garden wall running perpendicular to the proscenium, with the house and garden stage left (inside) and the lane and café stage right (outside), did not deal persuasively with the spatial ambiguities inherent in Molière's script. Louis Jouvet's mise en scène, on the other hand, provides a subtle examination of those very ambiguities.

Two recent critical discussions of *The School for Wives* complement Jouvet's reading of the play, although they take quite different approaches to its inside/outside dynamic. Focusing on the dramatic functions of the door, the window, and the balcony, Robert Nicolich shows how Molière has dramatized the ideas of enclosure and liberation:

Arnolphe has never considered the "leaks" in his otherwise "water-
tight" plan. It is on the balcony that Agnès sees and is first seen by
Horace. . . . Thus the balcony seems to play a role in helping vision
to defy all the material limitations of walls and door which en-
close . . . Molière has cleverly interwoven the stage setting, door,
window and balcony into the plot of *L'Ecole des femmes,* so that
these "props" would seem to have taken on somewhat of a dramatic
role of their own, in both on-stage and off-stage action. (376)[10]

Jouvet made extensive use of working doors, window, and balcony in his
mise en scène. In a radical departure from the stage tradition, he even
used them to stage the events that Horace narrates in his long speeches to
Arnolphe.[11] Jouvet showed Agnès at her window, throwing pebbles and
a letter down to the street below, and Horace moving a ladder up against
the side of the house. In addition, he invented a farcical staging for the
scene with the notary that made effective use of the inside/outside dynamic suggested by the garden walls: as the notary addressed Arnolphe,
Arnolphe climbed up and down a free-standing ladder, sometimes pausing
to sit on the top rung, to see if he could catch Horace lurking outside his
property.[12]

Ralph Albanese, Jr., offers a different kind of commentary on the
play's inside/outside dynamic: he uses the metaphor of scenic space as a
kind of expressionistic image of the situation and feelings of Arnolphe and
Agnès (he refers to neither a specific décor nor the implied scenic space
of Molière's script).[13] Where Nicolich emphasized the dialectic between
opening and closing (a dialectic that is potently figured by Bérard's opening and closing garden walls) and argued that a total and permanent
sequestration was an impossibility in such a world, Albanese sees only a
"hermetically sealed universe" dominated by the theme of "suffocation"
(*Le Dynamisme de la peur* 140–41). For Albanese, the stage itself is
invested with a "scenic fatality" that makes it an appropriate locus for
Arnolphe's tragedy:

For a man who, by virtue of the power of his gaze, maintains Agnès
in a state of submission, becoming the object of a spectacle is to be,
at a stroke, diminished in stature, to be transformed radically into an
object. From master-spectator, Arnolphe progresses to the stage
where he is the thing at which the spotlight is inexorably aimed; his

drama is precisely to be an actor who will forever remain a prisoner of the stage. (152)

Albanese imagines Arnolphe progressively becoming a helpless prisoner of the scenic space, changing through the course of the play from a spectator at the comedy of infidelity to a playwright/director trying to prevent his intended wife's potential infidelity and, finally, to a foolish actor trapped onstage in the drama of his own personal tragedy of betrayal. As the betrayed would-be husband, Albanese suggests, Arnolphe finds that he has less and less freedom of movement onstage: "The futility of these attempts at scenic mobility underlines the extent to which he suffers from a lack of space" (141). Albanese thus employs a modern critical vocabulary to restate, albeit in a significantly different fashion, a Romantic vision of Arnolphe's "tragedy" that has been current for at least 150 years.

On a purely literal level, Albanese is not correct when he states that Arnolphe suffers from a lack of physical space. In fact, Arnolphe moves around the stage quite freely, and nobody attempts to prevent his final exit. Indeed, Arnolphe believes that his own freedom of movement in and around the house gives him a decided advantage over Horace, who he wrongly believes to be almost as restricted in his movements as Agnès. It is only near the very end of the play that he appreciates the extent to which freedom of movement is an irrelevant issue. But Albanese is not talking about real scenic space or referring to specific mises en scène; nor is he talking about scenic space in the context of an imagined mise en scène: he is using the *idea* of scenic space much as Will Moore used the idea of the mask. For Albanese, the imagery of scenic space helps him describe his understanding of Arnolphe's experience, an understanding that has much in common with Jacques Arnavon's, who also sees Arnolphe's experience in essentially tragic (and Romantic) terms.

Albanese is correct in drawing our attention to the importance of the activity of spectating in the play's dramatic structure, although he again uses the metaphor of spectating rather than describing a specific activity of the actor playing Arnolphe. In performance, the actor cannot take full advantage of the comic possibilities for onstage spectating suggested in Molière's script (and exploited in Jouvet's mise en scène) if, at the same time, he is projecting to the audience Albanese's sense of Arnolphe's scenic claustrophobia. Arnolphe does not suffer from a lack of scenic space; he suffers because he cannot escape the attention of the spectators during those moments that he finds most acutely embarrassing, and he suffers because he believes himself to be "responsible" for the audience's intense interest in the proceedings, responsible because he himself has encouraged their interest at every step in the progress of the play's events. Although Jouvet extensively explores Arnolphe's pain both as "actor" and "director," as I will discuss, his choice of performance conventions, most significantly his emphasis on farce, serves to define the character's emotional experience more concretely than Albanese's comparatively abstract narrative of Arnolphe's metaphysical despair.

Inside and Outside: The Actor as Spectator

Commentators have remarked since Molière's time that Arnolphe's role has an unusually high proportion of lines that are spoken either as asides or soliloquies. Indeed, more than one tenth of the script serves as a vehicle for direct contact between the actor playing Arnolphe and the audience. In these addresses to the spectators, Arnolphe attempts to persuade his audience to share his perspective, to agree that women cannot be trusted to remain faithful to their husbands, and to approve of his chosen method of circumventing woman's "natural duplicity." As the action of the play progresses, however, Molière's script suggests that Arnolphe becomes more interested in encouraging the spectators to cheer him on in his battle with Horace. And, as events move finally beyond his control, Arnolphe turns to his audience for sympathy rather than support. Arnolphe never breaks his intimate connection with the audience and remains constantly aware of its presence in the course of his various conversations with all the other characters. Thus, Arnolphe is at all times both actor and spectator, a participant in the events of the drama who is also uniquely privileged to share an outsider's point of view in the very moment of the action. With a central character who is, quite literally, simultaneously a peripheral character, both inside and outside the dramatic action, *The School for Wives* constitutes a remarkable experiment in dramaturgy. Jouvet's mise en scène constitutes one of the most impressive explorations of this century of the complex interplay between character and scenic space suggested by Molière's script.

Arnolphe's relationship with the audience is dramatically complex. Unfortunately, however, readers have been too willing to take everything the character says at face value, paying very little attention to the special nature of the theatrical script as a text that always implies more than it explicitly contains. Arnavon's humanism-inspired desire to remain faithful to the letter of the printed text by ensuring that his décor provided scenic illustration for every word of dialogue was not, as we have seen, accompanied by an equal degree of sensitivity to the dramatic conventions in which that dialogue was grounded. An insufficient consideration of the comic structures of Arnolphe's relationship with the audience largely accounts for the number of critics and directors who, like Albanese, continue to read this play as a tragedy. (No first-rank French director has staged an unequivocally comic production of *The School for Wives* since World War II, although Vitez combined farce and tragedy.) The romantic notion that Molière transposed the pain of his personal life into the characters and events of his plays remains influential, even in Antoine Vitez's postmodern mise en scène; in those few instances in which a Romantic interpretation of the play has been avoided, a preoccupation with the social cruelties of the seventeenth century has resulted in mises en scène that are even darker in tone than those influenced by Romantic views of the relationship between the artist and his art.[14]

More than any other factor, Arnolphe's simultaneous awareness of both the spectators and the other actors releases the comic energy in the play. At all times, his perception of events is double; he is conscious of both his own responses to an event and the audience's potential evaluation of that event, an evaluation that, Arnolphe fears, will more often than not be expressed by laughter. The manner in which Molière theatricalizes Arnolphe's psychospatial relationship to the events of the drama creates an objective, scenic image of the character's double perspective and his unusually obsessive fear of being cuckolded; Arnolphe's relationship to the scenic space itself and the spectators in the adjacent auditorium thus dramatizes his particular paranoia.

Molière's script contains a number of soliloquies that provide the actor playing Arnolphe with a vehicle for creating and maintaining an open communication with the audience throughout the entire play. Each time the actor is left "alone" onstage by another character's exit, Arnolphe turns to address the audience (or, in Arnavon's "fourth-wall" mise en scène, to think aloud in their presence).[15] Approaching the audience in this manner allows Arnolphe (and the actor playing Arnolphe) to create the theatrical fiction that he shares, or believes that he shares, the audience's perspective on events. At the same time, the actor playing Arnolphe never ceases playing Arnolphe; he never pretends to become a part of the audience. Standing downstage, sharing his thoughts with the spectators, Arnolphe appears simultaneously as an actor and as a spectator who is privileged to comment aloud on the action of the play; he is an actor who is also an onstage spectator. In the seventeenth century, Molière played to two quite separate audiences: one small group of wealthy or otherwise privileged spectators who sat on the stage itself and the majority of the audience who sat or stood offstage. (Molière thus had the option of playing Arnolphe's soliloquies to the small group of onstage spectators, an option that was not available to Arnavon, Jouvet, or Vitez.) Because part of the audience was already onstage and, consequently, already part of the play, Molière had very little difficulty establishing Arnolphe as both actor and onstage spectator. In addition, this communication between Molière/Arnolphe and his audience was not hampered by the modern practice of darkening the auditorium, a practice that has done more than any other to effect a radical alteration in our perception of the activities of acting and spectating.

Several times in the course of the performance, Arnolphe addresses a quick comment to the spectators, an aside that serves to suggest that he is still, in the very heat of the moment, symbolically if not literally at center stage, capable of seeing events from the spectators' perspective. Even without an aside, Arnolphe can at any moment, simply by looking at the audience, indicate with an appropriate expression or gesture that he remains aware of their perspective.

At the beginning of the play, Arnolphe talks easily and at some length with Chrysalde in a conversation that can be played in such a fashion as to include the audience overtly; at the end of the play, at his final exit, Arnolphe is reduced to an inarticulate gasp or grunt, "Ouf," as events pass beyond his ability either to comprehend or influence them. His easy, fluent speech gradually becomes inarticulate as his only pupil demolishes his educational theories before his very eyes and the eyes of the spectators. Arnolphe's confidence in the spectators' willingness to see things from his perspective, which is the basis for his belief that he shares their perspective, gradually crumbles in the face of their laughter as he finds himself in the awkward position of the pupil learning a painful lesson. By the end of the play, fully aware of his own foolishness, Arnolphe discovers that he has turned into the very object of derision he so mercilessly mocked in the opening dialogue. Having acknowledged the presence of the audience from the very beginning of the play, he can hardly pretend that there are no witnesses to his defeat. Molière thus creates a dramatic mechanism that allows the actor playing Arnolphe to harness the audience's laughter to heighten the theatricality of a given moment, a mechanism that demands the very highest acting skills in that it places almost the entire burden of the play on a single actor. As a result of this structure, productions of *The School for Wives* succeed or fail principally on the strength of the performance of the actor playing Arnolphe.

Jouvet was fascinated by the character of Arnolphe as a young acting student and auditioned (unsuccessfully) in the role for the Conservatoire; he later played the part with the Théâtre d'Action d'Art, a company made up of theater students and of which he was a founding member (Knapp, *Louis Jouvet* 11–13). He had to wait almost twenty years, however, to play the part on a professional stage in a now legendary performance that adroitly exploited the self-conscious theatricality of Molière's script. Bernard Dort relates how Jouvet managed to appear simultaneously to be both inside and outside the character, manipulating his own presence-as-actor as a significant motif in the mise en scène:

> At his first entrance, he introduced us to this bewigged old man, covered with ribbons and frufru, with the face of a clown, as a marionette. But this marionette was puffed up with pride at playing an important character: that of Arnolphe, to be exact, who believes that he has dealt himself all the trump cards, and who affects a self-assured manner, with more than a little exaggeration, like a second-rate actor playing the King in a tragedy. . . . Then, the marionette progressively came to pieces, by fits and starts, and the laughs turned into long, painful, grotesque hiccups. Arnolphe began to sweat—the perspiration ran down his clown make-up, dissolving the white and the red; and here was Jouvet, pulling out a large white handkerchief from under his breeches, beginning to dab at his face and wipe under his wig. He even patted his whole body . . . as if to reassure himself that he was still there, that he was still the man he believed himself to be. For that matter, the spectator was not at all sure of what he was faced with: Arnolphe winning, Arnolphe losing, or Jouvet himself, a spectator at his own character's crushing defeat. . . . There was something genuinely vertiginous about this: not only an oscillation, a continual to-and-fro between the tragic and the comic, between the pathetic and the ridiculous, but also a perpetual exchange between the hero and the actor, between the past and the present, text and body, control and chaos. ("Sur deux comédiens" 30)

Here, Dort evokes Jouvet's adept articulation of Molière's inside/outside dynamic with remarkable eloquence and attention to detail; he also helps us understand the degree to which Jouvet's performance is itself constructed as a site of cultural intertextuality. In the same way that Bérard's scenography recalls and manipulates many different visual icons that we see as emblematic of French seventeenth-century culture, Jouvet's performance appears to be at least partially constructed as a consciously fashioned montage of images of actors and acting. Jouvet's adoption of the hiccup, for instance, as a means of expressing Arnolphe's increasingly unhappy reactions to Horace's exploits, makes clever use of Molière's own reputed difficulties with this embarrassing condition. In a sense, then, Jouvet is not only offering his audience a performance of Arnolphe and of Jouvet-playing-Arnolphe; he is also offering them a performance of Jouvet-playing-Molière-playing-Arnolphe.

In *Molière and the Comedy of Intellect,* Judd Hubert takes an approach to the play that has much in common with Jouvet's. Hubert adroitly draws a balance between the tragic, literary-philosophical view of the protagonist's experience and the theatrical potential for mocking that view in performance:

> Although classical canons proscribed the juxtaposition of serious and farcical traits, Molière did not hesitate to alternate grandiloquence with popular speech, as though Arnolphe could not decide whether to play the part of tragic hero or that of a bourgeois of Paris. This ludicrous contrast creates a feeling of discontinuity replete with comic effects. (67)

Molière's personal ambitions and failures as a tragic actor are well known, and Hubert here suggests how Molière may have found a way to introduce brief sequences of blatantly tragic acting into otherwise comic mises en scène. Indeed, as Jouvet's staging attests, *The School for Wives* is constructed on the basis of what Hubert calls the "ludicrous contrast" between the serious and the farcical. The theatrical vitality of that contrast, however, depends on the audience's ability to distinguish between what is represented and the mode of its representation. The dramatic structure of *The School for Wives* suggests that Molière was confident that his audience would not be confused by serious matters communicated in the medium of farce, or vice versa.

Molière's stunning satire of tragic acting in *The Versailles Im-*

promptu, which was composed as a response to criticisms of the implausibility of *The School for Wives,* depends entirely on his belief in the audience's ability to distinguish between the tragic nature of certain events and the techniques of tragic acting. In effect, *The Versailles Impromptu* offers a semiotic analysis of seventeenth-century tragic performance insofar as it reveals and critiques the mechanisms used to construct tragic significance. A great deal of the comic energy of that play is, in fact, generated by persuading the spectators to adopt an analytical perspective that leads them to see the rhetoric of tragic performance as artificial and therefore, Molière asks them to agree, laughable. By this means, Molière achieves a kind of realism. He presents artifice as artifice. Thus, in plays like *The School for Wives,* he manages to convince his spectators of the truth of his own representation precisely by calling attention to its theatricality. In *The School for Wives,* he calls the spectators' attention to his own presence as actor as well as to his blatant juxtaposition of different and usually antithetical genres. In *The School for Wives,* in what may be read as an early example of historicization, he presents tragic acting and tragic characterization as already unmasked, already revealed as unnatural, by showing them as historically determined procedures. Jouvet's, and later Vitez's, own citations from seventeenth-century theater may, then, perhaps be seen as extensions of Molière's own practice.

Arnolphe's oscillation between the positions/functions of spectator and actor is one of a series of dramatic mechanisms used by Molière and later exploited by Jouvet to mold the audience's response throughout the play: abrupt modulations of tone from the serious to the farcical, a carefully patterned repetition of scenes between Arnolphe and the other characters (particularly Horace), and the conventional fantastical resolution. Since Arnolphe's role is central to the play's structure, an examination of his multiple identities as actor, director, playwright, and spectator in the context of Jouvet's mise en scène may illuminate these other mechanisms.

From his first entry with Chrysalde, Arnolphe is explicitly identified as a spectator who enjoys watching other men suffer as a result of their spouses' infidelities. Arnolphe himself supplies the theatrical metaphor: "In conclusion, everybody sees them as subjects of satire/and what's wrong with my laughing at them like a spectator?" (1.1.43–44). With the garden walls in the closed position, Bérard's design creates a space that is principally defined by Arnolphe's spectator function. Throughout the first scene, Arnolphe and Chrysalde stand outside the garden walls in the town square as Arnolphe takes his closest friend into his confidence. We learn about Arnolphe's educational project, about Agnès and her history, and about Arnolphe's plans for her future. At the end of the story, Arnolphe reveals that Agnès lives in the house that occupies the center of the stage, "that other house" (1.1.146), which reminded Jacques Copeau of a fairy-tale castle: "that tall tower in which the little Agnès is sequestered, which gives her the aura of a princess of legend" (55).[16]

As Molière's exposition proceeds and our attention is drawn to the house and its contents, Bérard's décor appears as a space within a space, where the two spaces are separated only by the garden wall. This enclosed, private space framed by the town square with its elegant arcade represents, at a literal level, Arnolphe's property and, at a metaphorical level, Agnès's love and affection. Agnès's house provides a powerful visual focus by virtue of its central location, its extreme verticality in relation to the other scenic elements, and its double framing. The house is framed by both the proscenium arch and by the arcade that surround it on three sides, so that the arcade becomes just as significant as an extension of the proscenium frame than as an element of representational scenery. The arcade is further identified as an area from which to observe onstage events and is used for that purpose by both Arnolphe and Horace. Like the proscenium, it marks the limits of the playing area while emphasizing that the playing area itself is a space constantly under observation. Thus, Bérard's scenography for *The School for Wives* suggests a dramatic world dominated by the activity of spectating.

The arcade also serves as a constant reminder to Jouvet's Arnolphe of his rival's potential presence; as he sits atop the ladder during the scene with the notary, Arnolphe cannot see Horace, although he knows that he must be there. (Jouvet had directed Horace to lurk outside the walls in an earlier scene.) In Molière's time, with a significant number of aristocrats seated on stage, many of them potential Arnolphes or Horaces, Arnolphe's fear of being watched by Horace undoubtedly offered Molière/Arnolphe superb opportunities to theatricalize his ambiguous relationship with the audience.

After Chrysalde's departure, Arnolphe addresses the audience directly for the first time, assuming that the spectators share his opinion of Chrysalde as a man stubbornly fixed in his opinions. Arnolphe's direct communication with the audience depends on the absence of any perceived discontinuity between stage and auditorium, on the contiguity if not the congruence of the spaces that he and the spectators occupy. As he moves toward the house at the end of his soliloquy, Arnolphe invites us to enter the garden to observe the results of his unique educational system, all the while maintaining the established contact with the audience. At this point, Molière begins a farcical sequence that introduces Arnolphe's two incompetent servants, Alain and Georgette, and lets the audience know, if they ever had any doubt, that Arnolphe's plan is doomed to failure. The moment Arnolphe begins to activate the final stage of his plan, Molière's dramatic structure seems to suggest, the plan turns into a farce. Arnolphe's mood deteriorates throughout this first farcical sequence, as he begins to suspect that the spectators might, perhaps, be laughing at him rather than at the stupidity of his servants. Having, for the moment, finished with his servants, Arnolphe prepares to introduce his pupil to the audience.

Although Molière's placement of the first scene with Agnès in the town square may produce problems for directors concerned with a realistic treatment of scenic space, showing Arnolphe conducting his interview with Agnès in public offers interesting possibilities for exploring his overconfidence. After all, Arnolphe shows Agnès first to the theater audience, not to his friend Chrysalde. Bringing Agnès out into the garden/town square may also suggest that the house has outlived its usefulness as a place in which he can conceal Agnès from the world now that he has resolved to declare his romantic intentions and celebrate his betrothal.

Agnès's entrance is one of the most remarkable moments in the play. Arnolphe has spent several minutes trying to get into the house, but instead of going in as soon as the door opens, he decides to remain outside and conduct what he has proclaimed as his most secret enterprise, educating Agnès, in the town square. This apparently unrealistic location may partially be explained in terms of the staging techniques available to Molière at the time he wrote the play, but there is nothing to prevent a twentieth-century production from adopting the staging suggested in the script.[17] Jacques Arnavon resolved this implausibility by staging Arnolphe's entry at the garden gate; thus, by gaining access to the garden, Arnolphe was effectively inside. The unrealistic scale of Bérard's house precluded any possibility of staging a scene inside its walls; furthermore, since the house was situated in the very center of the town square, a realistic representation of domestic space, either inside or outside the house, was out of the question. Wherever Jouvet staged Agnès's first scene, the scenic space could only represent a public space, because the public—that is, the spectators—had already been "invited in" by Arnolphe to inspect his pupil.

Arnolphe carefully stages the presentation of Agnès so that we may observe her without having sufficient time to look closely and critically. He carefully instructs the audience to pay attention to what he regards as the significant details and limits his conversation to confirming what he wants the audience to hear. Having introduced us to his pupil and her guardians, he turns to the spectators, convinced that they have seen what he wanted them to see, confident to the point of challenging the members of the *galant* society in his audience:

> Heroines of today, Learned ladies,
> Advocates of sentimentality and fine feeling,
> I challenge, all together, all your verses, your novels,
> Your correspondence, love letters, all your learning,
> To match that true and innocent ignorance.
>
> (1.3.224–48)

Up to this point, Arnolphe has enjoyed success: his pupil has performed well, and even his idiotic servants have not proven seriously incompetent. Horace is, however, about to enter and begin to undermine Arnolphe's achievement and self-confidence.

Since Molière's time, critics have complained that the long scenes between Arnolphe and Horace are overly static because they consist almost entirely in the relating of offstage events. Such readings, however, place too much emphasis on the development of the plot and fail to appreciate that the significant dramatic action does indeed occur onstage. These scenes in which Arnolphe listens to Horace's accounts of his maneuvers to outwit the unattractive and foolish Monsieur de la Souche allow a gifted *farceur* (and Molière was acknowledged the best of his time) to improvise a series of complex responses to being caught as an onstage spectator at the comedy of his "ignorant" bride-to-be's willing seduction. (Not only is Arnolphe the most talkative character in the play; he is also the character who spends the most time listening. When Horace is offstage Arnolphe talks; when Horace is onstage Arnolphe listens.) The comedy in these scenes depends on our double and Horace's single perception of Arnolphe: we know that he is both Arnolphe and Monsieur de la Souche; Horace does not. These so-called static scenes thus play an important part in the spectating motif in addition to providing ample opportunities for comparing the two men as potential husbands for Agnès.

The conversations between the two would-be husbands take place in the town square and invariably focus on the question of how to gain access to the garden and house. As they discuss the problem of gaining entry, Bérard's décor, with its princess-in-the-tower aspect, suggests an interpretation of the garden wall as a burlesque of the medieval architectural imagery of seduction. The wall that separates the two spaces, the outside from the inside, is both a physical object and a metaphor, although the heavily caricatured convergence of the two swinging walls strongly privileges a metaphoric reading. For both Arnolphe and Horace, and even Agnès herself, the wall represents different things at different times. For Agnès, it is merely a garden wall until she desires to move freely in the space outside the wall; meeting Horace establishes the wall, for the first time, as the barrier between inside and outside Arnolphe's school. Similarly, Horace attaches no symbolic importance to the wall until he, too, perceives it as a barrier to satisfying his desires. As Nicolich reminds us (and as Jouvet shows in his mise en scène), Horace and Agnès succeed in circumventing the wall by using the door and window. Until he learns otherwise from Horace, Arnolphe never considers the possibility that the door and window of his property are potential breaches in his security system; he had trusted the walls and door even when he had been less then fully confident in Alain and Georgette's abilities. Because he is the proprietor of the schoolhouse, and because Alain and Georgette are his servants, Arnolphe tends to interpret the walls and door as symbolic guarantors of his sole right of access, assuming, of course, that he can persuade Alain and his wife to open the door. As he invites the spectators to join him in the garden (Jouvet has the walls swing apart to reveal the garden), however, Arnolphe begins to discover another "wall" within: Agnès. From this perspective, the action of *The School for Wives* might be described as Arnolphe's failure to penetrate Agnès's "defenses." He can enter the garden, but he cannot stimulate her affections or persuade her to take his love for her seriously; keeping the pupil locked up in school does not lead to her falling in love with the teacher. While Arnolphe has no difficulty gaining access to Agnès but discovers that access is not enough, Horace, on the other hand, wins her affections with ease, even though the walls prevent him easy access to her physical presence.

Arnolphe's and Horace's different responses to the barrier of the garden wall help clarify a fundamental difference between the two men. Horace is not afraid to act, to commit himself to asking for what he wants; he is not self-conscious when declaring his emotions either to Agnès or to Arnolphe. Arnolphe, however, remains a self-conscious, self-mocking spectator who cannot act effectively. Horace's meetings with Agnès are characterized by gallant conversation and the exchange of gifts; Arnolphe's conversations with her are singularly one-sided: he preaches or forces her to read aloud the "Maximes du Mariage." Whether giving instruction or observing the discomfort caused by that instruction, Arnolphe fails to transcend his role as parent, tutor, or spectator; he is incapable of forging an emotional empathy with her. Molière gives him ample opportunity to display a degree of sympathy for Agnès equal to his spontaneous offer of financial support to Horace, but Arnolphe ignores her pain at the death of her little cat, just as he refuses to mitigate the harshness of the "Maximes."

In the end, Arnolphe is the only loser in the play, a victim of his own self-consciousness. His profession of love for Agnès is painful for him and hilarious for us because he is so aware of the extent to which he can only turn himself into a spectacle. Indeed, at the moment when he feels his emotions rapidly escaping all hope of control, Arnolphe seems to stand outside himself, an onstage spectator who sees to what extent he has become an object of derision: "To what extremes can passion drive a man!" (5.4.1598). Arnolphe, who has laughed all his life at men in this very position, abjectly begging for the love of a woman who has no interest in him, cannot fail to anticipate the laughter of the audience.

Chapter 6

Antoine Vitez: An Archaeology of Grand Siècle Performance

Transparency of spoken discourse versus opacity of gesture—that is the recipe of Vitez.
                                                                —Anne Ubersfeld

Contesting Orthodoxies

In 1978 at the Avignon Theatre Festival, Antoine Vitez presented a tetralogy of four plays by Molière on successive evenings: *The School for Wives, Tartuffe, Dom Juan,* and *The Misanthrope.* The production was very well received and became a major turning point in Vitez's career. One critic, Edmond Radar, suggested, with only a small degree of hyperbole, that the Vitez mise en scène was the most significant event at Avignon in a decade:

> A theatrical event the likes of which we had not seen for ten years. Avant-garde and entirely literary. . . . Avant-garde: Vitez's dramaturgy emphasizes a gestural symbolism open to dream, to the unconscious, to the demands of the flesh. Entirely literary: the four texts performed were the object of a close reading that sought to illuminate them as if they were living works about which everything had not yet been said. First and foremost, the ways in which they could shed light on [questions of] our own time. (40)

After Avignon, the Vitez tetralogy toured extensively in Western Europe before going to Paris in 1979 as part of the Festival d'Automne. The plays were all performed on the same set, using the same props and furniture; the actors wore the same costumes in all four plays. By using the same scenography for all four plays, Vitez broke with the modern tradition that grew out of the realism-inspired practice of creating a new scenography to give expression to the unique features of each individual play.

139

Arnavon, Antoine, and others who shared their views had argued for a number of decades against the use of "repertory" scenery in the staging of Molière's plays. Over time their views prevailed, and more and more theater artists, including those who rejected the realist aesthetic, designed new sets and new costumes for productions of plays by Molière and other authors from the classical period. As we have seen, directors such as Jouvet and Planchon achieved impressive results, not only in terms of staging persuasive readings of particular plays but also in terms of developing new ways of approaching overly "familiar" texts. Vitez chose to turn away from the kind of mise en scène advocated by Antoine and later brought to a kind of perfection by Planchon. Instead, he turned to the self-consciously theatrical mode that originated with the experiments of Copeau at the Vieux-Colombier and was further developed by Barrault and Vilar.

Vitez also broke with another important tradition in staging his Molière tetralogy: he elected not to use actors who were the same age as the characters they played and instead used a company of twelve young actors. Vitez himself was the sole exception: born in 1930, Vitez was the oldest actor onstage by many years. During the European tour and in Paris, Vitez often played Laurent and the Exempt in *Tartuffe* as well as the Statue of the Commander in *Dom Juan*.[1] Vitez made no attempt to make the obviously older characters in the plays appear physically older than their younger counterparts; the actors used neither makeup nor gesture to create the illusion of an older body. By refusing to accept conventional notions of realist physical characterization, Vitez managed to encourage his spectators to reconsider received ideas about the plays. Stéphan de Lannoy, for example, observes that in the case of *The School for Wives*, a young Arnolphe circumvents the traditional ageist prejudice (a prejudice to which the critical tradition largely subscribes) that suggests that Arnolphe is too old to expect to marry such a young woman: "There is nothing at all improbable about the plans for their wedding" (51). Another commentator, Judith Miller, observes that with Vitez's casting, "Horace . . . is but a slightly younger version of Arnolphe, not his opposite but instead a slightly distorted mirror image" (74). Another significant effect of casting a young actor in the role of Arnolphe, however, is that the spectators are no longer invited, as they were in the case of Jouvet, to see the actor playing both "Molière" and Arnolphe, or to read Jouvet's well-known relationship with Madeleine Ozeray, his Agnès, as a contemporary analogue of Molière's relationship with Armande. With a young

Arnolphe, *The School for Wives* can no longer be read as an autobiographical play.

In yet another departure from modern practice, Vitez had his twelve actors play all of the roles, making little effort to conceal the doubling. Instead, Vitez explicitly used doubling to provoke comparisons and suggest similarities between characters in different plays. For example, Richard Fontana played Horace and Tartuffe; Didier Sandre played Arnolphe, Cléante, and Oronte; Daniel Martin played Chrysalde and Orgon; Jany Gastaldi played Elmire and Célimène;[2] Nada Strancar played Georgette, Dorine, and Arsinoë; and Dominique Valadié played Agnès, Marianne, and Eliante.

This doubling would have had little effect, however, if Vitez had not also taken the radical decision to stage the four plays as a tetralogy. By grouping four of Molière's plays together and staging them with the same small group of almost unknown actors, on the same set and with the same costumes and props, Vitez effectively shifted the focus of attention away from the single play. Where previous directors had labored to isolate what was theatrically unique about each play, seeking to explore (if not explain) details of character and plot, Vitez worked to draw the spectator's attention to what the four plays had in common. In so doing, he submerged what had traditionally been taken for autonomous characters in a flood of recurrent dramaturgic and scenographic motifs. With Vitez's mise en scène, Molière's four plays became not only a series of explorations of related dramatic themes but, more important, four expressions of the same gestic, semiotic, theatrical energy (Vitez's as much as Molière's). While the plays clearly referred to the world outside the theater— Molière's age-old themes remained easily readable—Vitez relentlessly reminded the spectators that the four plays were quintessentially *of* the theater. As a result, Vitez offered his spectators the very thing that Arnavon so despised, a *morceau de théâtre*. Indeed, the theater itself was the real subject of Vitez's mise en scène: instead of seeking to re-create the seventeenth-century environmental referent of Molière's plays as the other directors I have discussed had done, Vitez elected to reconstruct the languages of the seventeenth-century stage, making no claim to the accuracy of a re-creation grounded in the archaeological researches of an Antoine or in the historiographical researches of a Planchon. What Vitez offers us is, in effect, less a recreation than a reinvention of Grand Siècle performance.

Vitez's understanding of what can be accomplished in the mise en scène of a classic text rests on the presumption that no indisputably authentic restoration can ever be achieved. Directors who display the intellectual rigor of an Antoine, an Arnavon, a Jouvet, or a Planchon are, of course, conscious of the degree to which their respective mises en scène represent partial and, indeed, provisional readings of individual plays. Planchon, as we saw in chapter 3, revised and refined his reading of *Tartuffe* over the better part of two decades. What is significant in the present context, however, is that none of these directors seeks to emphasize the partiality, the fragmentariness, the frankly avowed subjectivity of his own reading. Instead, each presents his work in such a manner as to draw attention to its completeness; each sees his mise en scène as a complete realization in the modern mode of dramatic and theatrical ideas that originated with Molière in the 1660s. That is to say, each believes that his mise en scène is responsive to the demands of Molière's text in a modern way. This belief, however, is grounded in the culturally enshrined presumption of the intelligibility of the classic text.

Vitez, on the other hand, believes something quite different:

> The works of the past are ruined architectures (*architectures brisées*), shipwrecked galleons, and piece by piece we bring them back to the light of day without ever restoring them (for in any case, we no longer know how they were used), but to make something else out of the pieces. (Kaisergruber and Vitez 9)

The archaeological imagery of this passage, while striking in its own right, seems especially appropriate in the context of the Avignon festival, at which the tetralogy was first performed. At Avignon, the production was staged in the Carmelite Cloisters (Cloître des Carmes), a performance space that, like the mainstage venue of the Palace of the Popes (Palais des Papes), once served an entirely different function. In these "theaters," plays are performed on platform stages set against obviously ancient architectural facades. Surrounded by the ruins of these convent and palace walls, the classic play can be performed in a space that is itself of an even earlier vintage. Molière's "ruined architectures" and the ruined settings complement each other, with the result that the Avignon performance venues provide a scenography for many plays of the Grand Siècle that is more historically realistic than anything a modern theater can hope to create. At Avignon, there is no need to create the illusion of another time and place in history; the walls and courtyards of ancient Avignon *are already* of another time, already imbued with history. And like the classic texts, as Vitez tells us, they too are now being used to make something else.

Familiar Script, Unfamiliar Gestures

In her 1981 book, *L'Ecole du spectateur*, Anne Ubersfeld suggests that theatrical performance comprises two quite distinct arts: the art of mimetic representation in which the actors, director, and designers invoke a world of absences, an offstage reality, for the spectator; and the art of performance (39). The art of performance, according to Ubersfeld, appears in the body of the actor and, somewhat more problematically, in the mise en scène itself, in the sense that stage lighting and décor can provide a pleasure that derives from lighting and décor alone. Aspects of theatrical performance that are apparently pure expressions of the theatrical impulse itself are rarely discussed in the context of the mises en scène of classic texts for two reasons: they cannot immediately be related to the text on which the performance is based, and more important, they are the essentially indescribable manifestations of the impulse to perform itself; they have, in a sense, nothing at all to do with the specific script that is being performed.

Later in the same book, Ubersfeld argues that Vitez's work on gesture (*geste*) as both an acting teacher at the Conservatoire National d'Art Dramatique and as a director represents his most important contribution to French theater (200). While Vitez's enormously successful career in the 1980s (first as artistic director of the Théâtre National de Chaillot and later as Administrateur-Général of the Comédie-Française) suggests that Ubersfeld's 1981 assessment stands in need of some qualification, commentators such as Michel Corvin and de Lannoy agree that Vitez's use of the gesture is a key feature of his Molière tetralogy. Jean Mambrino goes even further to argue that Vitez's insistence on the *jeu* (a technique of performing, also a moment or segment of performance) places the actor's body at the very focal point of the theater event: "Vitez puts the burden of spectacle solely on the actor's body, whose *jeu* becomes the ultimate touchstone—a splendid austerity that brings to mind Copeau's vision and his '*tréteau nu*'" ("Carnet de théâtre" 639).[3]

With Vitez, however, the term *geste* or the slightly broader term *jeu* do not imply the same kind of relationship between actor and text that characterized mise en scène from Antoine to Planchon. Indeed, Vitez's *jeu* frequently takes precedence over Molière's dialogue and seems to oppose directly the traditional understanding of character and event based on three centuries of reading and performance. During *The School for Wives,* for instance, Vitez shows Horace landing on Arnolphe's shoulders as he leaves the house through a window, after which Arnolphe circles the stage a number of times with Horace still sitting on his shoulders. This *jeu* adroitly conveys Vitez's sense of Arnolphe's predicament at that point in the dramatic action (4.5), but it also plays against Molière's script insofar as the script offers no hint of such a *jeu,* and Arnolphe's dialogue takes no account of Horace's weight on his shoulders. By showing Arnolphe struggling under the physical burden of another actor's weight, Vitez creates a visual image that comments on the dramatic action, although it is not specifically authorized by any detail in Molière's script.

This *jeu* of Arnolphe's offers an example of what Ubersfeld refers to as Vitez's characteristic "opacity of gesture" in the passage that serves as epigraph to this chapter. She does not mean to suggest that the gestures of Vitez's actors are opaque in themselves, only that they are opaque in terms of their relationship to the classic script, a relationship that cannot be seen in terms of realization or illustration. By its very nature, such a *jeu* depends for its effect on its obviously self-conscious theatricality—it is explicitly and exclusively a *jeu de théâtre*—but it is impossible to relate the *jeu* to anything other than a general sense of the Arnolphe-Horace relationship as a relationship that is defined in terms of a rather abstract (because it is purely *of the theater*) hostility. Unlike Arnavon and Jouvet, Vitez seems relatively unconcerned with realist notions of character (e.g., his casting of young actors in almost every part obviates any psychosocial examination of generational conflict based on realist notions of character and motivation) and tends to focus on characters as mere elements in a dramatic, even scenographic relationship.

Vitez's interest in the abstract dramatic patterns of human interaction is reflected in his emphasis on a highly physicalized *jeu* as a privileged mode of representing those patterns. His intense focus on *jeux* that are difficult for the spectator/reader accustomed to a realist poetics to integrate with Molière's dialogue results in the creation of a semiotically rich performance text that is nevertheless often unreadable (in the Barthesian sense) as an interpretation of a specific play by Molière. Corvin suggests that a large proportion of Vitez's *jeu* may be interpreted only retrospectively, after the spectator has seen all four parts of the tetralogy; even from such a perspective, however, Corvin believes that much of Vitez's *jeu* will remain indecipherable (28). The unreadability of Vitez's *jeu* thus limits the spectator's ability to analyze the mise en scène as a simple realization of Molière's text. Vitez's emphasis on a *jeu* that is often unrelated to specific moments of Molière's script (indeed, Molière's scripts have, in a sense, been assimilated into a new script that Molière did not write—the Vitez tetralogy) tends to draw the spectator's attention away from Molière's characters as they have been traditionally perceived in order to focus it on Vitez's own dark vision of the human condition (which is not necessarily antithetical to Molière's), a vision that is forcefully communicated by the violent, eroticized gestures of Vitez's young actors.

Edmond Radar salutes Vitez not only for what he takes to be his intellectual and/or literary understanding of the scripts but also for his skill in creating a mise en scène with the purely theatrical seductiveness of an Artaudian Theater of Cruelty:

> Body language signs the impatience of desire in a hallucinatory dumbshow. There are leaps forward, pirouettes . . . the ecstasy of caresses, hand-to-hand combat, expressively agitated hands rejecting torturous separation, calling for a hallucinated embrace. Investigations of the theater of cruelty exploring relationships of breath, cries, and language alive to obsessions of desire seizing the rational animal and leaving it like an abandoned prey. . . . Gesture, the sign of sociability, now signifies the hallucinatory eroticism that is excluded from social intercourse in the normal course of things, and [is] surely [excluded] from the worldly ceremonies of the seventeenth century. . . . [Vitez] shows us fragile beings . . . he rediscovers the passion, the sorrow, the torments of a life [Molière's] that, feature by feature, give shape to the face we will recognize as his for all time. The face? The mask behind which a tortured self screams and implores. He does not achieve this by caprice or fantastic innovation; Vitez achieves it by making us listen more attentively to the text, a text that everybody feels they know and consequently no longer hear. (40–41)

To describe Vitez's gestural text, Radar invokes the eroticism often associated with Artaud's Theater of Cruelty. Invoking Artaud also brings to mind Artaud's war cry of "No More Masterpieces," which directors have often cited in justifying large-scale cuts and other adaptations when staging a classic text. Remarkably, Vitez manages to create a multilayered gestural text that at times overwhelms the spectator with an Artaudian density of physical performance disconnected from the playwright's text while, at the same time, his mise en scène remains connected to the playwright's text to an often startling degree.

While Vitez's work owes more, as we shall see, to the example of Meyerhold than to that of Artaud, Radar's perspective is useful because it draws our attention to the degree to which the *jeu* of Vitez's actors, the purely theatrical element of the performance, takes precedence over the mimetic concerns traditionally read into Molière's script. Vitez's eroticized *jeu* is the very opposite of what an audience expects from the performance of a seventeenth-century play. Instead of presenting an idealized version of the social manners of the Grand Siècle, Vitez offers the spectator a stage populated with violent, inelegant figures moving in a macabre dance that Radar interprets (and Vitez concurs; see "Quatre fois Molière" 183) as Molière's dramatic projection of his personal suffering and skepticism.

Gesture and Farce

At the beginning of Vitez's *School for Wives,* which is also the beginning of Vitez's tetralogy, Arnolphe walks to downstage center, strikes the stage floor with his cane, and raises his left hand to salute the audience. He maintains this pose during the opening lines of the first scene, paying no attention to Chrysalde. In the context of a larger discussion of Vitez's use of the *bâton,* Corvin suggests a multilayered interpretation of Arnolphe's first gesture (222). On one level, Arnolphe's gesture is explicitly theatrical in that it echoes the three taps (*les trois coups*) on the stage floor that traditionally signal the beginning of a theatrical performance in France. On a second level, the gesture is symbolic in that it announces Arnolphe's authority as master of the house (and of the bare stage that represents both house and town square in this production). On a third level, Arnolphe's pose recalls familiar portraits of Louis with his right hand resting on his cane (although the portraits do not show Louis with his left arm raised like Arnolphe's) and thus suggests his aspirations to nobility. In addition to these interpretations, however, the gesture serves as an introduction to the nature of the *jeu* that Vitez will employ throughout the tetralogy.[4] By having the actor strike his cane on the stage floor and hold his arm gesture through several lines, Vitez initiates the practice of having the actors play "against" the text. Neither Arnolphe nor Horace, for example, puts on a hat at the suggestion "Mettons donc" (3.4.852), a refusal to adhere to the stage direction implicit in the dialogue that Arnavon and Jouvet would certainly have abhorred (Corvin 195).

Vitez's actors play against the text in another more complex manner when they enact events that have already happened, thus creating what Corvin calls "a veritable superposition of time frames" (212). In act 3, scene 4, for example, as Horace recounts an earlier meeting with Agnès, he reenacts that meeting for Arnolphe as if he were experiencing once more, in the act of telling, precisely what he felt and thought during the meeting with Agnès: "Although he knows how the story ends . . . [Horace] is, moment by moment, the man who weeps, who rubs his skull, then laughs and gambols, depending on the various signifiers that pass through him" (Corvin 199). Vitez treats each of Horace's *récits* in a similar fashion by transforming the narrative of offstage events into what is, in effect, a play-within-a-play performed for the benefit of Arnolphe and the spectators in the auditorium. Corvin suggests that by removing the barriers between *récit* and physical representation, Vitez creates the theatrical equivalent of a Cubist painting for the spectator:

> Saying and doing become reconciled, unified in the spectator's perceptions: it is the spectator, not the character, who lives the action/text that is in the process of making itself. Character is no more than one aspect of this ensemble. One might say that Vitez operates like a Cubist painter, simultaneously showing all aspects of the *jeu* in a spatio-temporal shortcut. (235)

With this Cubist treatment of *récit*, Vitez not only suggests an innovative response to the traditional criticism of these sections of Molière's text as inherently undramatic; he also suggests that the relationship between the classic text and its mise en scène may be approached in a manner quite different from the classical models of illustration and translation that Carlson describes. Indeed, Vitez's Molière tetralogy offers a particularly rich example of what Carlson calls a "supplementary" mise en scène in that the tetralogy contains a significant number of *jeux* that are neither suggested by the script nor illuminated by it.[5] One example of such a *jeu* is described by Corvin, who isolates what he sees as a recurring fetishistic *jeu* with the shoes of the female characters (Agnès's dress is also fetishized), notably between Don Juan and Elvire (1.3) and Alceste and Célimène (4.3); in *The School for Wives*, Vitez has Arnolphe remove his shoes in act 5, scene 3, only to have Agnès put them back on a very short time later (218). In giving him back his shoes, Agnès also hands him back his *bâton,* which, in Corvin's opinion, suggests that both gestures may be interpreted as gestures of submission. While Agnès's submission may be readily integrated in a combined reading of Molière's script and Vitez's mise en scène, the intense eroticism of the fetishized *jeu* departs from the norms of *bienséance* usually associated with Molière's theater.

Throughout the tetralogy, Vitez eroticizes the *jeu* to an extent that is unusual even in twentieth-century stage production, with the result that he opens up an explicitly sadomasochistic perspective on the relationships between characters of all sexes, principally symbolized by the various uses of the *bâton.* This Sadeian perspective is equally strongly suggested by the frequency with which the female characters are treated as objects of pleasure by the men, to be looked at, punched, stroked, pinched, dressed and undressed at will. Vitez suggests that his treatment of the female characters directly reflects Molière's own problems with women as those problems are reflected in Molière's texts. Vitez thus appears to endorse the nineteenth-century tradition of interpretation that sees Molière transposing the vicissitudes of his emotional and sexual life into his drama. It is just as likely, however, that the sadomasochistic *jeu* developed by Vitez derives from Vitez's own conviction that "obscene farce" informs every play, if not every scene, written by Molière.

Although Vitez firmly believes that the dramatic structures of medieval farce help give Molière's plays their characteristic shape, his reading of Molière is essentially tragic. Judith Miller sees the dramatic action of each of Vitez's four mises en scène following a parallel downward curve as the protagonist moves toward a real or metaphoric death:

> In each play the marginal hero, a kind of exalted fool, attempts to live out an impossible passion in a rigidly-structured and passionless society. Passion is, in fact, the great deception, the final impostor. Salvation, according to Vitez, takes the form of an empty-headed woman or an omniscient but indifferent god. Intensity exists only in the "honest man's" determination to maintain order. In this world of controlled violence, the exceptional man finishes his flirtation with a real or metaphorical death by literally running, falling or staggering to it at the end of each play. (74)

As his tetralogy unfolds in performance, Miller describes the color scheme shifting to suggest the darkening of Molière's vision: "rose-umber in *The School for Wives*, rose-wine in *Tartuffe*, kelly green–brown in *Dom Juan*, and verdigris-black in *The Misanthrope*" (80). Similarly, the stage lighting evokes a darkening world. Vitez carefully sets the action of each play in the context of the natural morning-to-evening cycle in order to preserve the neoclassical unity of time, but by ending each play after dark (he uses candlelight rather than stage lighting effects to signify that darkness has fallen), he unavoidably evokes the metaphysical void that surrounds or engulfs the protagonist.[6]

Vitez's essentially tragic vision of Molière's protagonists, grounded in a psychoanalytical analysis of the playwright's personal antagonism toward women and God, finds expression in a series of mises en scène that subsumes Molière's text into a collage of post-Absurdist, post-Existentialist *farce tragique* and highly self-conscious postrealist scenography. Vitez's treatment of scenic space is both a direct citation of seventeenth-century scenography and an adroitly articulated deconstruction of the *écriture scénique* that characterizes the work of Arnavon, Antoine, Planchon, and the entire tradition of realist set design. Throughout the tetralogy, Vitez persistently undermines appearances with his ironic citation of trompe l'oeil scenery and his actors' intensely athletic *jeu*, which appears incongruous in their seventeenth-century clothing. Similarly, his insistence on playing against the traditional treatment of Molière's verse and dramatic structure (especially his technique of simultaneously dramatizing and narrating the *récits*) disturbs the audience's received notions about the formal perfection of literature from this period, notions that Jacques Arnavon was careful to reinforce. Vitez's mises en scène seem to insist that the social context suggested in a realist-inspired reading of Molière is almost irrelevant in the face of the metaphysical pain manifested in the playwright's oeuvre. At the same time, the fragmented, violent images of Molière's seventeenth century that Vitez offers have much in common with Roger Planchon's presentation of sociopolitical and cultural upheaval in the Grand Siècle.

Rethinking *Vraisemblance:* Reframing Molière's Dramaturgy

Vitez's main contribution to the twentieth-century mise en scène of Molière does not consist in the illumination of specific themes or in the solving of particularly difficult staging problems; rather, what Vitez has achieved is a radical reframing of Molière's dramaturgy. He has persuasively argued that Molière's theater is not only predominantly farcical in its origins and in its dramatic construction (an argument that Lanson had already proposed on purely literary critical grounds) but also that its farcical aspects can provide a powerful experience of theater in the late twentieth century.

More than any other French director of this century, Vitez has sought to remind his spectators of the artificiality and conventional nature of seventeenth-century stage dialogue. Unlike other directors who try to disguise the fact that the actors are speaking a poetic language composed in regular alexandrines, Vitez directs his actors to call attention to the artificial rhythms of the verse by pronouncing every syllable, including the mute *e*.[7] Consequently Vitez confronts his spectators with the material aspects of Molière's language, much as he confronts them with the corporeal nature of his actor's bodies. Vitez's strong emphasis on the poetic rhythms of Molière's verse runs directly counter to Arnavon's efforts to make Molière's dialogue sound like ordinary, everyday speech.[8] In Vitez's mise en scène Molière's language is used for musical effect as much as it is used as a medium of conversation. Yet Vitez's treatment of Molière's language should not be understood as a rejection of articulate, rational speech in the manner of Artaud, as Radar seems to suggest. Instead, Vitez's emphasis of the poetic form of Molière's dialogue calls attention to its conventional nature as a language of and for the stage, a quintessentially artificial speech that depends for its scenic power on its very artificiality. Vitez's exemplary achievement is to have historicized Molière's language by calling attention to its roots in neoclassical dramaturgy while, at the same time, showing some ways in which that same historicized language can be incorporated into a decidedly late twentieth-century mise en scène.

For Vitez, the Molière tetralogy project served as a kind of manifesto of his values as a teacher and director.[9] In a conversation with other respected French directors of Molière, Vitez stated that the idea of the tetralogy stemmed from two sources: his desire to bring together a majority of scenes that had provided the material for his acting classes at the Conservatoire as well as his desire to "say something about the theater" (Vitez, Lassalle, and Maréchal 21). He wanted the tetralogy, for example, to stand as a positive example for what could be achieved by a permanent company (in France today only the Comédie-Française has a truly permanent company). More polemically, he wanted to argue against what he calls a "sociologizing" mise en scène, best represented in the work of Roger Planchon. Vitez clearly acknowledges his own debt to Planchon's seminal work: "We are all descended from Planchon's *Dandin* and *Tartuffe*." At the same time, however, he maintains that Planchon's interpretive models are less than satisfactory: "There is an extreme idealism in a sociologically based mise en scène that sees works [of art] as slices of life. . . . One enters into . . . the scenario of the play as if it were a true story. But it is not a true story" (Vitez, Lassalle, and Maréchal 22, 21).

Rejecting Planchon's reading of Molière's comedies as explorations of the offstage realities of the seventeenth century, Vitez resolved to explore Molière's dramaturgy, specifically what he saw as Molière's innovative development of bourgeois comedy using the techniques of medieval farce:

> I could argue that every one of his works, almost every scene, is grounded in an archaic farcical structure that is very primitive. . . . I am interested in showing how Molière invents bourgeois comedy by building on that very structure. . . . The obscene archaic farce is manipulated, combined with something else. The characters . . . have a social history—they are not the creatures of a farce. As a director, my work is to look for ways of showing both things, either in succession or at the same time. (Vitez, Lassalle, and Maréchal 21)

Vitez wrote about his desire to show both bourgeois comedy and farce before the tetralogy was performed at Avignon. When his mise en scène appeared, however, it seemed to emphasize farce at the expense of bourgeois comedy, an emphasis that is also reflected in critical discussions of the production.

In a 1977 interview with Mambrino, Vitez revealed that Meyerhold had been the principal influence on his work as a director and that he saw his productions as a "rehabilitation" of Meyerhold's aesthetic:

> The essence of Meyerhold's thought [according to Vitez] resides in the notion of convention or, rather, of "conventionality," to give you an accurate translation of the Russian. For Meyerhold, realism itself has nothing at all to do with the real; it is but one of the conventions, one of the codes that allows us to translate the real. The essence of Meyerhold's thought is that there is no such thing as a "normal" *jeu,*

that there are only various kinds of *jeu*. . . . Meyerhold tells us that *vraisemblance* itself is nothing more than one kind of *jeu,* one kind of simulacrum. (Mambrino, "Entretien avec Antoine Vitez" 638)

Vitez's tetralogy of Molière plays clearly owes a good deal to this reading of Meyerhold, particularly the notion that realism, or *vraisemblance,* should be seen as just one of many mimetic options.[10]

The scenic space that Vitez created for his Molière tetralogy was designed to emphasize the fictive nature (or, to use Meyerhold's term, the conventionality) of not only Molière's text and the acting but also the scenography itself. At Avignon, the four plays were performed after nightfall on a bare platform set against the "ruined" arches of the Carmelite Cloisters. Later, Vitez invited Claude Lemaire to develop a new scenography for a tour of theaters with traditional proscenium stages. The problem that Lemaire faced of finding a way of recreating on indoor stages the effect of a mise en scène originally created for the Avignon festival is as old as the festival itself. For instance, when Jean Vilar was director of both the Théâtre National de Chaillot (then known as the Théâtre National Populaire) and the Avignon festival in the 1950s, he was obliged to find a solution to this problem every season. Vilar's solution, more often than not, was to attempt a re-creation of the darkness of the Avignon night by surrounding the stage with black drapes.[11] As at Avignon, modern stage lighting separated the actors from the surrounding darkness at the same time as it created an effective scenographic poetry of its own. Vilar's lyrical mises en scène undoubtedly owed much of their success to this relatively innovative reworking of Copeau's *tréteau nu* aesthetic (Vilar's debt to Appia is equally obvious).[12] Like Vilar, Lemaire also thought in terms of a bare platform stage, but her scenography creates cultural resonances that are quite different from anything we might associate with either Copeau or Vilar.

Lemaire designed a self-consciously self-referential theatrical setting that remained unchanged for all four plays. The playing area was backed by a Romanesque architectural facade decorated with reproduced segments of frescoes from a Pompeian villa that depicted, among other scenes, a Dionysian initiation rite that prominently featured Dionysus himself. As de Lannoy remarks, "The theater god himself seems to be giving his consent to the use of this décor on a stage" (48). In a meticulously detailed analysis of Lemaire's décor, de Lannoy also examines the way in which the fresco imagery represents both interior and exterior scenes, creating a powerful sense of the ambiguities of these pictorial representations of location while, at the same time, emphasizing the conventionality of the representations themselves (48–50). De Lannoy's discussion of Lemaire's scenic designs draws our attention to some of the aspects that seem to have most concerned Vitez himself. Vitez offers the following description of Lemaire's post-Avignon scenography for the Molière tetralogy:

> The stage represents an *exterior,* a public place. But what we look at is an interior, a stage: open doors, pools of darkness, shafts of light, apparitions. It is the *enchanted interior* that gives rise to the sense of an exterior. One might even propose this aphorism: *an exterior is an enchanted interior.* ("Quatre fois Molière" 178)

With its elegantly balanced phrases and provocative concluding aphorism, Vitez's statement is more evocative than descriptive. Rather than describe what the décor looked like, Vitez gives us a sense of how such a décor came into being, of the aesthetic requirements it was created to satisfy. In this brief passage, Vitez also helps us understand the value of flexible, compelling, "enchanted" scenic spaces, spaces that can have one identity and yet also evoke another (even opposite) identity. On such a stage, Arnolphe can place his chair wherever he pleases without raising doubts in the minds of the spectators about the *vraisemblance* of the physical location.

In addition to the architectural facade, Lemaire's décor included a backcloth that represented a cloudy sky and two doorways placed opposite each other, just upstage of the proscenium. The doorways served either as entrances to "houses" that were presumed to be in the wings or as entrances to the "room" that was represented by the stage itself. Other entrances and exits were made through doors and windows in the architectural facade. Furniture and props were confined to two simple chairs, a table, a stick, a book, a sack, and some candlesticks. The actors wore costumes and wigs that closely resembled everyday clothing of the mid-seventeenth century without caricaturing the period's taste for decoration, as so many traditional productions of Molière's plays have done.

One one level, the décor, costumes, and props remind the spectators of the theater for which Molière wrote the four plays of the tetralogy, a theater in which décor, costumes, props, acting styles, and so on, were quite different from anything a modern audience might expect. In a sense, the Lemaire/Vitez mise en scène recalls Antoine's recreation of *The Cid*, in which he tried to give his twentieth-century spectators a feeling for the performance conditions that informed Corneille's writing. Quite self-consciously, Vitez and Lemaire set out to "reinvent" a twentieth-century equivalent of the playing conditions of Molière's own theater: "We are reinventing, in a modest way, some ideas that are already very familiar, ideas that are primitive, essential: the company [of actors], [productions performed in an] alternating repertory, as well as the unities of time and place" ("Quatre fois Molière" 176, 182).[13] Their observance of the unities, in tandem with Vitez's emphasis on the poetic nature of the alexandrine, seems, at first, to constitute a reversal of the trend toward the modernization of Molière's dramatic and scenic conventions initiated by Antoine and Arnavon and continued by Jouvet and Planchon. In fact, however, Vitez modernizes Molière as much as Arnavon, Jouvet, or Planchon. What distinguishes Vitez's contribution to the mise en scène of Molière is his challenge to the time-honored identification of Molière as a realist artist: for Vitez, Molière's is not a realist dramaturgy.

At first glance, Lemaire's décor looks like a simple seventeenth-century décor with two functional doors downstage near the proscenium and a solid architectural facade backdrop. As the performance proceeds, however, it quickly becomes apparent that the facade, too, contains invisible functional doors and windows. In the closed position, these doors and windows are invisible, as they are disguised by the trompe l'oeil painting of the facade. In the open position, however, they disrupt the illusionist scene painting on the facade, thus calling attention to the fact that Lemaire's architectural facade is, in representing a piece of seventeenth-century décor, a piece of contemporary scenery and should be interpreted as such. Once we become aware of the trompe l'oeil techniques used in the facade, we cannot help but suspect that the stage floor has also been painted using illusionist techniques to look like the bare, untreated boards of a platform stage. Even the period clothing, which achieves the illusion of historical realism by refusing to copy conventional notions of how Molière's characters should be dressed, now seems calculated to draw our attention to the explicitly theatrical nature of the narrative to which we are giving attention. Lemaire's decision to make no obvious compromises in period line or texture to accommodate the actors' intensely physical, Artaudian performance now appears as a carefully crafted strategy designed to focus our attention on the contemporary actor's body rather than on the "period" costume.

By reinventing the theater of Molière's time, Vitez succeeds in creating a compelling piece of contemporary theater. He also reminds us that reconstructions and/or evocations of the realities of seventeenth-century cultural and political life are themselves illusions. As scenic illusions, Vitez seems to suggest, they come into being in the service of a contemporary agenda, an agenda that can never evade its own basis in ideology.

Corvin has suggested that in order to appreciate Vitez's Molière tetralogy, it is necessary first to overcome two deeply rooted cultural reflexes that result in us seeing Molière's plays in realistic terms (189). The first of these reflexes is the belief that each Molière play revolves around a group of characters endowed with psychological and/or sociological marks of an individuality revealed in a progressive dramatic action and explored through a central dominant thematic. The second cultural reflex is the belief that Molière is a trustworthy observer of the human condition whose work allows us to understand these individualized characters and, through them, ourselves. Clearly, Arnavon and Jouvet (although to a lesser extent) exhibit the cultural reflexes that Corvin describes. Taken together, the work of Jouvet and Vitez represents a moving away from treating Molière in predominantly humanistic terms in the theater.

In the tetralogy, Vitez was less interested in interpreting specific characters and themes in individual plays than in exploring Molière's dramaturgy through working simultaneously on a number of his plays. Indeed, his rehearsal schedule was designed to prevent too much attention being paid to any one play or character. First, he rehearsed each play in rotation for half a day; then, when the staging for all four plays was sufficiently developed, he concentrated on following each actor's characters through all four plays ("Quatre fois Molière" 181). But, curiously enough, Vitez does not seem to have made any interesting discoveries in these rehearsals, although he claims that performing the plays in the order in which they were composed reveals a great deal about Molière's development as a playwright (a thesis that also forms the basis for Jacques Guicharnaud's *Molière: une aventure théâtrale*):

From *The School for Wives* to *The Misanthrope,* the poet changed: he had written a tragedy-farce in the manner of the previous century—long monologues addressed to the audience, comic interludes, complaints, and that improbable dénouement at the end. *The Misanthrope* is more delicate: a tragedy of conversation, nothing hap-

pens . . . life as it was lived—the manners of the period, the moral vision of worldly individuals who are somewhat removed from the Court where important events take place. (182)

There is, however, nothing in these remarks that has not already been said innumerable times; indeed, they have long ago acquired the status of platitudes, and it is surprising that Vitez should offer them as discoveries. Acted against the same anti-illusionist décor as *The School for Wives,* his *Misanthrope* does not appear as a reflection of "life as it was lived" but as yet another manifestation of Molière's essentially antirealist theatricality. Vitez may have relied on the well-known details of Molière's life to provide a metanarrative compelling enough to forge the four separate plays into a coherent tetralogy at the level of plot and theme (Judith Miller reports that one early working title for the tetralogy was "Torture by Women and the Triumph of Atheism" [74]), but it is very difficult indeed to see his mise en scène as a biography of Molière.[14] If Vitez believes that performing the plays as a tetralogy reveals important insights into the changes in Molière's art and craft as well as his beliefs and opinions, his choice of scenography and acting style argue otherwise.

Lemaire's décor creates a scenic space that focuses the spectators' attention almost exclusively on the stage as a stage, identifying it as the area in which the actors perform. She thus turns away from the mimetic treatment of scenic space that characterized the work of Arnavon and his predecessors. Most realist directors and designers of the last hundred years have viewed scene design as an opportunity to comment on the action of the play and its characters from a sociohistorical or psychological perspective as well as a means of solving some of the problems posed by Molière's outdated theatrical conventions. Instead, following Vitez's Meyerholdian focus on the play of conventions in Molière's work, and in keeping with Vitez's conviction that Molière's plays are old plays and that Molière is not our contemporary, Lemaire developed a contemporary equivalent of the seventeenth-century *palais à volonté,* a setting that proved adequate, with the occasional addition of an accessory or two, for almost every play of the Grand Siècle.

While her twentieth-century *palais* accommodated itself to four different plays by Molière, it did not serve the same function it served in Molière's time. The new *palais* was not designed to lend *vraisemblance* to the dramatic action by suggesting, however symbolically, an appropriate location; instead, it was designed to suggest a reason for the twentieth-century mise en scène's lack of *vraisemblance:* for the duration of Vitez's tetralogy, the scenic space represented a place that existed *only in the theater.* Unlike a realist décor, Lemaire's did not refer the spectator to its offstage counterpart in the real world.[15] Instead, it emphasized the fact that Molière's plays belong to a different kind of theater, a theater with which twentieth-century spectators are not familiar, no matter how familiar they imagine themselves to be with Molière's texts. If her décor was in any sense realist, it was realist in that it presented the plays themselves as the cultural products of a previous era.

Realism and the Question of "Legibility"

In a sense, Planchon's *Tartuffe* represents the culmination of the realist tradition pioneered by Antoine and Arnavon, although Planchon's post-Brechtian realism was, as we have seen, quite different from the realism of Antoine and Arnavon. If Planchon can be said to have defamiliarized *Tartuffe* by offering a revisionist reading of Molière's narrative and by reframing Molière's well-known plot and characters in a scenography that called attention to some of the political realities of the Grand Siècle, Vitez, by the same token, can be said to have defamiliarized Molière's dramaturgy and its mise en scène in the modern era. Although Planchon's mise en scène problematized the realist representation of the past, it did not, like Vitez's, call into question the realist interpretation and performance of Molière's characters. After Vitez, the question of Molière's realism and the value of the realist mise en scène of Molière must be addressed in a somewhat different manner.

Arnavon proposed a realist mise en scène for both *Tartuffe* and *The School for Wives* in response to what he perceived as a problem of intelligibility. He argued that treating Molière's plays as "morceaux de théâtre" effectively made them incomprehensible as examinations of the human situation and, as a result, ineffective as moral lessons. A realist mise en scène would render Molière's comedies both aesthetically comprehensible and ethically salutary, he suggested, because the modern spectator already understood the conventions of realist dramaturgy and scenography (and because Arnavon himself believed that modern dramatic and scenic realism offered an objectively reliable representation of the world). Jouvet and Planchon, each in his own way, also employed realist conventions to make Molière's plots and characters intelligible to their spectators. Both of these directors differ from Arnavon, however, in one crucial respect:

they do not pretend that their mises en scène show what Molière's France actually looked like, and they do not attempt to convince us that we are observing an objectively accurate recreation of seventeenth-century behavior in an objectively accurate recreation of a seventeenth-century urban environment. Instead, they offer frankly acknowledged, mediated (i.e., theatricalized) representations of the Grand Siècle that are grounded in realist techniques. Jouvet acknowledges the explicitly theatrical artifice of Arnolphe/Molière's relationship with the audience in a scenography that derives from a realist analysis of *The School for Wives'* spatial system; Planchon calls attention to the theatricality of his own representations of the Grand Siècle in a mise en scène that investigates the behavior of Molière's characters using the psychological realism of Stanislavski and the critical realism of Brecht. For Arnavon, the objective representation of the past as the "true milieu" of Molière's dramatic actions remained an intellectually valid goal; for Jouvet and Planchon, such objective representations of the past are ineluctably compromised by the means of representation. Neither artist saw such a compromise in negative terms. Indeed, both of them created influential mises en scène by finding novel ways of negotiating that compromise. As a result, they were able to stage Molière's plays in an intelligible fashion that acknowledged them as products of an earlier culture and, at the same time, interpreted the behavior of that earlier culture from an admittedly modern perspective (it was precisely the presence of his own modern interpretation that Arnavon sought to conceal).

Vitez's tetralogy represents a radical break with the trend of mise en scène represented by Antoine, Arnavon, Jouvet, and Planchon, for Vitez was no longer concerned with intelligibility. As we have seen, Vitez believed that the great works of the past have survived, like "ruined architectures," only in a fragmented state. Whereas earlier generations of directors assumed that Molière's texts could be understood and that their task, as directors, was to make those texts intelligible in the theater, Vitez challenged the assumption that we can understand (that we have understood) Molière's texts. As Vitez said in *De Chaillot à Chaillot*, "The only thing that is truly other is writing" (52). Vitez refused to "naturalize" Molière's writing (or that of any other playwright) by refusing to make a mise en scène that would blend Molière's dialogue into a series of theatrical events to give spectators the impression that they were observing an essentially linear narrative. Instead, he worked to preserve the strangeness of Molière's text, to avoid disguising the text's otherness with his mise en scène.[16] As a result, Molière's text appeared dissected, disconnected, inorganic, a montage of fragments, as if Vitez had disassembled Molière in much the same way that Barthes had disassembled Balzac in *S/Z*. Vitez's unconventional treatment of Molière's dialogue, along with his treatment of *récit*, his rejection of traditional casting, and his use of a decidedly unrealistic acting style, all resulted in a radically unfamiliar Molière. Whereas Arnavon insisted that Molière was our contemporary, that his concerns were our concerns, that his moral vision was fully intelligible to us, Vitez seemed to suggest that Molière lived long ago in a different culture, had quite a different understanding of the human condition, and enjoyed and produced quite another kind of theater.

Many commentators and reviewers have expressed frustration with Vitez's aesthetic, and audiences were slow to respond with enthusiasm, although Vitez's work became more and more popular in the decade before his death in 1990. David Whitton remarks that spectators frequently left the theater during Vitez's performances and goes on to comment that "it is surely not philistinism to object when a theatrical performance invites the reflection that its ideal audience would be composed entirely of Ph.D.'s in performance theory" (279–80). Whitton's assessment of Vitez's work (and the work of other directors who employ similar techniques) as "intimidatingly intellectual" need not, however, be taken at face value. A spectator need not grasp Vitez's mise en scène in its minute details in order to comprehend the main thrust of his ideas. Vitez's challenge to the prevailing tradition of realist mise en scène, a tradition that continues to dominate despite decades of experimentation in nonrealist dramaturgy, is quite unmistakable.

Conclusion

> One is invariably struck, when looking at French society, by the overwhelming presence
> of the past and the degree to which this society turns to the past to legitimate the present
> and justify the future. The "modern" nineteenth century in many respects was not very
> modern at all. In spite of the many "revolutions" from 1789 onwards—political, social,
> and economic—French society held fast to familiar views of the world and one's business
> in it. Observers of French society ever since have noted how much of the ancien régime
> survived into the new, a survival that sustained a characteristically French tension between
> past and present, between tradition and modernity.
> —Priscilla Parkhurst Clark, *Literary France: The Making of a Culture*

From Antoine to Vitez, French directors have recoded Molière for modern audiences. As we have seen in the preceding chapters, this process has involved rethinking neoclassical issues of *vraisemblance* and *bienséances* in terms of modern dramaturgy and scenography. It has also involved an ongoing reflection on what Anne Ubersfeld called the "non-dit" of Molière's own culture—those elements of seventeenth-century French culture left unarticulated in Molière's text but which nevertheless inform Molière's creation.

From Antoine to Vitez, French directors have read Molière intertextually, continually reinscribing his texts in different contexts and recreating his seventeenth-century dramaturgy in a variety of different modes. Each in his own way has reimagined Molière's work as well as the culture that produced it (which we apprehend partially through Molière's own representations of that culture) in terms of the signifying practices of his own modern culture. For example, Arnavon's images of the Grand Siècle background of *The School for Wives* and *Tartuffe* derive from the Romantic histories of Jules Michelet and the Romantic novels of Alexandre Dumas, *père*. He then processed those images through the realist scenography of Antoine and late nineteenth-century realist dramaturgy and presented them to his audience as an authentic recreation of the milieu that Molière's characters would have lived in had they ever existed outside the theater.

161

Jouvet, by contrast, was not concerned with what the seventeenth century actually looked like. What mattered for him was the poetic and spiritual truth of the dramatic narrative. Consequently, his scenographic recreation of the Grand Siècle functioned like the settings for a fantasy by Cocteau or Giraudoux; for Jouvet, the imaginary was the real, and no objective verification needed to be obtained from historical documents or artifacts.

With Planchon, the historical context of Molière's text once again became important—only Planchon's interest in history was quite different from Arnavon's. Following his discovery of Brecht in the 1950s, Planchon developed a scenic vocabulary for representing the past that was quite different from the one developed by the Romantics and Realists of the nineteenth century. Planchon's Grand Siècle was a period of enormous social dislocation as well as of political and cultural achievements. French history for Planchon was no longer the history of Michelet or the Romantic novelizations of Dumas (one might argue that Michelet's history of France also takes the form of a Romantic novelization); it was the history of Braudel, Goubert, and their politically and socially conscious colleagues of the *Annales*.

For Vitez, finally, the theater and culture of seventeenth-century France existed only in fragmentary form, like the Greek civilization that produced Aeschylus and Euripides, Aristophanes and Menander; while the fragments could be reassembled, their original form and meaning could no longer be apprehended. For Vitez, the Grand Siècle was no longer a Golden Age whose mythical status had to be either affirmed (Arnavon) or challenged (Planchon). Instead, it was no more (but also no less) than an archive of cultural and theatrical motifs that could be adopted for modern uses. In a tetralogy of plays by Molière, Vitez offered a fantasia on what he saw as the obsessive themes and motifs of Molière's theater, rather than a conventional reading of four individual plays. In a montage of alternately farcical, grotesque, romantic, and even tragic sequences, Vitez offered representations of emotional, philosophical, and psychological trauma in the gestures and expressions of actors whose body language expressed a vision of the world that was recognizably modern. Yet because they were inscribed in a scenography that recalled an earlier era of theater, these *jeux*, for all their inescapable modernity, seemed to summon the ghosts of Molière and his actors, much like Jouvet's "inside and outside" portrayal of Arnolphe.

With each mise en scène, hitherto unfamiliar or even unsuspected aspects of Molière's dramatic universe took center stage, displacing traditional understandings of the play to a greater or lesser degree. These freshly revealed aspects had the effect of recreating Molière's cultural identity to the point where he began to look and sound like "our contemporary," in Jacques Arnavon's phrase. As the preceding chapters show, however, this contemporary Molière is different for every generation. For Antoine and Arnavon, Molière's dramaturgy mirrors the realist dramaturgy of their favorite contemporary dramatists; for Jouvet, Molière's dramaturgy marries the commedia dell'arte of Copeau to the poetic sensibilities of Giraudoux and other nonrealist dramatists of the interwar years; for Planchon, Molière's dramaturgy accommodates Planchon's commitment to a Brechtian cultural and political critique as well as his fascination with quasisurrealist *écriture scénique;* for Vitez, Molière's dramaturgy supplies an almost endless sequence of images that fuel a nonrealistic Artaudian dance of desire and unreason.

French directors from Antoine to Vitez have created modern theatrical events in which twentieth-century French artists enter into a dialogue with their predecessors. In a very real sense, the classics of the Grand Siècle haunt the modern stage. Modern actors learn many of the fundamentals of their art in classes that use fragments of classic text: speech, verse speaking, character analysis, and scene study classes all rely on texts from the classic repertoire. As we saw in the preceding chapter, Vitez's tetralogy originated in his acting classes. Jouvet, too, used Molière extensively in his own acting classes.[1] Jouvet's acting teacher, Jacques Copeau, relied exclusively on classic texts. Some years later, Vitez began his own training as an actor at the Théâtre du Vieux Colombier, where he took classes that had scarcely changed since the days of Copeau (Vitez and Copfermann 27).

In an analogous fashion, twentieth-century playwrights compete with classic authors. To a great extent, modern theater artists find their own distinctive voices in a dialectical exchange with their artistic ancestors, a process that, interestingly enough, rarely depends on a categorical rejection of the past. More often than not, as the work of the directors discussed in this study exemplifies, that process is one of folding the past into the present, the present into the past—without, for all that, dissolving the present in the past or the past in the present.

The major theatrical institutions of France, like their counterparts in other European countries, serve two major functions: they are both museums and privileged arenas of cultural experimentation. More often than not, the classic playscript is central to both functions as it represents a significant moment in the history of the nation's culture as well as an opportunity for the director to reflect on his or her own present historical moment. As Planchon reminds us, the stage director exists, in part, to serve as curator of these museums. But these national theaters are not museums in quite the same way as those buildings that house the great artworks of the past, for in the theater the past is never fixed. As the work of directors from Antoine onward shows, the past exists in the theater only to be recreated (and potentially reevaluated) from the perspective of today. The Grand Siècle and, indeed, Molière himself are not the immortal and immutable reference points that generations preceding Planchon believed them to be. Instead, they exist as powerful myths in modern French culture, and as Barthes and others have argued, myth is a uniquely persuasive form of speech. Planchon, Vitez, and other late twentieth-century directors have turned the very analysis of those myths into captivating theater, just as earlier generations embraced them to different degrees.

The cycle of experiment that began in 1907 with Antoine's *Tartuffe* has ironically come full circle: it began with a mise en scène designed to rescue Molière's writings from being reduced to mere *morceaux de théâtre* and evolved into a tetralogy that presented them as precisely that. The realist techniques of Stanislavski, Antoine, and others have fueled almost a century of experiment in reinterpreting and restaging classical texts. For the moment, no different approach to Molière's classic text has emerged. Although artists and writers have developed a considerable variety of nonrealistic aesthetics and techniques, late nineteenth-century dramatic and scenographic realism remains dominant in the theater, largely because the mainstream audience (influenced by photography and the cinema) has been reluctant or unable to acknowledge the extent to which late nineteenth-century realism and its derivatives present a mythic representation of the world.

Notes

Chapter 1

1. See also the Bray and Scherer edition of Molière's complete works, which contains discussions of significant performances of individual plays. Bray's other major contribution to our understanding of seventeenth-century French dramaturgy is *La Formation de la doctrine classique en France* (1927).

2. Moore's title clearly associates his project with that of the New Criticism, which at the time was positioned in the avant-garde of literary studies. Such an overt commitment to a mode of analysis so inextricably bound up with a certain notion of literature, of textuality, and of authorship probably made any engagement with the theater as an artistic practice and as a cultural institution almost impossible.

3. Among the most productive linkings of the "aesthetic" and the "ethical" in recent Molière criticism are Judd Hubert's *Molière and the Comedy of Intellect;* Ralph Albanese, Jr.'s *Le Dynamisme de la peur chez Molière;* and Jules Brody's two articles, "Esthétique et société chez Molière" and "*Dom Juan* and *Le Misanthrope,* or the Esthetics of Individualism in Molière."

4. Noteworthy exceptions to this trend include Jacques Scherer's *Structures de Tartuffe* (1974) and, more recently, Albert Bermel's *Molière's Theatrical Bounty* (1990). Both of these books are altogether exceptional in their sensitivity to the material problems of performance.

5. Curiously enough, the critical obsession with the *raisonneur* may be a response to the pervasive use of just such a moralizing character by the nineteenth-century members of the *école de bon sens* and authors of the *mélodrame* and the *pièce bien faite.* For an excellent history of nineteenth-century French theater, see Marvin Carlson's *The French Stage in the Nineteenth Century* (1972).

6. I have found the second edition of T. E. Lawrenson's *The French Stage and Playhouse in the XVIIth Century* (1986) especially useful.

7. Very few descriptions exist of those mises en scène, and those that are available are extremely problematic. Herzel's discussion of Molière's "natural" acting style, for instance, is considerably hampered by the absence of a reliable frame of reference. In addition, Herzel is constrained to rely on discussions of Molière's acting by various individuals, many of whom were not theater people. Herzel encounters a similar problem when he discusses the illustrations of several Molière productions by Brissart and Chauveau—he is forced to guess at the extent to which their representations can be relied on. The fact that Brissart and Chauveau do not show spectators on stage

165

(something we know to have been the case) severely damages their credibility as visual witnesses.

8. For a detailed discussion of Molière's natural acting, see Herzel's "Le Jeu 'naturel' de Molière et de sa troupe."

9. For a particularly trenchant discussion of the institution of Literature, see the first chapter of Terry Eagleton's *Literary Theory*. What Eagleton has to say about "English Literature" can readily be applied to "French Literature," a subject that first emerged, interestingly enough, in English universities.

10. Even in the seventeenth century Molière dramaturgy exercised a significant influence on English Restoration playwriting. Since the time of the Restoration translations of Molière's plays have been a staple of the English-language theater. As far as literary studies are concerned, scholars both in France and elsewhere have demonstrated an unflagging interest in his writings dating from the inception of the discipline of French Studies.

11. See Robert Nelson's "Classicism" for an excellent discussion of the ways in which Molière's plays have been read through Racine's. Nelson identifies what he calls a "classico-Racinian teleology" in Molière studies that stems from the tradition of seeing *The Misanthrope*, the most regularly neoclassical of the plays, as Molière's "best" play.

12. Nothing suggests that Molière ever gave any thought to the possibility that another director would want to stage his plays after his lifetime. Like every playwright of the period, he was concerned with guarding against pirated versions of his scripts being published, but there was no reason for him to have feared another company staging one of his plays in competition with one of his own productions.

13. There are, of course, well-known exceptions to this general rule. Even in Molière's time, authors who achieved no success in the theater often sought publication as a way of vindicating the quality of their work. As often as not, however, the academic correctness of such plays made up for what they lacked in theatrical inventiveness and stageworthiness.

14. David Maskell's recent *Racine: A Theatrical Reading* (1991) is the first English-language book-length analysis of Racine's tragedies grounded in the performance possibilities of the seventeenth-century tragic stage.

15. Bernard Dort is more often seen as France's foremost Brecht scholar than as a semiotician. He has, however, been in close contact with France's leading theater semioticians for most of his postwar career. Anne Ubersfeld and Patrice Pavis, for example, have been his colleagues in the Theatre Department at the Université de Paris III (Sorbonne Nouvelle) for many years. In any case, it would be difficult to overestimate Brecht's influence on the development of French theater semiotics.

16. No rehearsal drafts from the French classical period survive.

17. Perhaps one of the more obvious explanations for this phenomenon is the correct one: the director's contribution to the mise en scène of a classic text, particularly a well-known one, is not obscured by the presence of a living author and a contemporary dramaturgy. Indeed, in their 1988 book, *Directors' Theatre*, Bradby and Williams propose the director's assumption of the author function as a defining characteristic of "directors' theatre" (1).

18. Based on this definition of the classic which, she admits, privileges the French classical period from Corneille to Beaumarchais, Ubersfeld declines to acknowledge the plays of Musset, Lenz, or Büchner as classics on the grounds that their problematics are too close to those of her own period. In considering what remains and does not remain comprehensible or readable to us in the late twentieth century, Ubersfeld surprisingly elects to focus on the apparent content of the plays in question rather than on issues of form. Thus, we can understand *Lorenzaccio,* she argues, because the "social mechanism" that drives the plot is still transparent to us more than a century later. But other aspects of Musset's dramaturgy are equally relevant to this discussion. And surely the "social mechanisms" represented in the plays of Lenz and Büchner are not the only factors that account for the commonly asserted "modernity" of these authors. Despite these ambiguities of definition, however, her notion of the classic as having been written for others remains exceptionally productive.

19. For an excellent discussion of Brecht's use of scenic writing, see John Rouse's article, "Brecht and the Art of Scenic Writing."

Chapter 2

1. Along with Paul Ginisty, Antoine was co–artistic director of the Odéon for a few weeks in 1896.

2. See André-Paul Antoine's article, "Le Naturalisme d'Antoine," for a useful discussion of the genesis of what he calls the "myth" of his father's Naturalism and of the effects of that myth on the theater artists and historians of his own generations.

3. Like most theater historians of the last seventy-five years, Brockett and Findlay seem quite unwilling to see in Antoine anything other than the founder of the Théâtre Libre, and their comments on his work with the classics are frankly dismissive. In the end, they see Antoine's work as marking the final stage in the development of nineteenth-century scenic realism; for them, the nonrealist, poetic theater is more characteristically modern. As for French theater historians, the impressive two-volume history of French theater edited by Jacqueline de Jomaron, *Le Théâtre en France,* deals only with Antoine's innovative approach to Shakespeare. With respect to historians of directing, Bradby and Williams emphasize the importance of the classics in the rise to power of the modern stage director in their *Directors' Theatre,* yet apart from mentioning Antoine's work with the classics (7), they offer no discussion of his pioneering productions of those plays at the Théâtre Antoine or later at the Odéon. Similarly, David Whitton concentrates almost exclusively on Antoine's work with new plays in his *Stage Directors in Modern France.* Most surprising of all perhaps is Jean Chothia's *André Antoine,* a volume in the Cambridge Directors in Perspective series, which devotes a mere six pages to a discussion of Antoine's treatment of the French classic repertoire at the Odéon (155–60). Two of Chothia's six pages deal with Molière. Of the French historians of directing, Sylvain Dhomme mentions Antoine's productions of Corneille's *The Cid* and Shakespeare's *King Lear* and *Julius Caesar* only in passing in *La Mise en scène contemporaine d'André Antoine à Bertolt Brecht.* In a more recent study, *Théâtre et mise en scène, 1880–1980,* Jean-Jacques Roubine completely ignores Antoine's work with the classics, despite the fact that he is more interested in the question of staging classic texts than Dhomme.

4. At the time, the Comédie-Française used the same set for both *Tartuffe* and *The Miser* (Sanders, *André Antoine* 163).

5. Antoine acknowledged the importance of Arnavon's intellectual contribution to the production in a letter to *Le Figaro* on October 4, 1907 (Sanders, *André Antoine* 159). Antoine is not the only director to have staged one of Arnavon's notebook mises en scène. In January 1927, the Theatre Royal in Copenhagen staged Arnavon's *The Misanthrope,* directed by Egill Rostrup. Arnavon had first published his ideas about this play in *L'Interprétation de la comédie classique* (1914) and, at the request of the Theatre Royal, had agreed to develop a detailed proposal for a production (subsequently published by Arnavon in 1930). The successful Theatre Royal production was followed by a production at the Royal Dramatic Theatre in Stockholm (May 1929) that Arnavon considered even more successful than the one in Copenhagen (*Misanthrope* iii).

6. Maurice Descôtes, for example, does not mention Antoine's production in his *Grands Rôles du théâtre de Molière.*

7. The Académie Française awarded Arnavon the Prix Bordin for his *Notes sur l'interprétation de Molière* in 1923. Six years later, it honored his *Molière, notre contemporain* (1929). The fact that the arch-conservative Académie gave its approval to two works criticizing the Comédie-Française suggests the extent to which the French national theater had become aesthetically fossilized.

8. In 1963, Jacques Guicharnaud, one of the most respected *moliéristes* of this century, argued against Arnavon's contention that a twentieth-century mise en scène of *Tartuffe* should adopt twentieth-century staging conventions. Responding to Arnavon's discussion of Molière's first act, Guicharnaud writes that Arnavon

> rejected the traditional living room décor, but he seemed to forget that the *salle basse* [ground-floor family room], like the bourgeois living room or the vast antechamber, to which today's stage directors seem to have returned, remained the best means of simplifying the problem and of dissimulating, for the eyes of the spectators, everything that might be artificial about this entrance of Orgon and the circumstances surrounding it on the level of superficial realism. (32)

Guicharnaud, then, accepts Arnavon's basic point—that Molière's script raises questions of plausibility for today's directors and spectators—but insists that Molière's seventeenth-century stagecraft offers the best solution (curiously enough, Guicharnaud omits any discussion of Antoine's 1907 mise en scène). Unfortunately, Guicharnaud does not comment on the importance of Arnavon's distinction between unity of décor (representation of a single space in a single set), which Arnavon opposed, and unity of place (representation of two or more spaces by a single décor), which Arnavon championed.

9. Curiously enough, nothing in Arnavon's books suggests that he undertook any systematic research into the history of manners.

10. See Ralph Albanese, Jr.'s *Molière à l'école républicaine* for a detailed investigation of the ways in which Molière was used in the French educational system between 1870 and 1914, the period in which Arnavon received his formal education.

11. Descôtes gives an interesting account of why Voltaire and others in the eighteenth century also considered Molière a "contemporary" in his *Molière et sa fortune littéraire.*

12. Under Jean Vilar in the 1950s, and more recently under the guidance of directors such as Patrice Chéreau and Roger Planchon, the TNP has consistently adopted a less conservative political perspective than the Comédie-Française. However, with the appointment of Jean-Pierre Vincent and especially that of Antoine Vitez, both of whom had been artistic directors of different TNP theaters, as Administrateur-Général at the Comédie-Française during the 1980s, even the bastion of conservatism itself began to change.

13. The Théâtre National de Chaillot is the only major Parisian theater with a thrust configuration that can be, and frequently is, converted to an end-stage format.

Chapter 3

1. The most detailed account of Planchon's career remains Emile Copfermann's *Théâtres de Roger Planchon*. The only book-length study of his career in English is Yvette Daoust's *Roger Planchon: Director and Playwright*. Bradby and Williams include a discussion of Planchon in their *Directors' Theatre*, as does David Whitton in his *Stage Directors in Modern France*. Bradby's *Modern French Drama, 1940–1990* also deals with many of Planchon's productions and offers valuable comments on their cultural contexts.

2. An account of the first mise en scène can be found in Pierre Brunet's 1967 edition of *Tartuffe*. A brief illustrated account of the second mise en scène can be found in an unnumbered 1977 issue of *L'Avant-Scène*, edited by Alfred Simon. A richly detailed semiotic analysis of the second mise en scène by Tadeusz Kowzan is included in volume 6 of *Les Voies de la création théâtrale*. More recently, Michel Corvin has devoted a chapter of his *Molière et ses metteurs en scène d'aujourd'hui* to Planchon's second *Tartuffe*.

3. Merle suggests that Planchon is unique in describing Orgon as a high-level civil servant, but Scherer (*Structures* 201–3) and, more recently, James F. Gaines (200–203) have argued that Orgon's social standing and evident wealth imply that he is an official of the highest rank.

4. Bradby suggests that Planchon's adoption of Brechtian attitudes to the staging of classics marks a historically important shift away from the aesthetic values of the Cartel directors, with their traditional notions of "taste, beauty, and skill" (*Modern French Drama* 111). Planchon's relationship to the theory and practice of Brecht is discussed at length in Copfermann's *Théâtres de Roger Planchon* (esp. 95–182). A detailed account of Planchon's first experiments with Brechtian dramaturgy can be found in Pia Kleber's *Exceptions and Rules*.

5. Albert Bermel suggests that Allio's scenography "may have been commenting on" Antoine's (158 n. 2).

6. Unlike Antoine's and Arnavon's, Allio's solution to the problem of providing a number of different locations for the action did not include an exterior space such as a garden. His décor did, however, suggest a series of different locations inside the house.

7. As a result of this pigeonholing, Planchon's work as a playwright has, unfortunately, been undervalued.

8. Montloup's architectural fragments provide an interesting echo of Antoine Vitez's vision of the classic text as an "architectural ruin."

9. In Planchon's production, Flipote is one of Orgon's servants.

10. A spotlight comes up on the genital area of the painting during the opening segment from the de Sales book, thus focusing the spectator's attention on Planchon's juxtaposition of religious discourse and sexuality (Merle 40).

11. The skycloth may be read as a reference to seventeenth-century stagecraft akin to the chandeliers used by Louis Jouvet and his scenographer, Christian Bérard. Antoine Vitez also used a skycloth in his 1978 tetralogy as part of a décor that plainly sought to invoke the kind of scenic space in which Molière himself staged those plays.

12. In act 5, portions of the floor are removed during the police search of Orgon's house. Orgon is then thrown into one of the "pits" to await the Exempt's pronouncement.

13. Planchon thus identifies Dorine as a servant charged with household tasks and not solely as *servante* to Mariane.

14. For similar reasons, Planchon introduces a large number of servants into the cast of the play. These servants also function as a group of onstage spectators whose entrances and exits serve to emphasize the fact that moments of crisis for members of the family are equally moments of crisis for servants of the family: "The stage is . . . quite frequently filled with supernumeraries (servants) who come and stand with the family in the moments of crisis: groups come together, disband, make entrances and exits, thus accentuating the emotional dimsensions of the situation" (Millon 47).

15. The triptych of religious and regal images might appear to illustrate Jacques Guicharnaud's celebrated analysis of Orgon as a man who likes to serve his masters.

16. According to the 1682 edition, Molière himself cut some of the Exempt's *tirade* in performance (Couton 1:1370).

17. André Merle offers a perceptive comment on the instability of *vraisemblance* by comparing a *vraisemblance* grounded in the conventions of genre to one grounded, for example, in psychology:

There are two major kinds of *vraisemblance*. The first depends on what we call the rules of genre. . . . Here, *vraisemblance* designates the relationship between the work and literary discourse. . . . In the seventeenth century, a comedy is considered *vraisemblable* only if the juvenile leads marry in the final act. According to this norm, in *Tartuffe,* Mariane is the subject; Valère the object; Orgon, Madame Pernelle and Tartuffe are in opposition; Elmire, Cléante, Damis and Dorine are in support. But there is another *vraisemblance* that depends on a relationship of conformity between the work and a diffuse discourse that belongs to a social class. For the progressive middle-class intellectual of today, who has been formed by psychoanalysis, the *vraisemblable* structure of *Tartuffe* has become this: Orgon is the subject, and he is experiencing unusual feelings toward Tartuffe, who is the object; all the other characters are in opposition, with, of course, the exception of Orgon's mother, Madame Pernelle, who is in support. (45)

18. In 1668, Louis ordered the official destruction of all documents relating to the rebellion of the Fronde. Ralph Albanese, Jr., comments that Tartuffe picked a particularly bad time to remind Louis of the troubled early years of his reign: "At a time when Louis XIV's regime proclaimed its own cultural permanence, Tartuffe comes

on stage to expose—to the King himself—the socio-political heresy that was the civil wars" (*Le Dynamisme de la peur* 133). For an excellent discussion of the theatrical means employed by Louis's propagandists to create his identity as "Le Roi Soleil," see Jean-Marie Apostolidès's *Le Roi machine* and *Le Prince sacrifié*.

19. Planchon took over the role of Tartuffe in revivals of the 1962 production during the period 1963–71.

20. Planchon explores the sexual aspects of the scene far more "realistically" than Arnavon might ever have suggested. At the same time, Planchon's staging of the scene helps us appreciate, in retrospect, the enormous value of the particular way of looking at a Molière text that Antoine and Arnavon first explored.

21. Planchon clearly departs from the traditional staging of the scene that takes its inspiration from the engraving printed as the frontispiece to the 1669 edition of the play.

22. Jacques Scherer relates that Jouvet felt that one actor alone simply could not give the Exempt's final speech sufficient weight (*Structures* 205).

23. In Corvin's opinion, Planchon's staging amplifies the Exempt sequence to the extent that it becomes almost a sixth act (120).

Chapter 4

1. In his *Art poétique* (1674), Nicolas Boileau offered the following evaluation of Molière's work, the very terms of which reappear throughout Arnavon's commentaries:

Study the Court, and make yourself familiar with the City. Each provides an abundance of models. Molière's art would have achieved renown if he had illustrated his writings from that source, if he had been less interested in pleasing the people by so often turning objective character portraits into caricatures, if he had set aside buffoonery and embraced the beautiful and the fine, if he had not shamelessly blended Terence and Tabarin. I don't see the author of *The Misanthrope* in that ridiculous sack that Scapin covers himself with. (Qtd. in Mongrédien, *Recueil* 2:495).

2. Robert Nelson has forcefully argued against what he calls the "Classico-Racinian teleology" that has influenced our vision of the Molière canon. Because of this Classicist bias, Nelson suggests, "only four or five [of Molière's plays] are said to render the quintessential Molière" (172).

3. Judd Hubert's excellent chapter on *The School for Wives*, entitled "A Burlesque Tragedy," offers a good-humored discussion of Molière's admixture of styles that reveals this critic's exemplary sensitivity to the playwright's manipulations of tone.

4. Molière's text as we know it today is, of course, the product of many generations of textual scholars, each of which has modified the text in accordance with its own historically determined notions of seventeenth-century French artistic production. One salient example from *The School for Wives* can be found in Arnolphe's final line, which reads "Ouf!" in early editions but which was amended to a more tragic "Oh!" later on. In addition, of course, Molière's punctuation as well as his use of upper-case letters have been regularized from time to time in accordance with prevailing norms.

Fortunately, on the other hand, Molière's text does not present the range of problems that Shakespeare's editors have been obliged to grapple with.

5. Loret's account of the performance emphasizes what he took to be the purely frivolous nature of Molière's entertainment: "In ordinary rooms or in elegant salons, as an entertainment for ladies and gentlemen, they praise *The School for Wives,* which made Their Majesties laugh so much they had to hold their ribs. The play is absolutely delightful, not at all didactic. . . . It's a play that has been challenged in several quarters, but everybody goes to see it nonetheless. No serious subject ever attracted so many people" (qtd. in Mongrédien, *Recueil* 1:170).

6. Arnavon was, interestingly enough, not the first to see an affinity between Molière's dramaturgy and the kind of playwriting that was first popularized at the Théâtre Libre. Zola, in making his case for a new, experimental theater in the preface to *Thérèse Raquin,* had proposed Molière as a kind of model for the theater of the future: "We must move toward the future, and the future means the human problem studied in the context of reality; the future means the abandonment of all fables, it means the living drama of the double life of character and milieu, cut free . . . from the nonsense of conventions. . . . At this moment in time, we must have a broad and simple depiction of men and things, a drama such as Molière might have written" (qtd. in Bablet 11–12).

7. Indeed, Arnavon goes to unusual lengths to absolve Molière of responsibility for his play's flaws. He suggests that Molière adopted the dramatic conventions of his time merely as a gesture to his period and that his genius stood above and beyond the practices of the mid-seventeenth century: "He accepted them [the dramatic conventions]; a concession, perhaps, to the habits of his time, but which allowed him to impose what was essential, the astonishing satire that will amaze people and endure forever" (*L'Ecole des femmes* 32). Of course, this apologia also serves to draw our attention away from Molière's dramaturgy to the content of the "astonishing satire" that Arnavon sees as the true essence of the play.

8. Marvin Carlson reprints two assessments of Montigny's contributions to mise en scène in his book, *The French Stage in the Nineteenth Century.* The first of these is by Alexandre Dumas, *fils:* "It was Montigny who first had chairs changed in position by characters while they were speaking, who began ladies knitting during the dialogue when previously they never had anything in their hands but a fan or a handkerchief." The second account is by A. Thiers: "Montigny made the first reform by putting a table in the middle of the stage; then chairs had to be placed around the table; and the actors, instead of standing up to speak without looking at each other, sat down and spoke naturally among themselves as we do in real life" (124). Carlson himself offers the following assessment:

> Montigny directed the theatre [Théâtre du Gymnase] for thirty-six years, during which time it was the rival of the Comédie[-Française] itself in popularity, and the foremost theatre in Paris in the discovery of new talents and innovative staging practices. Both in his encouragement of the social drama of the Second Empire and in his directorial practices—his attention to realistic detail, his use of stage space, his long and careful rehearsal patterns—Montigny may in a real sense be considered the founder of the realistic theatre of the late nineteenth century. (130–31)

Carlson's article, "French Stage Composition from Hugo to Zola," which includes additional information about Montigny, offers a valuable account of the introduction of furniture and its influence on realist stage movement in nineteenth-century French theater.

9. "There is only one setting. Not that it would have been impossible to make all the set changes that common sense dictates with the use of special machinery. But the play requires twelve settings! And the audience would lose their patience with so many" (*L'Ecole des femmes* 54).

10. Curiously enough, although he offers no textual support, Arnavon borrows the traditional staging of this sequence, adding the proviso that the crying should not become overtly theatricalized.

Chapter 5

1. Descôtes records that the play was not highly thought of and rarely performed (to almost empty houses) during the eighteenth century. He quotes Voltaire, for instance, as saying that *The School for Wives* is "in every way inferior to *The School for Husbands*" (*Les Grands Rôles* 26). During the nineteenth century, the play served principally as a vehicle for launching the careers of young ingenues in the role of Agnès. As late as 1973, the play still served this function when the Comédie-Française produced it, under the direction of Jean-Paul Roussillon, as a vehicle for the young Isabelle Adjani.

2. Although it has frequently provided a forum for avant-garde theater, the Athénée—now called the Athénéé-Louis Jouvet—has always been a commercial theater. The theater's main auditorium is now called the Salle Jouvet; the second stage is named the Salle Christian Bérard.

3. Copeau is an enormously influential figure in French theater history, and his career is well documented. The most complete account in English of this career is John Rudlin's *Jacques Copeau*. Bettina Knapp's *The Reign of the Theatrical Director: French Theatre, 1887–1924* contains useful accounts of some of the productions at the Théâtre du Vieux-Colombier that involved Jouvet. Curiously enough, historians have focused almost exclusively on the early years of his career, as they have done with Antoine. Unlike Antoine's, however, Copeau's aesthetic did not undergo major changes.

4. Jules Romains's *Knock* was one of the great successes of Jouvet's career; he revived it as frequently as he did *The School for Wives* whenever he needed to offset financial losses on other productions. A good account of Jouvet's career in English can be found in Bettina Knapp's *Louis Jouvet: Man of the Theatre*. Two useful French biographies appeared in the 1980s: Jean-Marc Loubier's *Louis Jouvet* (1986) and Paul-Louis Mignon's *Louis Jouvet* (1988).

5. Sylvain Dhomme echoes Dort's assessment and suggests that Barrault's postwar work never developed beyond the parameters that were already established in the late 1930s (310).

6. Michelet's *Louis XIV et la révocation de l'Edit de Nantes* is largely devoted to a biography of Molière.

7. I attribute the scenography to Bérard since it was he who first visualized the various décors, although Jouvet is known to have designed the machinery that moved

the walls and other scenic elements. For a director of the period, Jouvet was unusually knowledgeable about the purely technical aspects of theatrical production and had taught design at Copeau's Vieux-Colombier school in the early 1920s. In addition, he designed the lighting for many of Copeau's productions and even invented a new kind of lighting instrument that bears his name.

8. André-Paul Antoine suggests that Bérard's décor was inspired by his father's use of mansions in his mise en scène of *Romeo and Juliet* during the 1910–11 season ("Le Naturalisme d'Antoine" 239).

9. As a result of his belief in the importance of historical accuracy in scenic detail, Arnavon's décor was based on the architecture of the mid-seventeenth century and not on what we today recognize as the characteristic style of Louis XIV's reign.

10. Like most scholars, Nicolich's commentary remains focused on the ways in which the various uses of the door, the window, and the balcony are implied in the dialogue. He does not discuss how these scenic elements have been (or might be) used in actual productions. For Nicolich, the door, window, and balcony, like the other elements of a mise en scène, exist only on an abstract, conceptual level, yet he discusses Arnolphe, Agnès, and Horace as if they were flesh-and-blood individuals.

11. Although he introduced many new ideas in his mise en scène, Arnavon retained the traditional practice of not staging the events that Horace narrates to Arnolphe. Arnavon did consider staging some of the events that take place in the interval between Molière's acts, events that Horace subsequently describes to Arnolphe, but decided against doing so on the grounds that staging an event before Horace described it would destroy the audience's sense of surprise (*L'Ecole des femmes* 223–24). In 1978, Vitez staged these same events while Horace described them and in the process opened up a radically new perspective on the theatrical possibilities of what has traditionally been seen as an essentially undramatic *récit*.

12. Brisson was highly critical of Jouvet's farcical staging in this scene: "A silly piece of gymnastics that creates a complication that leads to nothing. One feels here, as well as with certain other details, a seeking after novelty that rings false" (45). Judd Hubert has told me that he suspects that Jouvet may have agreed with Brisson, as Jouvet modified the staging of the notary scene in subsequent revivals of the production by introducing a second, mute notary who aped the gestures and expressions of his speaking counterpart.

13. Jean-Paul Roussillon's 1973 mise en scène at the Comédie-Française employed an expressionistic treatment of décor that suggested that *both* Agnès and Arnolphe were trapped in their situations (Maillard's articles reproduce photographs of and design drawings for the Roussillon scenography).

14. An interesting twentieth-century reflection on the relationship between Molière's life and art can be found in Mikhail Bulgakov's biographical novel, *The Life of Monsieur de Molière,* and in his play about Molière's difficulties with the authorities over *Tartuffe.* Bulgakov draws a parallel between his own situation in Stalinist Russia and Molière's under Louis XIV. Yuri Lubimov invoked similar parallels in his celebrated mise en scène of *Tartuffe* (see Jomaron, *"Le Tartuffe* mis en scène par Lioubimov").

15. It is important to remember that Arnavon is "staging" the play on a modern proscenium stage; he assumes that the actors will play their scenes behind the prosce-

nium and will do nothing to compromise the illusion that their characters are part of the self-contained world created by the mise en scène.

16. Unlike Arnavon, Jouvet felt no need to show another house onstage in order to justify Arnolphe's reference to the "other house." Jean-Paul Roussillon, on the other hand, did include a second house in his 1973 production at the Comédie-Française. The ground plan of Roussillon's décor is reproduced on the cover of *Comédie-Française* 19 (1973).

17. In his article, "The Décor of Molière's Stage: The Testimony of Brissart and Chauveau," Roger Herzel offers a detailed account of the setting Molière most probably used based on graphic evidence from Molière's contemporaries. Herzel regards *The School for Wives* as a transitional play because it marks the beginning of the playwright's interest in exploring events that occur inside his characters' houses (932). Herzel assumes that Molière was interested in scenic realism; he thus concludes that Molière was unable to solve the problem of moving back and forth between interior and exterior events and consequently was obliged to settle for having Arnolphe instruct his servants to bring Agnès outside.

Chapter 6

1. Didier Sandre, in an interview with Odette Aslan, reports that Vitez originally wanted to play both Arnolphe and Tartuffe (Aslan 25).

2. The casting of Gastaldi mirrors Molière's original casting of his wife. Vitez's other doublings do not reflect Molière's casting.

3. See Anna Dizier's *Antoine Vitez:* Faust, Britannicus, Tombeau pour 500,000 soldats for an extended discussion of Vitez's work with the body in rehearsal.

4. De Lannoy, for instance, sees Arnolphe's gesture as an emblem of the tetralogy's treatment of *jeu* and the actor's relationship to the audience (50).

5. Vitez translated a number of works from Russian, Greek, and German into French, including Sholokov's *Le Don paisible* [*And Quiet Flows the Don*], Sophocles' *Electra,* and Brecht's poetry. According to Vitez, this extensive experience as a translator exercised a significant influence on his ideas about mise en scène: "For me, the art of translation is absolutely analogous to my activities in the theater" (Vitez and Copfermann 51). Like a good translation, in Vitez's opinion, mise en scène must not seek to obscure the differences between production and text, between actor and character:

> One must very often tell the actors not to attempt either a comprehensive explanation or a comprehensive impersonation of a character, but to indicate with a few simple details that there exists a difference between the character [in performance] and its model [in the text]. . . . One indicates the disjunction [between the two] and the disjunction triggers the effect . . . of strangeness or *estrangement* (that's the neologism I invented) that Brecht calls for. (Vitez and Copfermann 56–57)

Because he seeks to remind the spectator of the difference between text and mise en scène, Vitez's understanding of translation is thus more akin, adopting Carlson's formulation, to mise en scène as supplement than it is to mise en scène as translation.

6. See Vitez's "Quatre fois Molière" (178–81) for a discussion of the tetralogy's time scheme.

7. See Dizier (64–68) for a useful technical discussion of Vitez's treatment of poetic dialogue.

8. By having his actors emphasize the regularity of Molière's verse, Vitez makes it possible to create powerful effects by disrupting the regular flow. Judith Miller, for example, describes how such a disruption functioned in the *Maximes* section of *The School for Wives:* "The actress playing Agnès, for example, pays no attention to the ends of lines or the sense of the verse. She delivers the *maximes* on 'the duties of a good wife' . . . as though her motor had gone haywire" (76).

9. When he was appointed artistic director of the Théâtre National de Chaillot in 1981, Vitez opened his first season with productions of Goethe's *Faust,* Racine's *Britannicus,* and his adaptation of Pierre Guyotat's *Tombeau pour 500,000 soldats.* In the context of this repertory of three productions, Vitez remarked: "A rotating repertory creates the impression of a statement of principle" (Vitez and Copfermann 24). The three 1981 productions were performed in rotating repertory in the same scenography (by Yannis Kokkos) and by the same actors, many of whom had performed in the Molière tetralogy. See Dizier for a detailed account of these productions and Vitez's rehearsal process.

10. Over the course of a series of conversations with Emile Copfermann collected in *De Chaillot à Chaillot,* Vitez returns time and again to what he sees as Meyerhold's influence on his work as both an acting teacher and a director (see esp. 43–47).

11. In *De Chaillot à Chaillot,* Vitez comments on Vilar's solution:

His solution was to recreate night and the open air in an enclosed theater, Nature enclosed by Culture. . . . The consequences were enormously significant with respect to the playing of the actors and the delivery of text. The acting was directed toward the public, a system of acting [that was] in large part hieratic, solemn, heroic, and born out of the restrictions of the open air and the Avignon courtyard. That lasted for a time. Vilar was successful for a quite a while. He could not keep it up because all systems lose momentum, people lose momentum. One cannot work forever in an indoor open air. (25)

12. An evocative and detailed account of Vilar's productions at Avignon can be found in Marie-Thérèse Serrière's *Le T.N.P. et nous.*

13. Vitez and Lemaire did not, however, attempt to recreate the actor/spectator relationship of Molière's theater.

14. Vitez gives one example of how his *écriture scénique* linked the four plays in an ongoing narrative with strategically timed sounds of thunder:

The School for Wives ends with a thunderclap (when Arnolphe, he who is guilty of having been in love, descends to his Hell), and there are rumbles of thunder in *Tartuffe.* . . . The thunder explodes with good cause in *Dom Juan,* then fades away, and the light of dawn comes up on the first scene of *The Misanthrope,* the day after the party. [There is] a final rumble in the dark beyond the stage as the torches make their entrance. ("Quatre fois Molière" 182)

15. De Lannoy suggests that Lemaire's décor functions as a critique of Grand Siècle ideology. He argues, for instance, that Lemaire's choice of Roman architecture and imagery reflects the popularity of Roman art as a source of inspiration for the court artists of Louis XIV's reign and should thus be interpreted as the director's and designer's implicit critique of the period's dominant ideology (49). Such a reading,

however, focuses on Lemaire's choice of graphic imagery to the exclusion of any consideration of the ways in which she blends architecture and imagery to create her scenic space.

16. In his innovative stagings of novels by Michel Tournier (*Vendredi, ou la vie sauvage* [Friday, or the Savage Life], Théâtre d'Ivry, 1973) and Louis Aragon, Vitez took great pains to retain something of the texture of the novels themselves. For example, *Catherine,* his version of Aragon's *Les Cloches de Bâle* (Festival d'Avignon, 1975), opened with the actors sitting around a dinner table, reading passages from the book and passing it to one another.

Conclusion

1. Edited transcripts of some of Jouvet's acting classes can be found in his *Molière et la comédie classique* as well as in *Revue d'Histoire du Théâtre* 39, no. 1 (1987).

Works Cited

Albanese, Ralph, Jr. *Le Dynamisme de la peur chez Molière: une analyse socio-culturelle de* Dom Juan, Tartuffe, *et* L'Ecole des Femmes. University, Miss.: Romance Monographs, 1976.

———. "The Molière Myth in Nineteenth-Century France." Trans. Patricia Pecoy. In *Pre-Text, Text, Context: Essays in Nineteenth-Century French Literature,* ed. Robert L. Mitchell, 238–54. Columbus: Ohio State University Press, 1980.

———. *Molière à l'école républicaine: de la critique universitaire aux manuels scolaires (1870–1914).* Stanford French and Italian Studies, vol. 72. Saratoga, Calif.: Anma Libri, 1992.

Antoine, André-Paul. *Antoine, père et fils: souvenirs du Paris littéraire et théâtral, 1900–1939.* Paris: R. Julliard, 1962.

———. "Le Naturalisme d'Antoine: une légende." In *Réalisme et poésie au théâtre,* ed. Jean Jacquot, 2d ed., 233–40. Paris: Centre Nationale de la Recherche Scientifique, 1967.

Apostolidès, Jean-Marie. *Le Roi machine: spectacle et politique au temps de Louis XIV.* Paris: Editions du Minuit, 1981.

———. *Le Prince sacrifié: théâtre et politique au temps de Louis XIV.* Paris: Editions du Minuit, 1985.

Aristotle. *Poetics.* Ed. and trans. Gerald F. Else. Ann Arbor: University of Michigan Press, 1967.

Arnavon, Jacques. Tartuffe: *la mise en scène rationnelle et la tradition.* Paris: Société d'Editions Littéraires et Artistiques, 1909.

———. *L'Interprétation de la comédie classique:* Le Misanthrope. Paris: Plon, 1914.

———. *Notes sur l'interprétation de Molière.* Paris: Plon, 1923.

———. *Molière, notre contemporain.* Paris: Editions de France, 1929.

———. Le Misanthrope *de Molière.* Paris: Plon, 1930.

———. L'Ecole des femmes *de Molière.* Paris: Plon, 1936.

———. *Le* Don Juan *de Molière.* Copenhagen: Gyldendal, 1947.

Aslan, Odette. "Didier Sandre: un parcours." *théâtre/public* 45 (1982): 24–28.

Bablet, Denis. *La Mise en scène contemporaine I: 1887–1914.* Paris: La Renaissance du Livre, 1968.

Barthes, Roland. *Critical Essays.* Trans. Richard Howard. Evanston: Northwestern University Press, 1972.

———. *Mythologies.* Ed. and trans. Annette Lavers. New York: Hill and Wang, 1972.

179

————. *S/Z.* Trans. Richard Miller. New York: Hill and Wang, 1974.

————. *Image-Music-Text.* Ed. and trans. Stephen Heath. New York: Hill and Wang, 1977.

Benhamou, Anne, et al. *Antoine Vitez: toutes les mises en scène.* Paris: Godefroy, 1981.

Bermel, Albert. *Molière's Theatrical Bounty: A New View of the Plays.* Carbondale: Southern Illinois University Press, 1990.

Bradby, David. *Modern French Drama, 1940–1990.* 2d ed. Cambridge: Cambridge University Press, 1991.

Bradby, David, and David Williams. *Directors' Theatre.* New York: St. Martin's Press, 1988.

Braun, Edward. *The Director and the Stage: From Naturalism to Grotowski.* New York: Holmes and Meier, 1982.

Bray, René. *La Formation de la doctrine classique en France.* Paris: Hachette, 1927.

————. *Molière: homme de théâtre.* Paris: Mercure de France, 1954.

Bray, René, and Jacques Scherer, eds. *Oeuvres complètes de Molière.* Paris: Club du Meilleur Livre, 1954–56.

Brisson, Pierre. *Du meilleur au pire.* Paris: Editions Gallimard, 1937.

Brockett, Oscar G., and Robert R. Findlay. *Century of Innovation: A History of American and European Theatre and Drama since 1870.* Englewood Cliffs, N.J.: Prentice-Hall, 1973.

Brody, Jules. "Esthétique et société chez Molière." In *Colloque des sciences humaines: dramaturgie et société,* ed. Jean Jacquot, 307–26. Paris: Centre National de la Recherche Scientifique, 1968.

————. "*Dom Juan* and *Le Misanthrope,* or the Esthetics of Individualism in Molière." *PMLA* 84 (1969): 559–76.

Brunet, Pierre, ed. Tartuffe: *dans la mise en scène de Roger Planchon.* Play by Molière. Paris: Hachette, 1967.

Bulgakov, Mikhail. *The Life of Monsieur de Molière.* Trans. Mirra Ginsburg. New York: Funk and Wagnalls, 1970.

————. *Molière.* Trans. Michael Glenny. In *Six Plays,* ed. Lesley Milne. London: Methuen, 1991.

Carlson, Marvin. "French Stage Composition from Hugo to Zola." *Educational Theatre Journal* 23, no. 4 (1971): 363–78.

————. *The French Stage in the Nineteenth Century.* Metuchen, N.J.: Scarecrow Press, 1972.

————. "Theatrical Performance: Illustration, Translation, Fulfillment, or Supplement?" *Theatre Journal* 37, no. 1 (1985): 5–11.

Chothia, Jean. *André Antoine.* Cambridge: Cambridge University Press, 1991.

Clark, Priscilla Parkhurst. *Literary France: The Making of a Culture.* Berkeley: University of California Press, 1987.

Copeau, Jacques. *Molière.* Paris: Editions Gallimard, 1976.

Copfermann, Emile. *Théâtres de Roger Planchon.* Paris: Union Générale d'Editions, 1977.

Corvin, Michel. *Molière et ses metteurs en scène d'aujourd'hui: pour une analyse de la représentation.* Lyon: Presses Universitaires de Lyon, 1985.

Couton, Georges, ed. *Oeuvres complètes de Molière*. By Molière. 2 vols. Paris: Editions Gallimard, 1971.

Daoust, Yvette. *Roger Planchon: Director and Playwright*. Cambridge: Cambridge University Press, 1981.

Descôtes, Maurice. *Les Grands Rôles du théâtre de Molière*. Paris: Presses Universitaires de France, 1960.

——. *Molière et sa fortune littéraire*. Bordeaux: Ducros, 1970.

Dhomme, Sylvain. *La Mise en scène contemporaine d'André Antoine à Bertolt Brecht*. Paris: Nathan, 1959.

Dizier, Anna. *Antoine Vitez:* Faust, Britannicus, Tombeau pour 500,000 soldats. Paris: Solin, 1982.

Dort, Bernard. "Antoine le patron." *Théâtre public, 1953–1966,* 299–302. Paris: Editions du Seuil, 1967.

——. "Les Classiques au théâtre ou la métamorphose sans fin." *Revue d'Histoire Littéraire de la France* 4 (1975): 155–65.

——. "Un Age d'or ou: sur la mise en scène des classiques en France entre 1945 et 1960." *Revue d'Histoire Littéraire de la France* 6 (1977): 1002–15.

——. "Sur deux comédiens: Louis Jouvet et Jean Vilar." *Cahiers Théâtre Louvain* 37 (1979): 29–34.

Eagleton, Terry. *Literary Theory: An Introduction*. Oxford: Basil Blackwell, 1983.

"L'Ecole des femmes." Review. *Theatre Arts* 36, no. 5 (1951): 23.

Elam, Keir. *The Semiotics of Theatre and Drama*. New York: Methuen, 1980.

Gaines, James F. *Social Structures in Molière's Theatre*. Columbus: Ohio University Press, 1984.

Genty, Christian. *Histoire du Théâtre National de L'Odéon (Journal de Bord), 1782–1982*. Paris: Fischbacher, 1982.

Gombrich, E. H. *Art and Illusion: A Study of the Psychology of Pictorial Representation*. Princeton, N.J.: Princeton University Press, 1961.

Gross, Nathan. *From Gesture to Idea: Esthetics and Ethics in Molière's Comedy*. New York: Columbia University Press, 1982.

Guicharnaud, Jacques. *Molière: une aventure théâtrale*. Paris: Editions Gallimard, 1963.

Hall, Gaston. *Comedy in Context: Essays on Molière*. Jackson: University Press of Mississippi, 1984.

Herzel, Roger. "Molière's Actors and the Question of Types." *Theatre Survey* 16, no. 1 (1975): 1–24.

——. "The Décor of Molière's Stage: The Testimony of Brissart and Chauveau." *PMLA* 93 (1978): 925–54.

——. *The Original Casting of Molière's Plays*. Ann Arbor: UMI Research Press, 1981.

——. "Le Jeu 'naturel' de Molière et de sa troupe." *XVIIe Siècle* 132 (1981): 279–83.

Holmberg, Arthur. "Les Plaisirs de l'île enchantée." Review of *Le Mariage forcé, La Princesse d'Elide,* and *Tartuffe* by Molière, Comédie-Française, April 8, 1981. *Theatre Journal* 34, no. 3 (1982): 400–401.

Hubert, Judd D. *Molière and the Comedy of Intellect*. 1962. Reprint. Berkeley: University of California Press, 1973.

Johnson, Barbara. "Teaching Ignorance: *L'Ecole des femmes*." *Yale French Studies* 63 (1982): 165–82.

Jomaron, Jacqueline de. "Le Tartuffe mis en scène par Lioubimov." *Travail Théâtral* 4 (1971): 158–62.

————. Ed. *Le Théâtre en France*. 2 vols. Paris: Armand Colin, 1989.

Jouvet, Louis. "Louis Jouvet et sa compagnie de *L'Ecole des femmes* de Molière." Jacket notes. In *L'Ecole des Femmes*. Paris: Disques Pathé, 1955.

————. "Doute." In *Louis Jouvet: exposition organisée pour le dixième anniversaire de sa mort*, 9. Paris: Bibliothèque Nationale, 1961.

————. *Molière et la comédie classique*. Paris: Editions Gallimard, 1965.

————. "Cours au Conservatoire National d'Art Dramatique 1949–1951 (extraits)." Edited transcripts of acting classes. *Revue d'Histoire du Théâtre* 39, no. 1 (1987).

Jouvet, Louis, and Robert Pignarre. "Problèmes de la mise en scène des chefs-d'oeuvre classiques (III): la comédie au XVIIe siècle." *Revue d'Histoire du Théâtre* 3, no. 4 (1951): 375–87.

Kaisergruber, Danielle, and Antoine Vitez. "Théorie/pratique théâtrale." *Dialectiques* 14 (1976): 8–16.

Kleber, Pia. *Exceptions and Rules: Brecht, Planchon, and* The Good Person of Szechwan. Frankfurt am Main: Peter Lang, 1987.

Knapp, Bettina L. *Louis Jouvet: Man of the Theatre*. New York: Columbia University Press, 1957.

————. *The Reign of the Theatrical Director: French Theatre, 1887–1924*. Troy, N.Y.: Whitson, 1988.

Kowzan, Tadeusz. "*Le Tartuffe* de Molière dans la mise en scène de Roger Planchon." In *Les Voies de la création théâtrale*, ed. Jean Jacquot, 6:279–340. Paris: Centre National de la Recherche Scientifique, 1978.

Lancaster, Henry Carrington. *A History of French Dramatic Literature in the Seventeenth Century*. 9 vols. Baltimore: Johns Hopkins Press, 1929–42.

Lannoy, Stephan de. "Molière à Louvain-la-Neuve: notes sur le décor et le jeu." *Cahiers Théâtre Louvain* 37 (1979): 47–60.

Lanson, Gustave. "Molière and Farce." Trans. Ruby Cohn. *TDR* 8, no. 2 (1963): 133–54.

Laplace, Roselyne. "La Scène est dans une place de ville." *Comédie Française* 123–24 (1985): 41–42.

Lawrenson, T. E. *The French Stage and Playhouse in the XVIIth Century: A Study in the Advent of the Italian Order*. 2d ed. New York: AMS, 1986.

Loubier, Jean-Marc. *Louis Jouvet*. Paris: Ramsay, 1986.

Maillard, Lucien. "A L'affiche: *L'Ecole des femmes*." *Comédie Française* 18 (1973): 6–8.

————. "A L'affiche: *L'Ecole des femmes*." *Comédie Française* 19 (1973): 6–7.

Mambrino, Jean. "Carnet de théâtre: *L'Ecole de femmes, Le Tartuffe, Don Juan, Le Misanthrope* de Molière à l'Athénée/Louis Jouvet." *Les Etudes* 349 (1978): 639–41.

————. "Entretien avec Antoine Vitez." *Les Etudes* 347 (1977): 631–54.

Maskell, David. *Racine: A Theatrical Reading*. Oxford: Clarendon Press, 1991.

Merle, André. "Tartuffe mis en scène par Roger Planchon." *Travail Théâtral* 17 (1978): 40–45.

Michelet, Jules. *Louis XIV et la révocation de L'Edit de Nantes*. Vol. 7 of *Oeuvres complètes: histoire de France*. Paris: Flammarion, 1896.

Mignon, Paul-Louis. *Louis Jouvet*. Lyon: La Manufacture, 1988.

Miller, Jonathan. *Subsequent Performances*. New York: Viking, 1986.

Miller, Judith Graves. "Vitez's Molière." *Theater* 11, no. 3 (1980): 74–81.

Millon, Martine. "Regards indiscrets sur une famille en chemise." *Travail Théâtral* 17 (1978): 46–49.

Mongrédien, Georges. *Recueil des textes et des documents du XVIIe siècle relatifs à Molière*. 2 vols. Paris: Centre National de la Recherche Scientifique, 1965.

————. *Daily Life in the French Theatre at the Time of Molière*. Trans. Claire Eliane Engel. London: Allen and Unwin, 1969.

Moore, Will. *Molière: A New Criticism*. Oxford: Clarendon Press, 1949.

Nelson, Robert J. "Classicism: The Rise of the Baroque in French Literature." *L'Esprit Créateur* 11, no. 2 (1971): 169–86.

Nicolich, Robert N. "Door, Window, and Balcony in *L'Ecole des femmes*." *Romance Notes* 12 (1971): 364–69.

Planchon, Roger. "I'm a Museum Guard." *Performing Arts Journal* 16 (1981): 97–109.

Radar, Edmond. "Molière selon Antoine Vitez." *Cahiers Théâtre Louvain* 37 (1979): 39–46.

Romero, Laurence. *Molière: Traditions in Criticism, 1900–1970*. Chapel Hill: University of North Carolina Press, 1974.

Roubine, Jean-Jacques. *Théâtre et mise en scène, 1880–1980*. Paris: Presses Universitaires de France, 1980.

Rouse, John. "Brecht and the Art of Scenic Writing." In *Brecht: Performance*, ed. John Fuegi, 77–87. Vol. 13 of *The Brecht Yearbook*. Detroit: Wayne State University Press, 1987.

Roussou, Matei. *André Antoine*. Paris: L'Arche, 1954.

Rudlin, John. *Jacques Copeau*. Cambridge: Cambridge University Press, 1986.

Sanders, James B. "*Le Tartuffe* d'Antoine (1907): essai de mise en scène rationnelle." In *Molière and the Commonwealth of Letters: Patrimony and Posterity*, ed. Roger Johnson, Jr., Editha S. Neumann, and Guy T. Trail, 583–90. Jackson: University Press of Mississippi, 1975.

————. *André Antoine, directeur à l'Odéon: dernière étape d'une odysée*. Paris: Minard, 1978.

Scherer, Jacques. *La Dramaturgie classique en France*. 1950. Reprint. Paris: Nizet, 1981.

————. *Structures de* Tartuffe. 2d ed. Paris: Société d'Editions d'Enseignement Supérieure, 1974.

Serrière, Marie-Thérèse. *Le T.N.P. et nous*. Paris: José Corti, 1959.

Simon, Alfred. Intro. and notes. Le Tartuffe, *Comédie en 5 actes de Molière, dans la mise en scène de Roger Planchon*. Paris: Editions de L'Avant-Scène, [1977].

Stoullig, Edmond. *Les Annales du théâtre et de la musique, 1907.* Vol. 33. Paris: Ollendorff, 1908.

Strindberg, August. "Author's Preface to *Miss Julie.*" In *European Theories of the Drama,* ed. Barrett H. Clark, 322–28. Rev. ed. New York: Crown, 1965.

Ubersfeld, Anne. "Le Jeu des classiques: réécriture ou musée?" In *Les Voies de la création théâtrale,* ed. Jean Jacquot, 6:179–92. Paris: Centre National de la Recherche Scientifique, 1978.

———. *L'Ecole du spectateur: lire le théâtre 2.* Paris: Editions Sociales, 1981.

Vitez, Antoine. "Quatre fois Molière." *Europe* 606 (1979): 176–88.

Vitez, Antoine, and Emile Copfermann. *De Chaillot à Chaillot.* Paris: Hachette, 1981.

Vitez, Antoine, Jacques Lassalle, and Marcel Maréchal. "Pourquoi Molière?" *théâtre/ public* 22–23 (1978): 20–25.

Whitton, David. *Stage Directors in Modern France.* Manchester: Manchester University Press, 1987.

Index